To Claire
love ya !
Sparky Lyle

THE YEAR I OWNED THE YANKEES

A Baseball Fantasy

SPARKY LYLE & DAVID FISHER

THE YEAR I OWNED THE YANKEES

A Baseball Fantasy

BANTAM BOOKS
NEW YORK · TORONTO · LONDON · SYDNEY · AUCKLAND

THE YEAR I OWNED THE YANKEES

A Bantam Book / April 1990

Produced by Ink Projects.

All rights reserved.

Copyright © 1990 by Sparky Lyle and David Fisher.

For information address: Bantam Books.

Library of Congress Cataloging-in-Publication Data

Lyle, Sparky.
    The year I owned the Yankees / by Sparky Lyle and David Fisher.
        p.   cm.
    ISBN 0-553-05750-2
    1. Lyle, Sparky.   2. Baseball—United States—Team owners—Biography.
    3. New York Yankees (Baseball team) I. Fisher, David. 1946–
    II. Title.
    GV865.L92A3   1990
    338.4'7796357'092—dc20
    [B]   89-49189
                                                                              CIP

Published simultaneously in the United States and Canada

PRINTED IN THE UNITED STATES OF AMERICA

B   0 9 8 7 6 5 4 3 2

TO ALBERT H. LYLE
Thanks for being Dad

I f this hadn't really happened, somebody would have had to make it up.

It all started a little over a year ago. I was sitting at home in New Jersey, with my wife, Mary, watching the semifinals of the *Jeopardy* All-Housewives $100,000 Tournament when the phone rang. Double Jeopardy had just begun, but at that point it didn't seem like an omen. Mary answered and spoke for a few minutes. Then she put her hand over the mouthpiece and said to me, "Sparky, there's a man on the phone who wants to know if you'd be interested in buying the New York Yankees."

My name is Albert Lyle. Sparky Lyle. *That* Sparky Lyle. The first man to have his picture on the cover of both *Sports Illustrated* and *Cosmopolitan*. The man who was blamed by baseball commissioner Fay Vincent for "changing the world of baseball as we have known it." Now I think it's time to tell my side of the story.

As just about everyone who reads the newspapers or watches television knows, last year I had the opportunity to fulfill the ultimate fantasy of every baseball fan—for one season I owned and operated a major-league baseball team. Not just any team either, but the New York Yankees, once the greatest team in professional sports. Now, a lot of what has been written about that season either isn't true or has been really exaggerated. For example, that *Newsweek* piece that called me "Baseball's Benedict Arnold" was filled with inaccuracies. And what happened to Lou Piniella was his own choice. And no matter how much has been written about it, the Tommy John experiment was not my idea, although I did go along with it and I'm glad I did. The *USA Today* story that said I was trying to sell advertising space on the backs of Yankee uniforms was completely false. The *National Enquirer* story that I considered replacing the high-intensity halogen lights at the Stadium with tanning lamps so fans could watch a ballgame and get a tan at the same time was ridiculous. And as for my part in the Duke Schneider controversy, the whole story has never been told before.

Some of the other stories are true. Sure, I made some mistakes. But before anyone makes a final judgment, I think all the facts should be known. So here, for the first time, is the whole story, exactly as it happened, of the year I owned the Yankees.

When I took the telephone from Mary I figured it had to be one of my former major-league teammates, probably Dick "Dirt" Tidrow, or one of my costars from the old Miller Lite All-Stars commercials, maybe Rodney "The Rocket" Dangerfield, playing a practical joke. But as I quickly found out, this was no joke. "Mr. Lyle," a pleasant voice said, "my name is Daniel Hunter, and I'm with the United American Holding Company. Is that name familiar to you?"

"Not really," I said.

"No matter. United American is a conglomerate with interests primarily in related areas of consumer products, light and heavy industry, timber, pharmaceuticals, and entertainment. I think you can say that, basically, we own things. Frozen foods, soaps, television and radio stations, western Colorado . . ." He paused, like he had told a joke and was waiting for a laugh. I didn't laugh. "Mr. Lyle?" he said.

"Look, Mr. Hunter," I told him, "if this is about a personal appearance you're gonna have to talk to my agent. He's got my schedule, and . . ."

"No, no, no," he said, laughing. I guess I had told a joke. "You see, we've decided to expand our interests, which is why I'm calling. Now, I know this is probably going to come as a shock, but actually, we were wondering if you'd be interested in buying the New York Yankees?"

"Sure," I said. "I'd love to. Will you take a check?"

Hunter laughed, but it sounded forced, like he didn't know how to laugh naturally. "Now, Mr. Lyle," he continued, "I know this is difficult for you to believe, but I am completely serious. The New York Yankees are going to be sold, and we would like you to purchase the team."

Mary yelled from the living room, "It's Final Jeopardy!" But Hunter had me interested. Somehow, I figured, he's trying to sell me something. I just couldn't figure out what, so I kept talking. "Does George Steinbrenner know about this?" I asked. As far as I knew, The Boss still owned the team. And even after the bloody anti-Steinbrenner riots and the embarrassing "Go George Go" campaign, he had no intention of selling.

"It's rather complicated," Hunter said, then began explaining the situation. In 1988 Congress had passed a series of technical corrections to the Income Tax Revision Act of 1987. A hidden provision of these corrections, introduced by conservative congressman Rudolph Woolward (R-Florida), provided that Section 384 of the tax bill would not apply to contributions made to any Delaware shipbuilding corporation whose principal place of business was Tampa, Florida.

This special-interest legislation, Hunter continued, had been submitted specifically to assist George M. Steinbrenner, whose shipbuilding company, American Ship Building, had suffered serious financial losses. The entire American shipbuilding industry had been devastated by a series of economic disasters, among them the end of the Iran-Iraq War, which brought some sort of peace to the Persian Gulf, the declining interest in vacation cruises, and the rising value of the dollar overseas, which cut deeply into imports. Amship, as Hunter referred to it, which had posted sales of $194 million and earnings of $1.26 a share a few years earlier, had fallen to $25 million in sales and a loss of $1.48 a share by 1987. The stock fell another 71¢ a share in 1988, and in 1989, when three-year losses exceeded $20,000,000 Steinbrenner had been able to convince his minority partners in the New York Yankees to trade their stock in that corporation for a substantial interest in Amship, enabling them to share in those very desirable net operating losses American Ship Building enjoyed, but necessitating the special exemption from the tax bill. "Is that clear so far?" Hunter asked.

"Mary!" I shouted. "Could you turn the TV down a little, please?" I began asking Hunter a lot of questions. It sounded like he'd said that Steinbrenner's shipbuilding company had enjoyed the losses. I'd never known anybody who enjoyed losing, and nobody enjoyed it less than George M. Steinbrenner III.

"Because of the U.S. tax code," Hunter told me, "there are good losses and bad losses." In certain situations losing money could be very good for a company, and this was one of those situations.

I began to understand. Steinbrenner's shipbuilding company had successfully managed to lose millions of dollars. I had to admit to Hunter that I'd never realized that The Boss was that good a businessman.

"Those losses have made American Ship Building an extremely attractive target for acquisition," Hunter pointed out, "and so we have initiated an improvement of long-term corporate prospects through management transition." Then he laughed, long and loudly, a banker's laugh.

"So where do I fit in?"

"We've offered Mr. Steinbrenner $890 million for American Ship Building and all of its subsidiary holdings, including the New York Yankees Corporation. It's an offer he can't realistically turn down. But we are particularly interested in those large net operating losses, which we can use to offset the substantial profits flowing from our forestry and television divisions. . . ."

"I guess you weren't such good businessmen, huh?" I said. "You made a profit."

"Yes," he said, meaning he understood my joke, then coughed and continued. "Now, the single American Ship asset currently capable of generating excess revenues is Yankee Corp. So we have to find a means of divesting ourselves of that asset."

So that's why they had called me. In this business losses were good and profits were bad. With my business smarts, I could be very good in that kind of business.

"Obviously," he continued, "we would want to keep Yankee Corp., in addition to the NOLs, so what we intend to do is have Mr. Steinbrenner sell the corporation before the new management team takes control, then recognize the gain for tax purposes and absorb the NOLs without really losing control of Yankee Corp. for any substantial period. I'm sure you can see what I'm getting at?"

Well, I knew he wasn't trying to sell me magazine subscriptions. The truth is I had no idea what he was talking about, but I was afraid that if I asked he was going to start explaining all over again.

"So. Our plan then, is to sell the corporation to an unrelated third party, with an option to reacquire at fair market value at the end of one fiscal year. If you so choose, we would like you to be that unrelated third party. Of course, you'll have to sign a recourse note, but that's really about all you'd have to do. Then the team belongs to you for one year. So?"

"Let me get this straight. You're offering me the New York Yankees?"

"The New York Yankees Corporation, actually. But essentially, that's correct."

This was too much. I mean, I had some friends who had Rotisserie League teams, but this guy was talking about owning the New York Yankees. "Why me?" I asked.

"That's an excellent question. You see, Mr. Lyle, in order to satisfy the applicable Internal Revenue regulations, we have to divest to someone who has had no prior financial relationship with United American. You. We decided it would be prudent to recruit someone with an expertise in the business. You again. And we wanted an individual no one could ever accuse us of controlling."

"Me."

"You. Apparently in the baseball business you've established a reputation of being quite uncontrollable."

"Thank you," I said. I decided to take that as a compliment.

"There was one additional matter, of course. I have to admit that none of the boys here at United American are actually baseball fans, but Mr. Marash, one of our principals, remembered that you received considerable attention for your habit of lowering your posterior into baked goods."

"I sat on cakes, right?"

"Precisely. The IRS would never believe we were in collusion with you. We're much too sophisticated for that. In short, you are the perfect choice to own Yankee Corp."

It all sounded too simple. I'm watching *Jeopardy* and somebody calls me up to sell me the Yankees? "Be honest with me, Mr. Hunter. How much is this going to cost me?"

"We estimate the fair market value of the New York Yankees Corporation to be approximately $225 million."

I thought about that for a few seconds. If I took a second mortgage on the house, floated a loan at the bank, hit on a few relatives, extended the limit on our credit cards, emptied the piggy banks . . .

I'd still be about $224 million short. "I admit it sounds like a good deal, Mr. Hunter," I said, "but I just don't have that kind of cash lying around right now. . . ."

Then he really laughed. His laugh sounded a lot like a cash register totaling a bill. "Oh, good heavens, Mr. Lyle, we certainly don't expect you to pay for the team. Oh, no, I don't believe anyone does business that way anymore. Taking money from you would be very bad management. No, what we intend to do is loan you the principal, at current interest rates, of course."

"Oh, now I see." I began doing a little figuring of my own. If Mary and I skipped going on vacations, if we didn't buy a new car every third year, cut down a little on the groceries, I could probably pay back most of the interest on the loan in, say, 180 years. "Look, I'm sorry, it really does sound like fun. But as much as I'd like to, I can't afford to buy the Yank—the corporation."

"Oh, you can't afford not to," he corrected me. "You see, this isn't going to cost you a thing. With a little luck, you might even make a few million or so in the process. Now, maybe this isn't worth the aggravation for only a few million, but . . ."

"Well," I said, "you know, I do have a little spare time."

"I'm sure the board will be glad to hear that. Now, what we propose to do is to have our institutional bond division loan you the money for the purchase, using the corporation as your collateral. In addition to paying prevailing interest rates for the loan, you will also have to give us an option to repurchase the corporation at the end of the fiscal year—I think you people refer to that as a 'season'—at its real market value as determined by an outside auditor, plus 10 percent, but under no conditions at less than the original purchase price. So you see, Mr. Lyle, you get to keep any profits earned by Yankee Corp., as well as any increase in its fair market value. If, for example, Yankee Corp. should be successful, if it should defeat the other thirteen corporations and win the so-called pennant, its value would obviously increase exponentially. . . ."

"Millions?" I said.

I finally hung up the phone about a half hour later. Mary was watching a *Rockford* rerun. "What was that all about, Sparky?" she asked.

"Maybe you'd better start calling me Albert," I told her. "I just bought the New York Yankees."

And that's how it all began.

The next few days were a blur of business meetings, press conferences, and parties, topped by that memorable ticker-tape parade down Broadway. The *New York Post* declared it, "V-G Day!" The *Daily News* referred to it as the "Yankee Liberation Day" parade. The *Times* reported "Steinbrenner Era Ends in Bronx." Whatever they called it, more than two million people lined the streets and leaned out of the buildings just to throw things at me. The last time I'd been part of such a great celebration had been in 1978, when we—when the Yankees had won our second consecutive world championship. But maybe this parade was even bigger. After all, Yankee fans had their team back.

The parade ended at City Hall. Several of my old teammates, Graig Nettles, Dirt, Catfish Hunter, and Mickey Rivers, had flown to the city to join the celebration and were seated on the reviewing stand. I remember, as I walked to the podium to give my brief statement, that Nettles leaned over and whispered, "I sure as hell hope The Boss doesn't hear about this. It's gonna really piss him off."

In my brief statement I told the fans exactly how I intended to run the team. "I'm going to be a hands-off owner," I said. "I'll be leaving the running of the ballclub in the hands of knowledgeable baseball people. They will be responsible for the running of the team. It'll be in their hands." For about a week after I made the speech everybody congratulated me. Then *New York Times* columnist Ira Berkow mentioned that it was exactly the same speech that George Steinbrenner had made when he'd bought the team from CBS in 1973.

The difference was that I meant it. My whole life, I've always meant what I said when I said it. I mean that. I didn't kid myself; I knew that my experience in management was somewhat limited, so I didn't expect to be able to move into The Boss's office and immediately start running the corporation. Being chief executive officer, or CEO, as we call it, of a professional sports franchise is an extremely complicated job. A major-league baseball team has an operating budget of more than $40 million annually, and can generate revenues of more than $75 million. The New York Yankees Corporation included major-league operations, minor-league operations, a staff of about 175 people not including players, an advertising and promotions department, ticket sales, publicity, the stadium operations group, a multimillion-dollar scouting department including a player development school in the Dominican Republic, a training and medical department, publications, concessions, a business affairs and accounting department, and a highly professional security force. No way would I simply be able to walk in the door and take over. I knew I had a lot to learn, and I expected it would take me at least seven or eight weeks.

The main problem I knew I'd have to overcome to run the corporation successfully was my lack of business experience. I didn't always own the Yankees. As my official biography in the media guide stated, I was born in Reynoldsville, Pennsylvania, a small town about 90 miles from Pittsburgh. My father was a contractor, and my first business experience was working for him. Once, I remember, he was renovating an old church and he wanted me to climb up to the top of the steeple and help my uncle paint the cross. I told him, "You got no chance of my going up there."

"But look at your uncle way up there," he said.

"I did," I said, "and that's why I'm not going up there."

My next experience in the business world took place at the Jackson China Company, the leading manufacturer of china dishes in Reynoldsville. After carefully reviewing my background and experience, they offered me a position as a mold runner. That meant I had to carry the molds for the plates from the batter-out to the jigger-man. I had to be there at five o'clock in the morning, and they paid me $116 every two weeks.

Besides that, when I was playing for the Boston Red Sox organization, I worked in their ticket office in the off-season. Specifically, I was in group sales promotion. My job was to go to see executives in their offices, and tell them that unless they bought a lot of tickets I'd have to come back.

After retiring as a major-league player I became a member of the Miller Lite Beer All-Stars and appeared in TV commercials. That was a tough job. While I was costarring with Rodney Dangerfield, for example, I sat under the klieg lights too long and burned my ear. And I've also worked as a VIP casino host at the Claridge Hotel in Atlantic City, New Jersey.

And that was my total experience in the world of big business—until I became the new "Boss of the Bronx Bombers."

But I knew about baseball. In baseball I had experience. My baseball career consisted of parts of two seasons in the minor leagues and fifteen seasons, or fiscal years, as we call them in the business world, in the major leagues. I was a left-handed pitcher, specifically a short reliever, a description that refers to my job, not my size. I was supposed to come into the game in the eighth or ninth inning and stop the other team from scoring any runs. Sometimes I did, sometimes I didn't. My basic philosophy as a relief pitcher was that whether I got them out or they scored some runs, it was still a whole lot better than being up on that church steeple with my uncle.

I played in the American League and the National League, on five different teams. I pitched for the Yankees in the one-game playoff against the Red Sox in 1978. I pitched in three League Championship Series and two World Series. In 1977 the Baseball Writers Association gave me the Cy Young Award, the award they give to the best pitcher in the league. When I finally retired after the 1982 season, I was fifth on the all-time list in appearances, fourth in wins among all relief pitchers, and second in saves. So I know what it feels like to be a major-league baseball player; I know what it feels like to be signed and traded and released, to be treated well and treated badly. The one vow I made when I signed the bill of sale for the Yankees was that I was going to treat my players the way I always wanted to be treated.

And when I vowed it, I meant it.

My best pitch was the slider, a pitch that curves in toward right-handed hitters, then suddenly drops straight down. It was my best pitch because it was the only pitch I ever threw during a game. Well, that's not totally true. In fifteen years in the big leagues I threw one curveball. I threw it to Reggie Jackson when he was with Oakland. Ever see a batted baseball cause rain? That ball may still be traveling.

I pitched for the New York Yankees for seven seasons, six of them after The Boss bought the team in 1973. In 1979 I published the diary I'd kept during the previous season. The book was called *The Bronx Zoo*, and it became a very controversial best-seller. It made George very angry. "It's an outright lie that I fired an office girl over a tuna fish sandwich," he swore to reporters. "I'm almost certain it was peanut butter and jelly."

The publication of the book, as well as the acquisition of free-agent reliever Goose Gossage, meant the end of my career as a Yankee. I pitched with the Texas Rangers for a little more than two seasons, then finished my career with the Phillies and White Sox. But the greatest times of my life in baseball took place while I was wearing the Yankee pinstripes. I'm not really a very sentimental person, but I really did feel something special when I put on the Yankee uniform. I guess it was pride, the feeling that I was good enough to help carry forward the tradition established by some of the greatest players in baseball history: Babe Ruth, Lou Gehrig, Joe DiMaggio, Mickey Mantle, Yogi Berra, Whitey Ford, Roger Maris. And I felt that surge of pride every time I put on that uniform. I think that pretty much all my teammates did, even Reggie Jackson. I know it sounds corny, but it's absolutely true—we felt we were special.

Somehow, though, that pride had disappeared during the last few years of The Boss's reign. Too many managers, too many arguments, not enough wins. I was determined to restore that pride. Or, as George M. Steinbrenner III had promised so many years ago, "to bring back the days of glory."

OCTOBER 20 ★

The baseball season ended officially two days ago when Ellis Burks's two home runs off Frankie Viola in the sixth game of the World Series brought the Red Sox their first world championship in more than six decades. The Yankees finished third, again, trailing the Red Sox by five games. The season is over; now the real work begins.

I walked into Yankee Stadium as owner of the New York Yankees for the first time, and took the elevator to the third level, the Executive Offices level that overlooked the playing field. I'd been in George Steinbrenner's office many times, usually to tell him why I wouldn't sign the contract he was offering me. But for the first time, I was nervous. All those other times I had felt secure in what I was doing.

I knew I had a huge job ahead of me. The situation in the Bronx had not been good for a long time. The Yankees had been competitive almost every season; in fact, during Steinbrenner's nearly two decades as owner they'd won more games than any other team in baseball. But in the last decade they'd won only one division title. Attendance, which had peaked at 2,633,701 in 1988, had fallen each year. And young kids growing up in the New York–New Jersey metropolitan area, the ticket buyers of the future, were growing up to be New York

Mets fans. Sales of replica team jackets, a reasonably accurate barometer of team loyalty among young fans and their parents, were running 3.5 to 1 in favor of the Mets. More important, in the vital lined-satin-jacket category, the more expensive jackets traditionally popular among Yankee fans, the Mets were leading almost 3 to 1. In the clubhouse Yankee pride had diminished to such a low point that players were asking to be traded and free agents were refusing to sign with the club, even when they were offered more money than they could get anywhere else. On the field the team was relatively solid, but the pitching staff consisted of prospects, aging veterans, and fill-ins.

So the job facing me was a tough one: make the team competitive on the field, restore pride in the pinstripes, and reinspire fan loyalty and enthusiasm.

I knew it was going to be difficult to do it all in one fiscal season. But I knew that even before I could get started one difficult task had to be accomplished—I had to get George Steinbrenner out of his office.

The Boss had locked himself inside and was refusing to talk to reporters, even as an "unnamed source." So everyone knew he was serious.

I unlocked the door with the key Daniel Hunter had given me when we'd closed the deal, and took two steps into The Boss's office. My feet sunk deeply and silently into the thick Yankee-blue-and-white carpeting covering the floor. George was sitting at his desk, bent over some papers. Behind him rows upon rows of photographs of Yankee managers during the Steinbrenner years were hung on the wall. There was Billy Martin, and Bob Lemon, and Billy Martin, Dick Howser, Gene Michael, Bob Lemon, Gene Michael, Clyde King, Billy Martin, Yogi Berra, Billy Martin, Lou Piniella, Billy Martin, Lou Piniella, Dallas Green, and Bucky Dent.

Just like in the old days, George didn't acknowledge my presence for a few minutes. I knew that that was his way of establishing superiority. Finally he sighed and looked up, and seemed genuinely surprised to see me. "Yes? What?" he said, sounding mildly annoyed.

The Boss had aged considerably since the last time I'd seen him. Too many lost seasons were etched into his face. His hair, which had always been perfectly barbered, was growing wild, like wheat in a windstorm. "It's Sparky, George," I said softly. "I'm here to take over the team."

"Oh? Oh, that," he said. "Didn't anybody tell you, that's all been straightened out. It was all just a big mistake."

"It's no mistake, George, I have all the papers right here. I own the Yankees now. I'm afraid you're going to have to leave."

"That's impossible," he said, his voice beginning to rise. "Don't you understand, I am the Yankees; the Yankees are me. Without me, there are no Yankees. Don't you see that?"

"Listen, Boss, I'm sorry . . ." And at that moment, I genuinely was.

He opened his eyes wide, and maybe it was my imagination, but in that dark room, a strange glow seemed to come from them. "No!" he shouted, "No! Listen to me, this is a mistake. Would The Boss lie to you? I can't go, my people love me. They love me, they do. Here, I'll prove it." He pushed a button on his intercom and barked, "Annie, get in here right this minute and tell Sparky that you love me. Now!"

"I'm going to have to call security," I said quietly, just like the doctors had advised.

He stared at me, that big bulldog jaw of his jutting forward, like the prow of a great ship, its lamplights glowing, cutting through a mist. "Ha! I know what you want, Lyle, but you're not getting it. You can hold out all season if you want to. . . ." As I stood there, he regressed into the past, to the time when I was still pitching for the Yankees, and refusing to sign my contract. "It won't work, you know. You can sit out the whole season, you can sit out the rest of your career, but you'll never beat me." He paused, then said in a voice ringing with defiance and threat, "Because I am The Boss. Do you hear me, I AM THE BOSS!"

The four-man security team came running in when they heard the shouting. One of them asked The Boss to leave the premises quietly. Steinbrenner immediately fired him, then quickly rehired him with a big raise, then just as quickly, fired him again. It was incredible, a classic example of the Martin Syndrome, as the psychiatrists have named it. When the security team finally decided to physically remove him, they discovered he had chained himself to his desk. It took them another few minutes to cut him free. Finally, they began dragging him out of the office.

It was a terrible thing to see. He clutched at his desk, somehow managing to grab hold of a team picture of the 1978 Yankees, his last championship team. He held it against his breast as they dragged him out of the office and down the hallway. For several minutes afterward I could still hear a faint voice shouting madly, "I am THE BOSS! I AM The Boss!"

And when that voice faded away I thought I heard another voice, or maybe a lot of voices, chanting, "Free at last. Free at last. Great God Almighty, free at last." Maybe that was just my imagination, or the whispers of the October breezes sweeping through the empty seats of Yankee Stadium.

And then there was an overwhelming silence. The Boss was gone. An era in baseball history was over. George Steinbrenner had left an office full of mementos, a broken chain locked around a desk leg, and two deep furrows in the carpet made by his feet as he was dragged out of the room. I smoothed out the furrows with my foot, but I decided to leave the chain where it was, as a reminder of what can happen to a major-league baseball team when too much power is held by the wrong person.

I took a long look around the office, my office. Then I went to work rebuilding the New York Yankees.

OCTOBER 22 ★

My first official act as owner of the Yankees was obvious. I had to send a message to the Yankee fans who had scattered all over America that times had changed. And I knew there was only one way to do it: I rehired Yogi Berra. After his Hall of Fame career as the Yankees' greatest catcher, Yogi had managed the team to the 1964 pennant, then been fired. The Boss hired him to manage again in 1984, but then fired him again at the beginning of the '85 season. After that embarrassment, he'd taken a coaching job with the Houston Astros and vowed never to set foot inside Yankee Stadium while Steinbrenner owned the team. I knew that Yankee fans would understand that Yogi's return was a symbol of my commitment to restore Yankee tradition.

I wanted him to replace Bobby Forgione as first base coach. Once, the only thing a first base coach had to do was pat baserunners on the rump and say things like, "Nice hit," "Don't get picked off," "One out," or "Two outs." Sometimes the first base coach would also be responsible for reminding the runner to watch the third base coach, who actually gave the signal that a play was on. But as baseball has become more technical, the job of the first base coach has changed. Now, when a player gets on base, the first base coach has to hold his batting glove, his wristband, his elbow pad, his shin guard, his gold chains, and whatever else he has in his pocket—plus pat him on the rump.

I called Yogi at his home in Montclair, New Jersey, first thing in the morning. "This is Yogi," I heard the familiar, gravelly voice answer. "My answering machine isn't working right now, but if you leave a message with me, soon as it's fixed I'll put it on the machine for you."

"Yog, it's Sparky Lyle. I hope I didn't wake you."

"Nah," he said. "I had to get up to answer the phone anyway." I laughed. "That's an old one. I already said it," he explained. "Besides, I didn't even have to get up. The truth is that I'm still lying down in bed."

"I'll tell you why I called," I said. "I want to ask you a question. Tell me honestly, how do you like being retired?"

He thought about it for a few seconds. "Well, I gotta admit it uses up a lot of my spare time."

"So how would you like to come back to work for the Yankees? I want you to coach first base."

"I don't know," he said. "Like I always say, a first base coach is like a bowling pin. The score just ain't his fault."

He meant that the first base coach didn't have a lot of responsibility. I decided to be completely honest with him. "I need you, Yog. I want Yankee fans to know that things are going to be different from now on."

"I'm not the Statute of Liberty, you know."

He meant that he wasn't interested in being used as a symbol. "Yog, listen to me. The Yankees need you." I knew that no one who had spent as much of his life wearing pinstripes as Yogi could resist that plea.

"How much do they need me?"

He meant, how much was I willing to pay him to become the Yankees' "Statute of Liberty," the symbol of the new era. "What would you say to $150,000?"

"I'd say, 'Thank you for calling.' "

He meant that that wasn't enough money. Eventually we settled on a two-year guaranteed contract for almost $600,000. That was more money than I had intended to pay a first base coach—let's be honest, Lassie could do the job—but this wasn't just any coach, this was Yogi Berra. And whatever it cost, it was worth it. Yogi was coming home.

OCTOBER 23 ★

I invited members of the media into my office for interviews this morning. I was actually looking forward to it. During my career I'd always gotten along pretty well with the writers. Of course, that was when they were still "the writers," before they became "the media." Basically, they seemed to like players who sat on cakes.

I'd been pretty friendly with New York beat writers like Red Foley, Phil Pepe, and Maury Allen. There were times when I'd give up a long home run to lose a ballgame and one of them would come in the clubhouse and ask, in that somber voice of doom you have to use in the locker room of the losing team, "So tell me, Sparky, did you hold that pitch in a special way to make it go so far?"

Not everybody got along so well with the writers. There were a lot of players who believed writers did only two things: They reported the details of the game, and they screwed the players. Thurman Munson used to tell them, "I know I can be an asshole sometimes, and I know I can be moody, but when I make the last out of a game or hit into a double play and it costs us a game, just leave me alone." And usually they did. Usually. But one day Maury Allen pressed a little hard and Thurman just honked up a big glob and, *hawonk*, he nailed Maury right in the forehead. It just hung there, then slowly dripped down. That ended the interview. I mean, it just hung there. Everybody on the team agreed that Thurman was wrong to spit at Maury, that he would have been much smarter to push him or punch him, but we were all behind Thurman, because he'd told the writers when to leave him alone. But it just *hung* there.

The only writer I didn't like was a little fellow named Henry Hecht. He wasn't a bad writer, maybe because he was so small he could get closer to the typewriter keys than the other writers, but I thought his ethics left something to be desired. Like ethics. We once caught him standing by a urinal listening to guys talking in the shitters. He was standing there as if he was taking a piss, but he was holding his notebook in his hands. He was eavesdropping. I wrote that story in *The Bronx Zoo,* and after the book was published he challenged me to a debate on television. A debate over whether it was ethical for him to eavesdrop in the bathroom? I told him I wouldn't debate him because he was so small there couldn't possibly be any extra room in his head for brains.

And, generally, I like small people. I even liked Earl Weaver.

We got even with Hecht, though. On two or three occasions we gave him phony stories. When we knew he was listening to private conversations we talked about ridiculous trades or made up stories about dissension on the team. He wrote several stories that were completely fictitious. When the paper ran them we'd read them out loud on the team bus for comic relief.

But that was when I was a player. Now, as an executive, as the owner, I knew I had to be more mature. So when the writers arrived I served them coffee, tea, and doughnuts. But no cakes.

I told them that I intended to make a lot of changes, but that the first thing I was going to do was nothing. "I think stability is underrated," I said. "I've always believed a winning team was better than the sum of its players." I liked the way that sounded so much that I said it again. "A winning team is better than the sum of its players."

Somebody whispered, I couldn't tell who, "How can a team be better than some of its players?"

Vic Zeigel of the *News* leaned over and asked the *Times*'s Dave Anderson, "Are you sure that's the *same* Sparky Lyle?"

I didn't bother to answer; I just kept talking. By that, I explained, I meant that the winning team is not always the one with the most talent, but the team that plays as a unit and has the most players contributing—and also has talent. It seemed to me that the endless juggling of players had prevented the Yankees from making the transformation from a group of individuals into a team. I intended to change that by stressing stability. "I want to let the players we have here play," I said, "instead of getting players who aren't here to play!"

Anderson told Zeigel, "I'm sure."

I then announced that I was officially shutting down the Columbus Shuttle. For too many years The Boss had been bringing up young players from the Columbus Clippers, our Triple-A farm club, then sending them back down, then bringing them back up. I remember an infielder we had, George Zeber, who spent a whole season on the Shuttle. The first time he was brought up he had his car shipped from Columbus to New York, but by the time the car got to New York, he had already been sent back to Columbus, so they turned the car around and shipped it back. But before the car got there, Zeber was recalled to New York. I think he was brought up and sent back five times that season, and his car never did catch up with him. I didn't think that kind of treatment helped the team or the confidence of young players. So, no more Columbus Shuttle. Only in case of injuries or emergencies would we bring up players from Columbus during the season.

And when we brought up a young player we were going to give him a real opportunity to play. The Boss never gave young players a chance to get used to playing in the big leagues. If they didn't produce immediately, they were gone, either back to the minors, or traded to another organization, or, worst of all, sent to a place from which few players ever returned, a place we always referred to as . . . Bossland.

Not only young players went to Bossland. Players who failed to hit in a key situation went to Bossland. Fielders who made errors that cost the team a game went to Bossland. Even a third base coach, Mike Ferraro, was once sent to Bossland. No one knew exactly where it was, but we knew it was very cold there, and lonely, and we knew it was almost impossible to escape from there. And we always knew when a player was in Bossland. Even though he was still visible, we knew it was only a matter of time until he disappeared completely. Sometimes they even had an overpopulation problem in Bossland. Among the people who were sent there were players like Jim Beattie, Ken Clay, Dave Pagan, Doyle Alexander, Bobby Meacham, M. L. Blanks, and Rafael Santana. Only Santana returned.

Steinbrenner also tried to send Dave Winfield to Bossland, but Winfield had a no-Bossland clause in his contract.

I also told the writers that we were no longer going to use the disabled list to keep players in reserve. Too many teams, including the Yankees, were creating mythical injuries to keep players nearby for fifteen to thirty days while they tried out other players. Apparently pro football teams had been so successful in using the injured reserve list that baseball teams decided to do the same thing; the baseball teams just didn't bother to announce it. "It isn't healthy for players who aren't hurt to be on the disabled list," I said, and I meant it.

And when a player was hurt, I promised, we would admit the full extent of his injury. The team looked foolish telling writers that a player had suffered a minor bruise and was going to be out for the remainder of the season.

Next, I guaranteed that we would no longer be trading prospects for older players. "The future is ahead of us," I pointed out confidently, "and if we keep trading away our young players, there'll be no tomorrow."

I saw Zeigel look at Anderson and nod his head.

I started mentioning some of the young players we'd traded away who were still playing in the big leagues for other clubs, people like Willie McGee, Fred McGriff, Doug Drabek, Jay Buhner, Dan Pasqua, Milt Gittens, Jim DeShaies, Mike Heath, Jose Rijo, Henry Cotto, Brian . . .

"All right, all right, Sparky," *Newsday*'s Marty Noble interrupted, "we've got to file our stories today." And everybody laughed.

"Well, you get the idea," I said. "Now you can forget it. We won't be trading our young prospects anymore. And we're going to concentrate on developing young pitching. So as of today we're releasing Jerry Atrics as our pitching coach."

Chris Kelly of the *Village Voice* leaned over and said to David Bell of *Newsweek*, "I didn't even know the Yankees had signed Atrics."

I finished by guaranteeing that we would be staying out of the free-agent market unless it became absolutely necessary. "We're through giving up our draft choices for players who aren't wanted by their own teams." Then I guaranteed that we would not be signing any more players who could only serve as designated hitters, saying, "I think the three we have are more than enough for any team."

I was really pleased with the way the meeting had gone. I thought I'd made a professional presentation of my plans to restore Yankee glory and bring our fans back to the Stadium. I had tried very hard to sound confident, because it was important that the writers take me seriously. Finally, I asked if anyone had any questions.

Every hand in the room went up. I called on Joanne Curtis of the *Jersey Bulletin*. Curtis was one of the leaders of a group of young investigative sports journalists who'd started referring to themselves as the "Full Court Press." She stood up and looked at her notebook and read her question. "Sparky," she asked, "does this mean you won't be sitting on any cakes this season?"

OCTOBER 25 ★

I had quite a surprise waiting for me when I got to the office this morning: Pete Rose. Pete and I had played together on the Phillies and, far as I was concerned, he was the epitome of what a ballplayer should be. He was always the first one at the ballpark and the last one to leave. Just watching him play made me try to play harder. We exchanged a Phillies high-five, then sat down to talk. He told me some amazing news—after spending most of the last two years going to collectibles shows, since being banned from baseball because of gambling, he'd decided to complete his education. "I've enrolled in college," he said, then he added, "but they wouldn't let me play football."

"What? They were afraid a guy your age would get hurt?"

He laughed at that, then shook his head, "They were afraid I'd hurt somebody." Finally he told me his real reason for being there. "If you make a change, I'd like to be considered."

I wasn't surprised. He'd been reinstated by the Commissioner last winter, but hadn't gotten a job. Because of his gambling history, most clubs were wary of him. "I really haven't thought about it," I said. That was true; Bucky Dent had done a good job in his second stint as Yankee manager. I just hadn't decided if I wanted to bring him back.

But before I could say all this, Pete put up his hands and said in that bulldog growl of his, "I know what you're thinking, but I want you to know that I've stopped gambling completely."

"Really?" That was great news. "On everything?"

"I don't even go to the track no more. If you don't believe me, I'd be willing to make a wager with you. Give you good odds, too."

"Pete, I thought you said you've stopped gambling."

"I have, but that don't include sure things."

OCTOBER 27 ★

I made the most incredible discoveries today. While I was cleaning out George Steinbrenner's desk, I found, among his autographed pictures of Richard Nixon, Spiro Agnew, Ferdinand and Imelda Marcos, Ivan Boesky, Ronald Reagan, Ed Meese, Roy Cohn, and Donald Trump, a branding iron with the Yankee symbol—Y on top of N—at the tip. As I held it in my hand I remembered hearing rumors that The Boss had desperately wanted to put his brand on his players, but had been talked out of it by Bob Lemon. Until this morning, I'd figured it was just some sort of silly joke. Now, as I held the branding iron in my hand, I wasn't so sure. And I wondered if that was the reason why players like Mickey Rivers and Judge Lewis never went into the shower after a game.

But the branding iron was just the beginning. As I dug deeper into the desk drawer, I accidentally pushed a little button and the bottom of the drawer popped open. It revealed a secret compartment. And in that compartment I found dozens and dozens of minicassette tapes and what appeared to be a miniature tape recorder. I got down on my knees and looked under the desk and, after searching for a few minutes, I found a button hidden in the thick carpeting. I pressed the button and the tape recorder went on. George Steinbrenner had had a secret taping system!

I searched the top of the desk for a microphone, but I never found it. I wondered if it could have been hidden in that team picture The Boss had clutched as they dragged him out of the office.

I locked the door and after several minutes figured out how to use the system. Then I began listening.

I was stunned. The tapes were the most incredible things I'd ever heard, or at least the most incredible things I'd heard since The Boss had invited me into his office after I'd won the Cy Young Award and told me he was giving me a $35,000 bonus. These tapes told the entire history of the Steinbrenner Era.

The first tape went all the way back to 1973, when Mike Burke, who was then running the Yankees for CBS, had put together a syndicate to buy the team. Steinbrenner had been the principal member of that syndicate. "So you can believe me, Mike," I distinctly heard George say—although this conversation must have taken place before he had this office, so I assumed it was recorded on another machine, and it was very scratchy—"I have neither the time nor the inclination to get involved with a baseball team on a daily basis. You know me; football's my game. But I think the Yankees are a good investment, and if I could just come out to the ballpark once in a while that would be enough for me." Then he had coughed, and asked, "It is called a ballpark in baseball, isn't it?"

I found one marked "1975." The quality of this tape was much better, and I could clearly hear The Boss say, "You know you can trust me, Charlie, there's no way in the world I'd be willing to pay that kind of money for a pitcher like Catfish Hunter. You just hold the line on his salary; he'll have to sign with the A's."

Several conversations later on the same tape I heard him telling someone, I never did figure out who, "If there's one thing I know, it's pitching. I'm telling you this kid Guidry isn't big enough or strong enough to last in the big leagues. He's just a pony; let's see if we can get a horse for him. . . ."

There was no question who he was talking to on a 1976 tape. I heard him say, really sincerely, "I'm telling you, Reggie, you sign with me and together we'll own this town. They'll change the name to Jacksonville."

I picked out an undated tape and put it on, and I immediately recognized Gene Michael's voice. "The Stick" has been a Yankee player, coach, scout, manager, and executive, and he was telling The Boss, "I don't know, George. It's a good offer but you, you have this reputation, you know, of being . . . difficult. Tough to work for."

"Oh, that," George told him. "Don't believe those old stories, that's just sour grapes from people who couldn't do the job. But that shouldn't worry you, because I've been watching you, Stick, and I know what you're made of. If I hired you and you didn't do the job, whose fault would that be? It would be mine, because I would have made a mistake in hiring you; and Stick, I don't make too many mistakes. I promise, you'll be running the show. I've been looking a long time for someone I felt confident in turning this club over to to run and I believe you're my man. You'll be absolutely free to make any moves you want. You won't even have to clear them with me. . . ."

Six tapes were held together with a rubber band, and someone had scribbled the initials "B. M." in Magic Marker on the side of one of them. I didn't have to listen very long to know who The Boss was talking to. "So here's what I thought we'd do to increase attendance," he was saying. "Next road trip we go on you pretend to have too much to drink, then you tell one of the writers something outrageous. I don't know, maybe something like, 'One's a born liar and the other's convicted.' You'll think of something, and then I'll make a big deal about firing you. I'm telling you, together we'll make the biggest headlines this town has ever seen. They'll have to change the name to Billytown. . . ."

Then I heard Billy's voice, agreeing. "I like it, I really do. One's a born liar, the other's convicted. Yeah, I like it."

"Wait, wait, there's more. Then, on Old Timers' Day—that's what, two weeks? I'll make a surprise announcement that I'm going to rehire you. Believe me, the place'll go crazy. We won't be able to print tickets fast enough. . . ."

Who could have guessed? I'd known that George was a great showman, but even I hadn't guessed how great a showman he really was.

I put on another Reggie tape. George was lecturing him. "It's all about selling tickets. Believe me, I'm right on this one. I mean, why do people go to hockey games? You think anybody really likes hockey? Grown men skating around? People go for the fights. Let me ask you, you ever been to a wrestling match?"

"Sure."

"Does anybody really care who wins? It's the battle, good against evil, the bully against the underdog. . . ." George hesitated, then said dramatically, "Reggie against George."

"You don't mean—but Boss, me fight with you? Nobody'd believe that."

I turned off the tape. I just couldn't listen to that anymore. What a fool I'd been. All of us, we'd all been fooled. We believed that Reggie and George, that Reggie and Billy, and Billy and George really didn't get along. It was just impossible to believe it had all been planned.

I found the Dick Howser tape crammed into a corner of the drawer. Contrary to what everybody had believed, it sounded like Dick really wanted to leave and George was urging him to return as manager. "I'd really like to come back and manage next year," Dick was saying, "but that real estate deal you set up for me in Florida is so tough to resist. . . ."

Among eight tapes identified as "1977 Team," I found one with my name on it. I put it on and heard myself thanking George for the Cy Young bonus. A few seconds later I heard the door close and then—and then he started laughing. He mumbled, I guess to himself, "Just wait'll he finds out I got him for $35,000 and I'm signing Goose Gossage to a six-year, $2.75 million contract." Then he laughed again, loudly.

There were about 200 tapes in all. On some of them I couldn't figure out exactly who he was talking to. On one tape, for example, he was saying, "Sure we can agree on what we're going to pay free agents. It's just good business. Besides, what are they going to do, take us to court?"

Several tapes sounded like repeats, only the people he was talking to were different. "Trust me, Yogi, no matter what happens, you're my manager this year. . . ." "Believe me, Bob, I wouldn't think of making a managerial change this year. . . ." "You're it, Billy, for better or worse. . . ." ". . . it, Billy, for better or worse. And this time I mean it. . . ." ". . . Billy, for better or worse. And this time, I really mean it. . . ."

There were several tapes of conversations with politicians, most of them just the usual discussions about contributions and elections. But there was one tape on which I heard him say, "I guarantee it, Ed, I'd never even consider moving the Yankees to the Meadowlands. The New Jersey Yankees? Come on. The Yankees belong in Yankee Stadium, and as long as I'm the boss that's where they're going to stay. Ed, you know you can trust me. . . ."

The entire history of George Steinbrenner's Yankees in a drawer. It was all right there, all the managers and pitching coaches and executives. Pitching coaches. Jeez, hiring pitching coaches filled nine complete tapes.

The quality of the more recent tapes was much better than the tapes made in the seventies. I think the one that surprised me the most was a conversation between The Boss and Dave Winfield. ". . . we'll own this town. They'll change the name to Winfieldville," I could hear George saying, "and you know I'd put up a plaque for you in Monument Park right now if I could. But let me ask you a question. Why do you think people go to hockey games?"

"Hockey games?" Winfield said.

I sat there wondering what I was going to do with these tapes. Release them to the writers? Send them to the Hall of Fame? Copy them and sell them to the public? It was just too much to think about. These tapes, I realized, belonged to history—and to me. So I opened my briefcase and dropped them in. Then I left for the day.

OCTOBER 29 ★

I decided to ignore "The Stanley Curse" and hire the original Chicken today. Fred Stanley played for thirteen seasons in the big leagues. Well, maybe it would be more accurate to say that Fred Stanley didn't play for thirteen seasons in the big leagues. Chicken, as we called him, was a utility infielder, meaning that his job was to sit on the bench and be ready to play when a regular got hurt. Chicken followed Stick to the Yankees and did a great job. Few players were better at sitting on the bench looking ready to play than he was.

Fortunately, when a utility infielder is forced to play, nobody really expects very much from him, and the Chicken more than lived up to expectations. But he was a great person to have on the team. In fact, his real contributions were made off the field. He kept people awake on the bench; he was one of the best bench jockeys in baseball, and he was an excellent sign stealer. He just kept the whole team loose.

Chicken studied the game, and he knew how it was supposed to be played. My wife, Mary, and I became close friends with Fred and his wife, Mrs. Chicken. The only problem was "The Stanley Curse." Whenever the Stanleys made the plans, something went wrong. Every time. If they made the reservations at a restaurant, either our reservations were lost or the restaurant burned down. If we were going to the theater, the star got sick. If we were driving somewhere, the car broke down. They were great about it, just sort of accepting it, and whenever something happened they'd say, "Well, it's just the curse again."

The curse never extended to the field, though. I mean, the man played as many years in the big leagues as Joe DiMaggio, and he had a lifetime batting average of .216. He must have been doing something right.

After Chicken retired as a player he had worked as a front office executive for several teams. I knew I needed a knowledgeable baseball man to run the team while I took care of the business, someone I trusted. I offered him the job.

He didn't want to take it. "C'mon, Spark, I know you. You're gonna want to run the whole show by yourself."

" 'Member what we used to say when we were playing, Chicken?" I said. "How if we ran the team we'd do things differently? Well, this is our chance. We can run the team. Take the job. You'll make all the baseball decisions. I'll only make suggestions once in a while. I'm not The Boss, you know."

Chicken finally agreed to take the job. I had my general manager. "It'll take me a few days to pack up the car and drive to New York," he said. "I should be there in four or five days."

Later that afternoon traveling secretary Bill Emslie handed in his resignation. When I had taken control of the corporation, I had made it clear to everybody on The Boss's staff that they were welcome to stay. I might have brought my own staff in with me, but I didn't have a staff. I have a wife who isn't a very good typist, and three sons.

A few members of the front office staff had retired, but just about everybody else had decided to stay. I knew how important it was to have a good staff, and I hoped that I could gain their loyalty. I knew that that would take time and I knew that I couldn't buy their loyalty. But I didn't have too much time, so I decided to do the next best thing; I decided to rent it. The first thing I did was give everybody a small raise.

I was sorry to lose Emslie. Bill had been a highly rated minor-league umpire who had refused to accept a promotion to the big leagues during the umpires' strike. Some less qualified minor leaguers did come up, and part of the strike settlement allowed many of them to stay in the majors. So Emslie and several other qualified minor-league umpires never got their shot. The Boss had hired him a few years later to be traveling secretary, even though he had no experience. Bill had done an excellent job—during his four years on the job the Yankees had never gone to the wrong city—and now he'd been offered a job as director of minor league operations by the Red Sox.

The Boss has been criticized for a lot of things, but I don't think he ever got credit for his ability to recognize good executive talent. The first time he saw Gene Michael playing shortstop, for example, he knew he really belonged in the front office. A lot of people in baseball owe their careers to him. He was the first person to hire them. Of course, he was also the first person to fire them. I heard that he used to tell people, as he fired them, "Think of it as an opportunity to move up to a better position." Only The Boss could make getting fired seem like a promotion.

So I needed a new traveling secretary. I had no idea where to get one. It's not a job people go to college to learn. The traveling secretary makes all of the team's travel arrangements, assigns hotel rooms on the road, hands out the meal money, and distributes the four free tickets each player gets for every game. But probably the most important part of the job is being able to take abuse. Whenever anything goes wrong, it's the traveling secretary who gets blamed. The plane is late, a hotel room isn't ready, the food is cold, war in the Mideast, whatever it is, it's always the traveling secretary's fault.

Players don't realize how spoiled they are. I know I certainly didn't when I was a player. I thought everybody just left their suitcases in front of their lockers and somehow they arrived in the next city. Baseball players don't even have to carry their own tickets. I remember, after I retired, running into Willie Stargell at an airport. Neither one of us had ever had to read an airplane ticket, so we stood there trying to figure out what all the numbers meant.

Finally my stationary-secretary, Annie, suggested we put an ad in *The Sporting News.* That's what we did.

NOVEMBER 8 ★

Chicken called this afternoon to report that the garage had finally gotten the part for his car and he'd be in New York in three days. I hope so; I need him. Running a major-league corporation is tough.

New contracts have to be mailed out to our players by the end of the month, and I can't even figure out what everybody's status is. I've had dozens of inquiries from other GMs about players who might be on the trading block. And the annual winter meetings begin in Maui, Hawaii, next month and I haven't even had time to buy a new bathing suit.

Yesterday was the first opportunity I've had to sit down with our crack director of player personnel, Dick Woodley, and go over the roster. I've got to start making decisions. . . . I've got to be ready to help Chicken make the decisions when he gets here, about what we have, what we need, and how we're going to proceed.

There are a lot of theories about the best way to build a baseball team. Steinbrenner was a football man, believing in a big squad with endless substitutes ready to come off the bench and make the big play. The Mets' Frank Cashen is a family man; he believes in building from the farm system. The Orioles' Herb Deutsch subscribes to the circus theory, believing that as long as you continually bring in new attractions the fans will come to the ballpark, so he signs at least one big free agent every winter. George Hicker of the A's is an astrology man, building his team on the star system. I guess I'd classify myself as a military man: I see the infield as the infantry, the first line of defense, a light-hitting probing force. The outfield is where you put the heavy artillery, the relentless power that continually bombards the opposition. The designated hitters and the bench are the air power that appear suddenly, destroy the opposition with a big bomb, then disappear. But the key to victory is the pitching staff, the supply lines. Their job is to make sure that we have enough arms to sustain the battle until our superior firepower can make the difference. Every baseball team, like every army, that has gone into battle without sufficient arms has been defeated.

Actually, Woodley convinced me that we're in pretty good shape, much better than I thought when I bought the team. It's amazing how different things look from the inside. We're set at catcher with Bob Geren and Don Slaught. Geren's average fell more than 100 points last year, but Woodley says they've isolated a flaw in his swing and corrected it. Over the last game of the season he hit .500, so we feel confident he can regain the punch he showed his first seasons.

Don Mattingly is still the best first baseman in baseball, although his bad back slows him down occasionally. The big problem is that next year is his option year and his agent wants to start negotiations for a multiyear deal now. I read in the papers that he was going to ask for a three-year deal at $3.99 million a year. I don't know Mattingly that well, but I've heard he's one of the nicest guys in the game, and I really believe that he'll understand why we can't give him that kind of money, and accept less. Left-handed DH "Rosey" Rogers can fill in at first base in an emergency, but he's awfully slow and I'd like to find a more reliable backup there.

Steve Sax is set at second base, and Alvaro Espinoza is the shortstop. The backup middle infielder is probably going to be 22-year-old Raoul Rojas. Rojas, the first graduate of the "High School for Performing Shortstops"—the Yankee Academy that The Boss set up in San Pedro de Macoris, Dominican Republic—to reach the majors, is the best young shortstop I've seen come along since Ozzie Guillen. He's got great range and good hands, and turns the double play very well; at bat he's got good power from both sides of the plate, and outstanding speed, and all the scouting reports say he'll eventually hit for a decent average. We just have to work on his bunting. Having Saxy and Espinoza gives us the luxury of bringing him along slowly.

There are a lot of candidates for third base. Hensley "Bam Bam" Meulens hit .268 with 18 home runs at Columbus, and he'll get a chance to win the job in spring training. Randy Velarde and the veteran Keith Reich, whom The Boss picked up from the Phillies in September, are both capable, but neither one of them has hit enough to win the everyday job.

Felipe Suarez is going to be the best left fielder in the American League. Getting him for Phelps and Polonia was probably the best deal The Boss ever made. He hit .285 last season, only his second full season in the big leagues, with 21 home runs. Most important, he still has four years before he can become a free agent, and two years left on his contract.

Roberto Kelly is the center fielder. His batting average fell a little last year, to .308, but he's getting stronger and all the reports predict he'll hit between 15 and 20 home runs when he adds a little more weight.

Jesse Barfield is the right fielder, at least for now, but Joe Verola's going to be a very good player. If we're going to commit ourselves to promoting talent from within our farm system rather than trading it away, we've got to give young players like Joe V a chance to play. Barfield hits home runs and is still the best defensive right fielder in the American League, but he strikes out too often.

Dave Winfield did a great job as the right-handed DH and fourth outfielder, but the question is, how much longer can we depend on him? His contract expired at the end of the season and we have to decide if we're going to pick up his option. At $1.65 million plus at-bat bonuses he's very expensive for a part-time player. Chicken is going to have to make a tough decision.

I firmly believe in the old saying: You can never be too rich, too thin, or have too much pitching. And the one thing I know we don't have is too much pitching. Greg Cadaret's 14 wins led the staff last year, but he needs to come up with another pitch to complement his fastball. I'm going to talk to him about mixing in an occasional slider just to keep the hitters honest.

Andy Hawkins is going to win his 12 to 15 games like he does every season. I think Eric Plunk is finally ready for a big year, now that he's throwing a slider to set up his heater. And Chuck Cary just needs to establish that the inside of the plate belongs to him to become a consistent winner. The fifth spot in the starting rotation is up for grabs. I think it'll be either Clay Parker or Hanko Tsumi, and the one who doesn't win the spot'll become the long reliever. Tsumi, whom The Boss got from the Hiroshima Toyo Carp for Dave Righetti in baseball's first international trade, is going to be a good one. He didn't pitch very well last season, but I've heard he had a tough time adjusting to baseball in the United States. I really believe if he can come up with a breaking pitch, maybe a slider, to go along with his great curveball, he can be a big winner in the big leagues.

The key man in the bullpen is burly right-hander Tums Taft, who finally established himself as the stopper last season. I guess by now everybody knows Taft's incredible story. After being released by the Giants two years ago he signed with the Mexico City Reds in the Mexican League. While he was down there he took up bullfighting, which, he claims, helped him overcome his lack of confidence and greatly increased his concentration. "After looking an angry bull in the nostrils," he said, "facing Jose Canseco with the bases loaded just didn't seem so terrifying." Maybe, but a lot of people think the weight he lost running away from the bulls was a more important factor. If Taft can keep his weight down, he should have another good year.

Frank Biondo is as good a setup man as there is in the American League East. He's big and strong. He throws a great slow change and went to the Instructional League to learn the slurper from Billy Connors. The slurper is thrown like a slerve, but breaks like a knuckleslider. A good slurper is just about impossible to hit, although it supposedly puts tremendous strain on the pitcher's shoulder.

I still think Bob Forsch can be valuable as a spot starter, or long reliever. I know what I've said about building with young players, but Forsch really is a young forty-four. There was a time in baseball when anyone over thirty was considered on the downhill side of his career, but that's changed. Players actually used to lie about their age, like movie stars. Then the over-the-hill age became thirty-five; when Warren Spahn was thirty-nine he was considered ancient. Then forty meant the absolute end of a career. But recently Graig Nettles played until he was forty-five and Darrell Evans hit 25 home runs when he was forty-four. And I'm told there were a few players in the Florida Senior League who looked like they could still play. I think we've begun to appreciate the importance of experience. So I prefer to think of Forsch as overflowing with experience rather than as forty-four years old.

Wily veteran Big John Nicholson will probably be our situation left-hander, coming out of the bullpen to face left-handed hitters in game-deciding situations. He appeared in 48 games last year, pitching a total of 18 ⅓ innings, and compiled a good 2.95 earned run average. As long as he doesn't have to face right-handers he's very valuable in relief.

There are several kids who pitched for Columbus who might make the staff. In addition, several attractive free agents will be coming on the market at the ESPN Major League Baseball Free Agent Auction at the winter meetings. I know I told reporters we'd be staying out of the free-agent market forever, but that was almost three weeks ago. I've come to understand that the key to establishing stability is being flexible enough to build a team we can be stable with. So we're going to be flexibly stable.

Basically, that's what the roster is going to look like this season. I really believe that with just a few changes we'll be able to compete from the opening bell. But as I've learned over a lot of seasons, the only thing you can be sure of in baseball is that you never know. A lot of things can change between today and Opening Day, and probably will. You just never know when some big kid with a blazing fastball, the heart of a lion, and a big-league dream will come out of a small American town like Reynoldsville, Pennsylvania, and force you to change your plans. At least, as Woodley says, you're always hoping you never know.

Besides, Chicken and the manager will have to make the final decisions. It'll be their team, not mine. I'm not The Boss. I'm just the boss.

NOVEMBER 10 ★

Since I took over the team everybody I've met tells me how much they love the Yankees, then offers suggestions how I should change things. I've told them all the same thing, I want to go slow. I don't want to make changes just for the sake of making changes. I'm not interested in cosmetic changes; if I'm going to change things, I'll change them for a good reason. Today, for example, I had a call from Clifford Campion of the New Jersey Sports Development Corporation. He runs the Meadowlands Complex where the football Giants and Jets, the basketball Nets, the hockey Devils, and Bruce Springsteen play. The purpose of the call, he explained, was to introduce himself, but then he asked me if I would at least consider thinking about discussing the possibility of moving the Yankees from the Bronx to the Meadowlands. Campion's a lawyer.

I told him I wouldn't even take the time to consider thinking about discussing that possibility. "The Yankees belong in Yankee Stadium, in the Bronx, New York," I said proudly. The New Jersey Yankees? "I don't think I can think about that."

"That's fine," he said politely. "At least you're not ruling it out. I'll get back to you on that with an outline of what might later be solidified into a working document as the basis of an agreement."

"Whatever you said," I said.

Probably the biggest surprise I've had is how many people want to change the Yankee uniform. Of course, most of them are designers. The Yankees' home uniform, white with thin blue pinstripes, with the cursive "NY" over the left breast, might be the best known uniform, except for the U.S. Army, in the country. Even the visiting uniform, gray with a blue "New York" across the chest, is a classic in its simple design. Why would anyone want to change it? Even The Boss didn't change it when he bought the team.

He did consider it, though. I remember in 1973 he showed us several variations of the road uniform. The most ridiculous was black, with white pinstripes. Black uniforms? Who'd he think we were, Al Davis's All-California Raiders? That was by far the ugliest uni I've ever seen, even uglier than the red uniforms the Cleveland Indians wore one Fourth of July, and even uglier than the black bermuda shorts Bill

Veeck made the White Sox wear one day. At least George had the good sense to leave the uniform alone.

I happen to be a firm believer in tradition. So much so that I'd like to start some new ones. And there are a few small changes that I might make in the uniform. For example, I'll probably put the players' names on the backs of their uniforms. And then I'd like to set up some sort of award system. I've always thought it would be a good idea to give baseball players some sort of award decal to wear on their uniforms, the kind of thing that football players stick on their helmets to show how many unassisted tackles they've made, or fighter pilots paint on the side of their aircraft to indicate how many enemy planes they've shot down.

I don't know what my baseball award should look like. Maybe I'd even have a different symbol for each achievement. Maybe a bat for every game-winning RBI or every 20 RBIs, while pitchers would earn a baseball for every win or save. I don't know where to put them yet—maybe on the hat or the shoulder, or even on the back of the uni. I know the clubhouse men wouldn't like it, because they would have to sew them on, but I think the fans might appreciate the color it would add to the otherwise drab white and blue uniform.

Of course Chicken'll make that decision when he gets here.

NOVEMBER 16 ★

I met with an agent for the first time in my official capacity today. Joe Verola's agent, David Braun, came in for an initial discussion of Joe V's new contract. I think that both of us knew no real negotiating was going to take place, but it was important that we meet each other. I wanted to know how much he was going to ask for, so I could offer him less; he wanted to know what I intended to offer, so he could ask for more. In the last few years contract negotiations have become the real game in baseball.

Supposedly, most owners feel that the main thing agents have done is make them nostalgic for the days before there were agents, but I have nothing against them. Just because I, personally, didn't need one; just because I always believed I was mature, intelligent, and determined enough to negotiate my own contract; just because I always knew I had my own best interests at heart, I didn't see any reason why other players shouldn't give away their money to people who had never played the game.

I understood that agents are a necessary evil. Like mosquitoes. Although, honestly, I never have understood why mosquitoes are necessary. But most agents are much smarter than mosquitoes. Besides, it was the owners who made agents necessary by limiting players to two choices—sign the contract they were offering or get a job as a mold runner at the Jackson China Company. Calvin Griffith, when he owned the Minnesota Twins, once told a player that if he didn't sign the contract he was offered, Calvin would be glad to get him a job at the local General Motors plant. One time the great Philly pitcher Bobby Ramsdell tore up the contact he had been offered, put the pieces in an envelope, and sent it back to the general manager. A few days later he got the same contract back, Scotch-taped together.

Negotiations weren't really fair. On one side of the desk was the well-educated general manager, an experienced businessman who held all the power, and who negotiated thirty-five to forty contracts each year; on the other side was the player, who may have had a high school education and who negotiated one contract every season.

Things have certainly changed. I always liked to negotiate by myself, face to face. Today it takes at least six people to negotiate a contract: the general manager, lawyer, and accountant for the club; the agent, accountant, and lawyer for the player—and that's when the player doesn't go to arbitration. Based on my experiences, I intend to pay my players what they're worth. And I don't mean, like Branch Rickey once told Ralph Kiner, "I know you hit 40 home runs, but we finished last, and we could have done that without you."

I was a tough negotiator during my playing career. I did sign my first contract with the Baltimore Orioles for nothing, but that was the best offer I got. After that, I held out several times. In fact, in 1974, I almost became baseball's first free agent. I played the entire season without a contract and had every intention of challenging the reserve clause that allowed clubs to renew a player's contract year after year. But on the final day of the season The Boss gave me what I had been demanding, $90,000 in salary and a $10,000 signing bonus. I structured it that way because I wanted to be paid $100,000, but I was afraid to ask for it because no team believed a short reliever was worth that kind of money. A lot of players were disappointed when I signed because I was going to be a test case—we were finally going to test the legality of the reserve clause. But George gave me what I'd been asking for, so I felt I had to do the honorable thing, and sign. I'd won. I'd held my position and I'd beaten The Boss.

The next year Andy Messersmith became a free agent and Steinbrenner signed him for $1.25 million. At least I'd won on principle. Which is sort of like a prizefighter winning a moral victory.

George rarely negotiated with players himself. He usually let his top aides, Al Rosen, Gabe Paul, or Lee MacPhail, negotiate contracts. I liked negotiating with George, because he was tough and smart and loved to win as much as I do. I think between George and Al and Lee and Gabe and Brad Corbett in Texas I probably heard every conceivable argument about why I should be paid less than I felt I deserved; basically they all could be summed up this way—it was for my own good.

When I was a young player they didn't want to pay me too much because I hadn't proven myself over a long period of time. After I had proven myself over a long period of time they didn't want to pay me because I was older and more vulnerable to injury. If I had had a good year they claimed they'd already paid me for what I'd done. If I had had a bad year they didn't want to pay me, because I'd been overpaid the year before. One season, after I'd had a great first half and a mediocre second half, Gabe Paul told me he couldn't give me the raise I wanted because my year had been a doughnut—it had a hole in the middle. "Come back after you've had a jelly doughnut," he told me, "and then I can give you what you want."

After another season, when Rosen refused to give me what I felt I'd earned, I told him I wanted to be traded. He told me that he'd tried to trade me, but that no other clubs were interested. I asked permission to make my own deal and he agreed, but added, "But if you find somebody who wants you, call us first so we can make a deal."

So I never needed an agent to tell me what I was worth. I had a wife.

But I was sympathetic to agents. I'd had too many friends of mine forced to sign contracts for much less than they should have been paid to feel any other way. I also knew I had something in common with the good agents. Both of us wanted to make sure my players, their clients, were paid what they were worth. First, I would have to tell the agents what I thought their clients were worth; then the agents would tell me what they thought my players were worth, and we would fight it out until I won.

Joe V's agent, David Braun, had established a reputation as a skilled negotiator who capably represented the interests of his clients. He represented Jose Canseco in the deal with Oakland that gave him partial ownership in the team. Joe Verola had had a good rookie year, hitting .278 with 8 home runs, 32 RBIs, and 15 stolen bases, in only 180 at-bats. He'd been paid a fair $90,000 in his first season. I figured we'd double that for his sophomore year. There were several reasons for that: It was only his second year; I didn't think it would be good for him to be paid too much money when he was so young; he couldn't demand arbitration; and finally, we only had two more years to stick it to him.

I poured Braun a cup of coffee and put it down in front of him. Then I settled comfortably into my own chair. "No, David," I said firmly, "I'm afraid not. That's ridiculous. It's completely out of the question. We can't afford that—it would completely disrupt our payroll. Do you know how many years I was in the big leagues before I earned that kind of money? I'm sorry, we just can't do it. Let him have another good season and then we'll see. He's been paid well for that season."

Braun's mouth fell open. When I'd finished he pointed out, "But I haven't said anything yet."

"I know," I agreed, "I'm just warming up. This is the first time I've ever done this."

"You really are crazy," he said, laughing.

I knew I had him then. That was an old trick George Steinbrenner had taught me. Once they think you're crazy you can get away with any kind of behavior. Then if you do something really crazy, that's just keeping in character. "Don't try to flatter me," I said sharply, "it won't work. I don't flatter easily. Of course, that's no reason you shouldn't keep trying."

"Look, Sparky," he said. "We understand that Joe's still a very young player. We just want to ensure that he receives fair compensation for what he's accomplished."

"I certainly agree with that," I agreed, "but I think it's important to remember that he's only played one full season. This second year is the key year. I think it's very important that we don't make him too comfortable. I've seen a lot of young players ruined because they let money go to their head."

"I can agree with that," Braun said. "We just want to make sure he's paid on a comparative basis with the other right fielders in the league."

"Oh, absolutely, but I know I don't have to point out to you that last year was a particularly bad year for right fielders in the top half of the Eastern Division."

We continued our discussion, both of us carefully saying nothing, for another hour. Then Braun left, both of us feeling we had accomplished what we had intended to do. Nothing. I had successfully not negotiated my first contract.

NOVEMBER 26 ★

The floodwaters are beginning to recede, Chicken reports, and the National Guard believes the roads will be passable in no more than a day. And a day after that, he told me, "I'll be there like clockwork. Just keep my desk warm."

We received over two thousand replies to our ad in *The Sporting News* for a traveling secretary. They came from people in every profession: stationary-secretaries, a doctor, numerous lawyers, several convicts due to be released on parole, a man with a split personality who said they both wanted to take the job, and many retired people. A lot of applicants offered to work for no salary. The thing that amazed me was how many people were willing to change their lives completely for an opportunity to work in professional baseball. As a player I know I sometimes took the passion people feel for the game for granted. There were times when I felt that being a major leaguer was just a tough job, and I forgot how many people would have given anything to trade places with me for just one day. These letters reminded me of that.

Naturally, we need to hire someone qualified to be the traveling secretary, and pay him a fair salary. Naturally. We've offered the job to a computer expert from Columbia, South Carolina, named Duke Schneider. Schneider did that study for the Padres last season that pointed out the impact of being on base on pitchers. According to that study, pitchers who were on base for a minimum of two batters gave up .3 runs more than usual in the inning that followed. The Padres had a lot of success last year walking the pitcher intentionally when he led off an inning, until the Braves finally showed the league how to counter that by allowing the pitcher to be picked off.

Schneider's letter of application outlined a very complex plan that included a computer study he had done of airline schedules. He believes he can save us a substantial amount of money with creative scheduling of our flights on road trips. He claims he can save us so much money on travel expenses that we would actually make a profit by hiring him. Best job application I've ever seen.

DECEMBER 6 ★

Today was the first day of the annual winter meetings. Chicken is scheduled to arrive in Hawaii this afternoon. They finally decided his car had sustained too much water damage to be repaired, so he rented one and drove to the airport for a connecting flight.

Baseball's winter meeting is much more fun than I thought it would be. Who knew, for example, that Cincinnati owner Marge Schott had such great legs? This meeting is baseball's convention; it's the time that contacts are made, players are moved, jobs are obtained, and tans are gotten. This afternoon I attended my first clubowners' meeting. When I was a player, we used to say that this was where all the owners got together behind locked doors to figure out how they were going to screw the players. So naturally, I was pretty excited about seeing what really took place.

Precisely at 12:30 the big wooden doors of the conference room were closed and locked and Seattle Mariners president George Zelma gaveled the meeting to order. "It's a real pleasure to see all of these familiar faces," he said, "and to welcome our new partner." He nodded toward me. "As you all know, we meet here once again to figure out how best to screw the players. . . ."

Everybody started cheering. People stood up and started slapping other people on the back. I couldn't believe it. It was exactly as we . . . as the players had imagined. When the meeting continued I sat there in absolute silence, staring straight ahead, listening to a series of proposals. And to my surprise, some of the suggestions really did make sense.

Milwaukee Brewers owner Bud Selig was chairman of the Compensation Committee. "I have no fear in stating unequivocally that the greatest problem we are facing today is spiraling compensation," he began. Several other owners banged their fists on the conference table in agreement. "And after extensive research it has become apparent that the primary cause of the constantly increasing salaries we are paying is the reckless use of statistics. We've all seen it. The players absolutely insist on using statistics to get more and more money from us. It's time we begin using those same statistics ourselves." His committee had agreed, he explained, that steps should be taken to keep batting averages down, as well as to decrease the number of wins and saves compiled by pitchers. Selig's first recommendation was that baseball crack down "hard," he said, "on lenient official scorers. Let's make sure a hit is a hit. It's important to remember that errors work for us in two ways. They take points off the hitter's batting average while simultaneously lowering the defensive player's fielding average, two statistics that we can put to positive use during contract negotiations and mandatory arbitration."

After a long, technical discussion it was unanimously agreed that the Office of the Commissioner would hire an official scorer in each major-league city, to be paid $250 per game. "For years," the commissioner's announcement would read, "scoring decisions favoring hometown players have prevented objective comparisons of statistical accomplishments. With this decision, we are attempting to guarantee a uniform application of the often complex scoring rules, as a service to the loyal baseball fans of America." In reality, the official scorer would be encouraged to credit errors whenever possible. Scorers allowing too many hits would not have their contracts renewed.

Atlanta Braves owner Ted Turner was assigned to inform the commissioner of his decision.

"Next," Selig continued, "pitchers. I suspect everyone here is just as fed up as I am with the fact that we are simply giving away victories, which continues to plague us during negotiations. Currently, all a starting pitcher has to do is complete five innings to receive credit for a win. Now, I have a study here"—he took copies of a report out of his briefcase and distributed them around the table—"that shows, quite graphically, the drastic change that would result if we changed that rule to six innings." I looked at the chart. A descending line dramatically illustrated how the number of victories awarded to starting pitchers decreased at each ⅓ of an inning. Raising the minimum number of innings a pitcher must complete in order to receive credit for a win to six would cause a 12 percent decrease in the number of victories compiled by starting pitchers. That would have a significant impact in contract discussions. Well, after spending my entire career saving the hides of starting pitchers who managed to struggle through five innings, then seeing them receive most of the credit, this did not seem like an unfair proposal to me. Who decided that five innings was enough to gain credit for a victory? Where was it written in stone?

"We're also working on modifications of the save rule for relief pitchers," Selig added.

Now, let's not get carried away.

"The salaries of relief pitchers have risen faster than those of any position player," Selig continued, "and we find that by changing the current, complicated system for awarding saves to a much simpler rule—the relief pitcher must face the potential tying or winning run—we can immediately decrease the number of saves awarded by almost 28 percent. We estimate that this will impact upon salary . . ." He suddenly looked at me and stopped. "Of course, Sparky, you might not agree with this. . . ."

The room was absolutely silent. Everyone was looking directly at me to see what my reaction would be. Was I still a player, or was I ready to understand the economic realities of the game? This was the corporate version of facing George Brett with the bases loaded, two out, in the bottom of the ninth inning. I took a deep breath, then said, "Well, I'd like to know exactly what that would translate into in terms of financial benefits."

Everybody breathed. A few people laughed nervously. Once again, the room was filled with noisy chatter. Margie Schott winked at me.

Selig summed up his presentation by reminding clubowners that they could save hundreds of thousands of dollars per club each season in salaries if the scoring rules were modified, reducing the number of .300 hitters, 20-game winners, and relievers with 30 or more saves, while the game itself would not be affected at all.

When he finished, we gave him a standing ovation.

The Mets' Nelson Doubleday, chairman of the Baseball Committee, stood and began the next report. "This past season," he began—I'd never known he was so tall—"we increased the tension in the winding around the core of the baseball two sprockets. The result was an 8 percent increase in the number of home runs, which is identical to the increase during the 1985 season. However, the 1985 increase coincided with an 11 percent increase in attendance, which may be at least partially attributable to the rise in power output. This past season, though, attendance increased only 3.2 percent. So it's the recommendation of the Baseball Committee, in conjunction with Bud's salary report, that for the coming season we decrease the tension in the baseball"—he paused and took a deep breath—". . . five sprockets."

"My God!" Jesse Tarlov, representing the *Chicago Tribune,* owner of the Cubs, blurted out, "five sprockets!"

"Do we dare?" Charlie Bronfman of the Expos wondered aloud. "That's . . . that's quite a change."

"Five sprockets," Doubleday repeated firmly. "This will lead to an estimated 11 percent decline in home runs this coming season, without adversely affecting attendance."

There was a lot of discussion about the proposal, most of it debating the relationship between offense and attendance, but eventually it was decided that the baseball would be four sprockets less lively in the coming season.

Once again, I sat in complete shock. For years I'd heard the rumors that the owners made the baseball livelier to increase scoring, or deader to cut down on scoring, but there had been no real proof. It seemed like *Sports Illustrated* ran a boring story about laboratory testing of baseballs every season, but no one paid any attention. As a pitcher, I knew that every baseball felt different, and I believed I could feel the difference in the tension of the cover or the height of the strings from year to year. But I was so naive. So naive. When I asked about it I was told that it had to do with new sewing machines being installed in the factory in Haiti, or a drug that had been given to cows to make their hides softer, or that another shift of seamstresses had been added to the production line and their fingers weren't tough enough. And I believed that. I believed it. What a fool I'd been.

I knew I could expose the truth with one phone call to a reporter. But what good would it do? The other owners would simply deny that the discussion ever took place. The minutes of the meeting, I suspected, wouldn't mention it. And I would instantly become an outcast among owners, unable to obtain waivers on a player, left out of trade discussions. I realized I owed it to loyal Yankee fans to say nothing.

Los Angeles Dodgers owner Peter O'Malley, chairman of the Expansion Committee, made the next presentation. "And speaking of expansion," he said, as he stood up, "I see that some of us have added a few inches since last year." Several owners chuckled good-naturedly. The National League is committed to expansion, O'Malley said; the only questions to be answered are which two cities will be invited to join the league and when expansion will take place. Applications had been received from fifteen cities, he reported. The leading contenders were Tampa–St. Petersburg, with a brand new domed stadium located right off the interstate; Mexico City, with its huge baseball-loving population and growing television market; Washington, D.C., with its small local population and TV market but large congressional lobby; Buffalo, New York; Denver, Colorado; Honolulu, Hawaii, with its beautiful women; Charlotte, North Carolina; the Meadowlands area in New Jersey; Phoenix, Arizona; Vancouver, Canada; Louisville, Kentucky; and Great Plains, South Dakota, with its O'Malley cousin as mayor.

"Each applicant has paid a $25,000 good-faith fee and filed a detailed report," O'Malley explained. "Copies of these reports are available to anyone interested. We asked them to supply things like the most recent population figures for a radius of 50, 100, and 200 miles from the site of the ballpark, complete ballpark specifications—including any plans to construct a new stadium or add to the existing facility—the television-rights situation in the local market, potential competition for leisure-time dollars, environmental impact statements focusing on the potential for damage being caused by excess traffic or crowd congestion, a complete study of local tourist activity, an analysis of the local road system and plans for any improvements, a complete airline and airport study, the anticipated level of support from local merchants, an analysis of start-up costs in the immediate area, any additional inducements, benefits, or reasons we should award that city a National League franchise, and a certified check for the $25,000.

"After an extremely detailed review of all the applications, we've narrowed it down to four cities. These are Tampa–St. Pete, Mexico City, Charlotte, and Buffalo. . . ."

"And, uh, what was the primary criterion the committee used to make these selections?" Orioles owner David Burnett asked.

"The usual," O'Malley replied. "These were the four left after the bidding was done. So far they've agreed to pay each one of us three and a half mil."

O'Malley concluded his report by announcing that negotiations were continuing with those four cities, and that the deadline for filing additional applications had been extended another six months. At the end of that time, he said, the new final deadline for applications would be set.

William "Will" Edgerton, representing Anheuser-Busch, owner of the St. Louis Cardinals and chairman of the Attendance Committee, spoke next. "As each of you is well aware," he said in a crisp, lawyerly voice, "for several years now baseball has faced a serious problem concerning alcohol consumption in our ballparks. Unfortunately, that problem has gotten worse. I'm afraid I must report that for the fourth consecutive year beer sales in stadiums have declined. The result is a substantial loss of revenue."

There was a low murmur around the table. Somebody said, "I need a drink," and several other owners laughed nervously.

"The study we commissioned last year suggested four or five areas in which improvements might be made. These include adding more salt to lower-priced items like peanuts, popcorn, and hot dogs; decreasing the size of the container; showing additional suggestive advertising on ballpark scoreboard screens; and considering the introduction of near beer with a 3.2 percent alcohol content, meaning fans can drink more. My committee believes we should immediately commission a study to examine the recommendations of this prior study before making any decisions.

"Also, as you all know, alcohol and beer consumption at ballparks continues to cause additional problems. A few years ago, you remember we had problems with people dropping beer on the heads of people sitting below them. Fortunately, we were able to solve that problem with our public relations campaign that proved beer was good for the hair. The problem now is that people are dropping beer on the ground. In fact, we have a quite detailed study proving that the more they consume, the more they spill on the ground. This results in very sticky footing, which is of serious concern to our liability insurers.

"There is a new cleaning compound on the market. It's called New

Brew Cheer. It not only eliminates the sticky footing, but replaces the odor of stale beer with the heady aroma of fresh beer."

"Excuse me," Burnett interrupted, "but let's be honest. Is this Brew Cheer really necessary?"

"Absolutely," Edgerton replied. "It will enable us to announce to the reporters waiting outside this room that Major League Baseball has renewed our efforts to clean up problems created by alcohol and beer consumption in our ballparks."

The meeting continued for another two hours. I sat there without saying one word. I was a raw rookie in this league, and they were throwing curveballs like I'd never seen before. This was a side of baseball I'd never seen before: the inside. For example, the owners agreed to reduce the number of grandstand seats by redesignating them reserved seats, for which they could charge an additional $1.25 per seat. And at the recommendation of the Merchandise Committee, seven teams agreed to make slight modifications to their uniforms and team logos, "[T]o present a more consistent image as baseball moves into the twenty-first century"—as well as greatly increase revenues from replica jerseys and hats by making everything in existence outdated. The Licensing Committee strongly urged teams to consider creation of mascots, pointing out that sales of mascot dolls represented a potential profit center that had never been fully exploited. The Television Committee announced that NBC had made it clear that it would not permit interleague play, although they reserved the right to change that decision if ratings started falling. The Public Relations Committee recommended that female umpire Trish Todd immediately be signed to a major-league contract, pointing out studies that showed an immediate increase in female attendance at pro basketball after the NBA had signed two female officials.

The meeting might have continued into the night, but we had to stop at 5 o'clock to allow everyone to get ready for the free agent auction. George Zelman asked everyone to stand, "For a moment of silence in honor of our dear departed colleague, George M. Steinbrenner III." Then the meeting was adjourned.

The ESPN Major League Baseball Players Association Free Agent Auction was inspired by ESPN's success in televising the pro football and pro basketball college drafts. That cable network had gotten really good ratings for both events. They wanted to do the same thing for baseball, but because high school and college baseball players aren't as well known as college football and basketball players, there was little interest in televising baseball's amateur draft. Supposedly it was the well-known player agent Doug Newton who suggested the free-agent auction.

The auction was broadcast last year for the first time, and was a huge success. It has a very simple format: Three weeks before the winter meetings any free agent can announce his intention to participate in the show, for which he is guaranteed two first-class round-trip tickets to the site of the meetings, plus a wonderful array of prizes, including a lifetime supply of Dial Soap and Johnson Wax, an Amana Radar Range, a selection of Mary Kay Cosmetics for the woman in his life, a Relax-a-Lounger, and a chance to pick one key that might start a brand new Pontiac Firebird. He gets to keep all the prizes whether he gets bought or not.

Any active major-league free agent is eligible. The only thing he has to do is set a minimum acceptable contract price.

The show itself is a black-tie affair, hosted by Joe Garagiola, assisted by Miss Vanna White. The announcer is Don Pardo. The theme song, "Make Me the Pick of Your Life," was written and is performed by Barry Manilow. The way it works is very simple: As each player is introduced, Vanna leads him to the Grand Stand. The owners, sitting onstage in The Bleachers, then bid on any player they want to sign. All bids are binding.

This year, Coke is sponsoring a contest in conjunction with the show. Viewers at home have to try to guess which free agent is going to get the best contract. The person coming closest to the actual contract, without going over the guaranteed salary, wins $25,000.

The free agents who have agreed to participate so far have all been near the end of their careers. The big stars can afford to negotiate privately. The participants in this year's auction included Rick Cerone, Rick Dempsey, Mike Heath, Bob Tewksbury, Bill Smyth, Danny Heep, Tony Pena, Gary Carter, Larry Parrish, Jim Morrison, Ray Robinson, Chris Speier, Thad Bosley, Jim Sundberg, Goose Gossage, Hal Goldman, Mark Mackay, Jerry Reuss, Greg Minton, and Bobby Meacham.

The auditorium was completely filled as I took my seat in The Bleachers. I didn't intend to do any bidding. I just didn't think any of these players were capable of helping the team, and the one thing I didn't want to do was give Yankee fans the impression that I was going to continue the tradition of signing older players.

After Barry Manilow had finished singing the theme song, and Joe Garagiola had completed his opening monologue—"So he asked me, with a name like Garagiola, how come I never stole a base?"—Don Pardo announced the first player to be auctioned: "Our leadoff player is one of baseball's favorite catchers. A twelve-year veteran who has played in four All-Star games, one playoff, and one World Series, while winning three Gold Gloves for defensive excellence, this former Pirate, Cardinal, and Red Sox has compiled a fine .263 lifetime batting average and has become a fan favorite thanks to his winning spirit and unorthodox catching technique. . . . Ladies and gentlemen, please give a warm welcome to Toe-nee Peen-ya!"

Pena climbed the steps to the top of the Grand Stand and spoke with Joe for a few minutes. He said that he had completely recovered from his back injury and expected to have his best season ever in the big leagues next year. Joe asked him to turn around several times so we could judge his weight, then asked him to bend over and touch his toes to prove that his back no longer bothered him. "Okay, owners," Joe said, "here he is, a proven big-league catcher. And he can be yours for"—the band played some suspense music and numbers whirled on a tote board until a bell sounded—"a minimum salary of only $325,000 per year for two years. All right, who'll start the bidding?"

The bidding on Pena was much more exciting than I thought it would be. Under normal circumstances Pena probably would have received invitations from several teams to come to spring training on a look-see basis. No guarantees. But after almost five minutes of lively bidding the Chicago White Sox, urged on by the enthusiastic studio audience, offered Pena $360,000 for two years, although only the first season would be guaranteed.

After Eddie Einhorn of the White Sox announced his bid, everyone waited nervously as the huge clock on the stage ticked off the required thirty seconds. There were no more bids. At the chime, Garagiola turned to Pena and said, "Okay, Tony, you've heard the offer. The Chicago White Sox have bid $360,000 for two years, but they'll only guarantee the first one. You've got thirty seconds to either . . . accept or decline." The clock started counting down another thirty seconds as Pena thought about his decision. Some fans in the studio audience shouted suggestions, but Joe asked, in a whisper, "Please audience, don't help him." Finally, time ran out. "Okay, Tony," Joe said, "have you made your decision?"

He nodded his head. "I have," he said, "I'll take it." The audience erupted. Tony's wife ran onto the stage and hugged him. Seconds later his two kids came out and joined their parents. Then Joe spoke to the whole family, wishing them all a great season in Chicago, and finally Vanna escorted them off the stage.

The show was a lot more exciting than I would have anticipated. There were moments of real happiness, for example when the fine pinch hitter Thad Bolsey got an unexpectedly nice deal from the Reds, and moments of great sadness, particularly when no one met Jerry Reuss's salary minimum. That was tough, watching Jerry stand there as the clock ticked off the last few seconds of his life as a player. Garagiola handled what could have been a bad time very well, reminding everyone that Jerry had had a great career, that he was still eligible to sign a contract after the show, and then asking the audience to "join with me in saluting a great guy, Jerry Reuss, at what might be the conclusion of a great career. Come on, let's have a real big-league salute for him." I think he also gave him an extra case of Johnson Wax. Then Vanna led him offstage and into retirement.

I bought Jim Sundberg. I was just as surprised as everyone else about that. I still don't quite know how it happened. But everybody who was bidding seemed to be having so much fun that I decided to put in an occasional low bid just to remind Yankee fans that I was working in their behalf. I was a little nervous when I made my first bid, for Ray Robinson, and fortunately, I was quickly outbid. But I felt much more comfortable when I made my second bid, and I was even more relaxed when I made my third bid. I had been right, bidding was a lot of fun.

When Sundberg was presented he looked like he was in such good shape that I couldn't help bidding. I knew we didn't need another catcher, not with Geren and Slaught, but he was just too good a buy at $240,000 for one season. So when he opened at that price I bid for him. So did several other teams. Haywood Sullivan raised the bidding to $250,000. I figured, what's $260,000 for a catcher with Sundberg's experience? Sullivan topped me at $275,000. A lot of teams are carrying three catchers these days, and I knew that Sundberg could probably play a little outfield for the Yankees if we needed him. I bid $290,000. Sullivan bid $300,000. I couldn't let the Red Sox beat me. I bid $310,000. Sullivan, a reserve catcher his entire career and the father of a reserve catcher, probably knew reserve catchers better than anyone in the game, and he wanted Sundberg. He bid $325,000. I looked right at Sullivan—and he was staring at me. "Three thirty-five," I said clearly.

Sullivan never took his eyes off me. "Three fifty."

I could feel my adrenaline flowing. This wasn't just an isolated battle over a player, this was the Yankees against the Red Sox—just like it had been throughout my career—the Red Sox, who had traded me to the Yankees. "Three . . . sixty," I said.

Sullivan frowned and waved his hand towards me, a gesture that said clearly, take him. I'd won. Again. I smiled broadly and leaned back in my chair. Onstage Sundberg was accepting my offer and being congratulated by his family. And that was when I realized I'd just bought a reserve catcher for $360,000. Boy, this game is much tougher than I'd thought.

I bid on a few more players, but I was very careful to bid low, and Sundberg was the only player I won. Well, at least we finally had the third-string catcher I knew we might need.

And we'd beaten the Red Sox.

DECEMBER 7 ★

During a recess in the meetings this afternoon I went into the sporting-goods show to see what new products were being introduced. Improving baseball equipment was as much a part of the game as doubleheaders used to be. Every season sporting-goods manufacturers promote an entire range of new products guaranteed to raise your batting average, lower your earned run average, or make you a better defensive player.

The emphasis this season seemed to be on the application of modern technology to traditional equipment. Several manufacturers were showing spandex uniforms. Caps were being made in a wide variety of sweat-absorbing materials. One of them had a band inside that you filled with water to keep cool, and another had a solarized brim that outfielders could use instead of sunglasses. There were at least a dozen new types of spikes. Elastic bands were very popular, and besides improved wristbands, elbow bands, and headbands, manufacturers were showing knee bands to prevent turf burns caused by sliding on artificial surfaces, and even a shock-absorbing foot band that cushioned the blow if a batter fouled a ball off his instep.

I was amazed how many different things had been done to the bat. I mean, how do you improve a bat? There were bats with deep wedges cut out of the top of the barrel, bats with curved handles, computer-designed bats made with grooves cut in the handle to conform to the owner's grip, bats treated with resin that allowed the batter to see exactly where on the bat the ball had hit, and electronic training bats that measured the speed of the swing, the degree of arc on the swing, and the power generated by the combination of bat speed and weight. There was even a practice bat with an extra-wide barrel that had a large oval hole in it—if the ball went through the hole without touching the bat, the batter had swung correctly.

An entire aisle was filled with video playback systems and software packages guaranteed to improve batting, pitching, and fielding performance. There was even a software package for managers that set up hypothetical situations and, after the user had made his decision, showed the statistical results of each option.

There were all types of new products to promote safety, including an antimagnetic batting helmet that completely absorbed the force of a baseball traveling up to 100 mph, and an electronic warning track that consisted of several speakers installed in the outfield fence to warn outfielders they were coming too close by announcing, in that Japanese-English used in watches and new cars, "You coming very near. Watch out!"

But the highlight of the show was the gloves. It seemed like everything conceivable that could be done to a baseball glove had been done. There were leather gloves and plastic gloves and rubber gloves; gloves with three fingers, four fingers, five fingers, and six fingers; gloves with a solarized webbing so fielders who weren't wearing hats with solarized brims wouldn't need sunglasses—apparently prescription webbings were available—and gloves in every color of the rainbow. There was a catcher's glove with a miniature loudspeaker that was supposed to improve a pitcher's confidence by amplifying the thud of the pitch smacking into the pocket. There was a glove with a simple radar system that triggered a warning signal when two fielders were on a collision course. But the glove that interested me most was the cellular glove being introduced by Mizuno. This glove had a two-way telephone system built into it which allowed coaches in skyboxes to communicate directly with fielders in order to properly position them. As I tried on that glove, and pounded my fist into the patented "Venus Flytrap" pocket, I thought, what a shame they hadn't invented this glove when Reggie Jackson was still playing.

I played three seasons with Reggie. There were a lot of people who thought I didn't like him. That wasn't true; I didn't mind him. I didn't like the way he treated some people, but he was all right off the field. What I did mind was the fact that he was constantly getting pitchers in trouble by playing out of position or misplaying singles into doubles. Reggie Jackson proved the importance of correctly positioning out-fielders to me. So I made arrangements with the Mizuno representative to provide a demonstration of the cellular glove in spring training.

DECEMBER 9 ★

By the time the meetings ended this afternoon I was no longer a raw rookie in the tough game of corporate baseball. A lot of things that had happened had surprised me, and maybe made me tougher. I knew that I was a very different corporate player than I had been when I first arrived in Hawaii. I was going home with a different attitude, a new catcher, and a decent suntan.

DECEMBER 11 ★

Chicken finally got to New York today, just in time to mail out contracts. We offered everybody the legal minimum as defined in the last Basic Agreement. This is known in business as opening negotiations. It is also known as a waste of paper. But the rules state that any player not receiving a legitimate offer postmarked by five P.M. today becomes a free agent and can negotiate with any team. Imagine that.

That means that if someone took control of the local post office of a major-league team and prevented mail from getting postmarked, they could effectively destroy that team. I can't imagine anyone going to all that trouble just to win a few ballgames, though.

But I am glad The Boss never figured that out.

DECEMBER 18 ★

I hired my first manager today. It was a much more difficult decision than I thought it would be. During my career I played for maybe twenty-five different managers, and the only thing they had in common was that eventually every one of them got fired. Billy Martin got fired seven or eight times all by himself. Every manager I played for was unique: I played for Dick Williams, who would angrily criticize his players in public, and Ralph Houk, who wouldn't criticize one of his players if reporters stuck sharp pencils under his fingernails. I played for Billy Martin, who called every pitch from the dugout, and for Bill Virdon, who believed bunting was a felony. I played for Dallas Green, who had more rules than a South American dictator, and Bob Lemon, whose only rules were win and have a good time. And I played for Dickie Soll, who would tell reporters, "We had a bad middle half," but was a genius when it came to handling pitchers.

Probably the one thing I learned from all of them is that there is no magic formula. There is no right way and wrong way. The best thing a manager can do is get his team ready to play, put his players on the field, and try not to get in their way. Casey Stengel used to say he had ten players who loved him, ten players who hated him, and five undecideds, and that the whole key to his success was keeping the undecideds away from the ten who hated him.

I never believed managers made much of a difference once the game began. Most strategy in baseball is obvious. There's a reason a bunting situation is called a bunting situation. I've always thought that the most important part of a manager's job is knowing when to press his players and knowing when to leave them alone. Billy was the best I ever saw at treating each player as an individual and knowing how to motivate them; Pat Corrales was the worst.

Corrales was tough to play for. For example, the weather in Arlington, Texas, home of the Texas Rangers, was always the same—100°, 100 percent humidity, no chance of rain. As Yogi once said quite accurately, the heat is hotter there. One night Corrales called me into his office and started complaining that the pitching staff seemed sluggish. "No shit, Sherlock," I said respectfully, then pointed out that he made us stand in the outfield for forty-five minutes shagging batting-practice flies during the hottest part of the day, while the position players only had to stand in the heat for the eight or ten minutes they were actually hitting, "So," I suggested, "why don't you let the batboys do the shagging so the pitchers can go inside and cool off?"

"No way," he said flatly. "You guys go stand out there with everybody else."

I started to tell him that everybody else was us, but I knew he'd never understand, so I just walked out of his office. I was pretty upset about his attitude. Nobody was trying to get out of doing their work. Major-league baseball players are usually pretty serious about staying major-league baseball players; but he just wouldn't listen to reason. He believed that there were only two ways of doing things; his way and the wrong way.

I was still angry when I went out to the field. I was standing in the outfield, shagging flies in the hot sun, when a fan hollered to me, "Hey Sparky, how about a ball?"

I don't quite know what clicked on, but it did. "That's all you want?" I said. "A cheap baseball? How about this whole uniform?" With that I took off my hat and I scaled it into the stands. Then I heaved my glove into the stands. Then I took off my uniform jersey and flipped that to the fans. My spikes went next, one at a time, then my stirrup socks and my sanitary hose. Then my belt. And then . . . and then I took off my pants and threw them into the stands. Then I . . . saw Pat Corrales running toward me as fast as he could, screaming, "You get back in that clubhouse right now! Get in there right now!"

"Well, Jeez, Pat," I said, "it's about time you changed your mind. How come when I wanted to do that fifteen minutes ago you wouldn't let me?" And Corrales told me. That was when I realized how important it is for a manager to have a sense of humor.

Eventually I had to pay the fans about $40 to buy my uniform back.

All except the socks; I let them keep the socks. Hey, anybody who wants my socks after I've been wearing them in 100° heat, they can have them.

Picking a manager was tough. If it were a skill that could be learned, George Steinbrenner would have been great at it, because he certainly had enough practice. I wanted to take my time before making a decision, because I was determined to end the Yankees' "Manager-of-the-Month" policy forever. So I wanted to make sure that the person I picked would be there for a long time. Or at least the whole season. But the local reporters started writing that I was indecisive, claiming that I was afraid to make a decision. So I had to make a decision.

My first decision was that I would not rehire Bucky Dent. Bucky had done a good job holding the team together during his second tour of duty in the dugout, and I liked and respected him. But I felt that I had to bring in my own man as a signal that this was the beginning of a new era in Yankee history.

I knew I wanted to hire a manager who had been a major-league player, because I felt that that experience was invaluable. I wanted a man with a sense of humor, because I'd seen how important it was to be able to keep a team loose. I wanted a man who knew the game, who had a lot of self-confidence, who wasn't going to panic when things went wrong, who knew how to run a pitching staff. And, like all owners, I wanted a man with the guts to look me in the eye and tell me I was wrong, and the wisdom to know when I didn't want him to.

There was only one person I knew who could do all those things; unfortunately, I couldn't take the job because I was too busy running the organization. Secretly, I'd always suspected that every owner really wanted to get down in the dugout and manage his team. Now I knew that for sure.

I probably considered 150 candidates for the job. I spoke to baseball people I respected like Graig Nettles and Ron Guidry and Ralph Houk to get their suggestions. Finally, it became apparent that there was really only one candidate right for the job. So I decided to bring back Lou Piniella for a third term as Yankee skipper.

I knew a lot of people were going to object. I didn't care. I'd been a teammate of Piniella's for six years. I knew how smart he was; I knew how intense he was; I knew he'd learned how to handle players; and I knew he had experience. I also knew he was available. He became available several months ago, when Reds owner Marge Schott fired him for referring to her dog as "Baseball's most rabid fan."

The only thing I was afraid of was that his pride had been so badly damaged by Steinbrenner that he wouldn't take the job. "Hey, Lou," I said when he answered the phone in Tampa, Florida, "this is Sparky. I was . . ."

"I'll take it," he said.

DECEMBER 20 ★

We received official notification from the Players Association that four of our players—Don Mattingly, Tums Taft, Roberto Kelly, and Felipe Suarez—had agreed to accept binding arbitration. Players who agree to go to arbitration are considered to be signed, although the reason we have to go to arbitration is that they won't sign. At the arbitration hearing the team makes one offer, the player makes his demand, and a neutral arbitrator has to decide who has come closer to the player's actual retail value.

Negotiating contracts used to be a simple process: The team would send me a contract and I would reject it. They would call me ungrateful and I would call them cheap. They would threaten to trade me, and I would threaten to sit out the entire season. Then they would threaten to let me sit out the entire season and I would threaten to demand a trade.

Sportswriters would then begin to write stories claiming that this time, after they'd seen the old holdout game played hundreds of times, this time it was for real. This time the player and the club were really serious. Then spring training would begin and the club would announce that they were making their final offer, and I would reject it and refuse to report. Two weeks would pass, sometimes more, and the club would make an absolutely final offer, which I would reject, but I'd go to Florida anyway. Finally, when I felt I had to report to get into shape for the season, I'd work out a deal with the club and nobody would ever mention my holdout again. At least until the next spring, when the holdout game would start all over again.

That was the real rite of spring—the right to hold out. Now everything is so formal, so complicated, so legal. So expensive.

But when I looked at the A&W Plumbing calendar on my desk, with the picture of a beautiful girl wearing only a Santa Claus hat, one thought came into my mind. Well, two thoughts, actually. But the more important one was that it was exactly two months until pitchers and catchers reported to our complex at Ft. Lauderdale and the business of baseball was conducted on the playing field. That led me directly to a prayer I once thought I would never make: Come on, February!

JANUARY 6 ★

Our new traveling secretary came into the office for the first time today. Annie buzzed me and whispered, "Duke Schneider is here."

"Send him in," I told her.

Annie chuckled. It was that laugh of a secretary who knows her boss is about to make a fool of himself. Again.

I didn't understand why she was laughing until the door opened and Duke walked in. I noticed immediately that she was a girl. "You're a girl," I pointed out.

"Thank you," she replied.

"No, that's not what I meant. What I mean to say is . . . you're a girl!" And not just a girl, but a very pretty girl. About five feet eight inches tall, athletic-looking, but still slightly more shapely than one of those old green Coke bottles, with long black hair and very high cheekbones. Exactly the kind of looks capable of turning a contending baseball team into a second-division club.

She stuck out her hand. "Duke Schneider," she said. "I've been a fan of yours since I was a little girl."

"Thank you," I said weakly, "but . . ."

"My father was a fanatical Brooklyn Dodger fan." She smiled. She had perfect teeth. Naturally. "I can't tell you how excited I am to be working for you and the New York Yankees. Working in professional sports has always been my dream."

"Miss Schneid . . . Duke, listen." There was no way she could be traveling secretary. Just what I needed, one beautiful woman traveling with thirty men. I could see the cartoon in *The Sporting News* already, and *The Sporting News* didn't even carry cartoons. Now all I had to do was tell her. "Duke, look, I know we offered you the job, but . . . I want to be honest with you, when we hired you I didn't realize you were a woman."

She looked hurt. "I think I understand," she said.

"So you see why this just isn't going to work out?"

She took a deep breath. "Mr. Lyle, I just want to make sure I understand this. Are you telling me that because I'm a woman I can't do the job?"

"No, absolutely not. I'm sure you can do the job. It's just that I don't think it's a good idea for you to take the job. You know, being on the road with all those men. Going into the locker room. Living in hotels. Listening to that language. Believe me, you don't want that job."

"Yes," she said firmly, "I do."

"Excuse me?"

She stood straight up and squared her shoulders. "Mr. Lyle, are you familiar with the term 'sex discrimination'?"

"Now come on, wait a second," I said, raising a hand in protest. I had visions of lawyers and lawsuits, and of lawyers in expensive suits that I'd paid for. "I never, ever discriminated against sex." I paused and thought about that for a minute. That wasn't exactly what I'd meant to say. "You know what I mean. Look, Duke, we'll find another job for you with the Yankees, I promise, but you just wouldn't work out as the traveling secretary. I mean, Marge Schott has a man as traveling secretary, and she's one of you."

"Mr. Lyle," she said evenly. "I was hired to be traveling secretary and I am fully capable of fulfilling the responsibilities of that position. I don't want to take this to court any more than you do, but I will. Believe me, I will. And I'll win, too. Statistically, the odds favor me approximately 5.83 to 1."

No matter what everybody said later, at that moment I didn't think I had a choice. This wasn't a story somebody had made up; this was real life. And in real life discrimination cases can get very expensive. "Your office is right down the hall," I told her.

"Thanks, boss," she said.

"And don't call me that," I practically shouted.

JANUARY 14 ★

Since getting back from the winter meetings I've been toying with the idea of creating a Yankee mascot. The concept of a Yankee mascot isn't really as silly as it seems. In fact, most people don't know this, but the Yankees actually had a mascot once. It was created for The Boss by a New York company named Harrison and Erickson. The character's name was Dandy, and he looked like he had escaped from a comic strip: He had a huge belly, a large round nose, a mustache that unfurled, and a hat that spun around, and he wore a Yankee uniform. A lot of people thought he looked a little like me.

The day before he was supposed to make his debut at Yankee Stadium in 1980, Lou Piniella got into a fight in Cleveland with the Indians' mascot, Basebug, causing The Boss to complain, "These characters don't belong in the ballpark."

A lot of people thought he was talking about me.

So Dandy was banished to the upper deck. He walked around the upper deck with a security guard for two seasons. At the end of the second year Steinbrenner fired the security guard, and the kid inside the Dandy suit said his mother wouldn't let him walk around the upper deck at Yankee Stadium wearing a furry Yankee outfit and a hat that spun around without security. That kid had one smart mother. Dandy ended up in the storage room at the Stadium, and was eventually cut up into little pieces.

But I liked mascots. I remember the Twins had Twinkie the Loon, the White Sox have both Ribbie and Roobarb, Toronto has B.J. Birdy. . . . Birdy was baseball's clumsiest mascot. Once he opened his beak to kiss a female fan and accidently swallowed her wig. The Expos have Youpie. The Phillies have the popular, profitable Phanatic. The Dodgers have Tommy Lasorda.

So I thought it might be fun to have a Yankee mascot. The question was, what kind of mascot would be right for New York City? A Big Apple? A Con Ed man? A con man? A giant cockroach? And then it hit me: A Big Boss. It was certainly something that everybody in New York could relate to. Then I started wondering, what would a Big Boss look like? I'll have to admit, it didn't take me long to figure that one out.

I made a note to talk to Chicken about it as soon as he got back from the police station, where he was busy reporting that his car had been stolen.

JANUARY 20 ★

Trades are made for five reasons: one, to improve your ballclub either by addition or subtraction; two, to get rid of an expensive contract; three, to make your fans believe you're actually trying to improve the club; four, to get publicity during the off-season; and five, because it's fun.

Number five is probably the most important reason. I didn't collect baseball cards when I was growing up, so I never experienced the thrill of making a deal for a card you really needed; but owning the Yankees gave me the chance to do it for real. And I can tell you, it's great. I never realized how easy it is to make a trade, or how much fun it is, until I actually made one. I liked it so much I'm going to do it again as soon as possible.

Trading is easy. Everybody in baseball knows that the success of a team depends on a core group of players, and that the extra players— the third-string catcher, the utility infielders, a couple of pitchers—are interchangeable. Most trades involve these extra players, and the only thing they really have to do is not improve suddenly and make the person who traded them look bad.

During my career I was traded four times, and I saw countless other players traded. Most players hated being traded. I remember when I was with the Phillies, they traded a young pitcher named Bob Walk to Kansas City. He was devastated. He sat in front of his locker crying. The Phillies organization had tried hard to project a family image—they kept telling us we were all part of the "Philly family," or maybe they'd prefer to call it "The Philly Phamily." Bob Walk believed all that, so he felt like he was being kicked out of the family. It was like they were telling him that there was this other son that they liked more than they liked him. You know, drop by over Thanksgiving.

I guess I was a little different. That probably wouldn't surprise anybody who knows me. A player can look at a trade in two ways— either the team that traded you didn't want you anymore, or the team that got you really wanted you. I preferred to be wanted. In fact, every time I was traded I believed it was for my own good. When the Red Sox traded me to the Yankees for Danny Cater, I figured it was a blessing because I just didn't get along with the Boston manager Eddie Kasko. The trade was made during spring training. I was so happy I went over to general manager Dick O'Connell's office, which was located in a mobile trailer, to thank him for giving me a chance to pitch in the big leagues and for trading me to a contending team that needed a left-handed reliever. The trailer door was locked, so I started banging on it; meanwhile, O'Connell, who was inside, thought I was mad at him for trading me, so he wouldn't unlock the door. The harder I banged the more convinced O'Connell became that I wanted to bury him. I have to admit, I was getting pretty angry that he wouldn't let me in to thank him. Finally, I just stood there banging on the glass door, screaming at him, "Thank you! Thank you very much!"

I practically demanded the Yankees trade me after The Boss signed free agent Goose Gossage. I knew with the Goose in New York I wasn't going to pitch often enough to be effective, and the less I pitched the less effective I was going to be. The Yankees did me a tremendous favor by trading me to Texas without asking my permission. Because, under the rules, since I had ten years in the major leagues, five with the same club, I had the right to veto any deal. So even though Texas traded for me, they didn't own me. Legally, or baseball legally, I was a free agent. The Rangers had to give the Yankees the players they'd traded for me whether I signed with them or not. Eventually I signed with the Rangers for three years guaranteed at $300,000 a year, plus a ten-year broadcasting contract at $50,000 a year.

As far as I'm concerned that proves the importance of paperwork to me.

The Rangers eventually traded me to the Phillies, who agreed to pay me $350,000 *not* to broadcast for ten years, probably the best contract any announcer ever received. If I could have gotten the same deal not to pitch, I'd probably still be in the big leagues.

The Phillies traded me to the White Sox. By that time about all I had left as a pitcher was my reputation.

So I didn't have anything against being traded. Most players didn't feel that way, though. One thing I never liked was the way that managers told players they had been traded. The manager would say things like, "Okay, all current members of the Yankees take one step forward. Not so fast, Lyle." Of course that's not really true, but it just as well might have been. The moment a team got rid of you they stopped caring about you. I found out the Rangers had traded me when I got to the ballpark and found all my equipment in a big pile in the middle of the room. I'd been traded to the Phillies for Willie Montanez, who'd gotten to the ballpark early and had thoughtfully cleaned out my locker for me. My friend Jim Kern broke the news to me in that gentle way typical of pro athletes: "Hey, Spark," he said, "can I have your parking space?" Several other players then crowded around me to wish me luck and ask permission to use my free tickets to the ballgame that night.

One of the things I knew when I took the Yankee job was that I would be sensitive to the feelings of ballplayers, particularly ballplayers that I traded.

I'd refused to consider making any deals until Chicken had gotten here. One of the main reasons I hired him was because he is a great judge of talent. I can remember sitting near him in the dugout during the early innings of a lot of ballgames, watching him look out onto the field wistfully and say, "I wish I could hit like him," or "I wish I could field like him," or, "I wish I could run like him." And I usually agreed with his assessments. So as soon as he settled into his job, once all the insurance papers from the fire had been filed, we began going over the roster to decide where we needed to make changes.

There are a lot of clichés in the language of baseball: "The game is never over until the last man is out." "Baseball is a game of inches." "A team has to be strong up the middle to win." "A smart manager never spits into the wind." "Some of the best deals are the deals you don't make." "No team is as good as it looks when it's winning, or is as bad as it looks when it's losing." And probably the only one that really makes any difference, "You never have enough pitching." Chicken and I decided that if we were going to deal, we were going to get pitching.

Unfortunately, the owners and general managers of every other major-league team had reached exactly that same decision about a decade ago. I guess they'd all heard the same old cliché.

As I've learned, every trade begins with a telephone call. My phone had started ringing even before we'd smoothed the furrows from George's feet out of the carpet. The first thing everybody said was "Congratulations." The second thing they said was "Who are you interested in moving?" From that point on I was constantly on the phone with other owners and general managers not talking about deals.

The most important thing to remember when you want to make a deal is not to let the person you're speaking to know that you want to make a deal. That way he can't take advantage of you. The more reluctant you are, the better deal you can make. Naturally, that means a lot of potentially good deals fall through because everybody refuses to talk about them; but it's better to make no deal at all than make a bad deal. For example, people still blame former Mets general manager M. Donald Grant for trading Nolan Ryan to the Angels for Jim Fregosi, but you never hear anybody blaming that former Yankees general manager George Weiss for trading Mickey Mantle to the A's for Gus Zernial—because Weiss didn't make that trade!

Nobody ever admits that they've called you to talk about a trade. Believe me, more general managers I've never met seem concerned about my health than my family does. But eventually every conversation gets around to dealing. The first thing a general manager tells you is what he won't do: "Not that I'd ever consider moving Eric Davis, but if I did, what would you say to Mattingly and Taft?"

Obviously, I had to learn to speak the same language: "Are you kidding? There is absolutely no way in the world I'd ever consider moving Mattingly. If I traded Mattingly the fans here'd dip me in tar and tie me to a third rail. And even if I'd consider it, I'd have to get more than Davis."

In addition to these telephone calls, a surprisingly large number of deals begin in the newspaper. A general manager will be speaking to a local reporter and very subtly drop a hint: "You can't quote me on this, but we're trying to get rid of Bobby Fielding." The reporter will quote an "inside source," allowing other general managers to call and laugh about the ridiculous rumor they've heard. Then the discussions begin.

The first deal we made sent Don Slaught to the Giants for the good middle-inning reliever Roger Shelley and minor-league infielder Brian Gibson. That trade began when Mike Lupica mentioned in his notes column in *The National Sports Daily* that I'd owned the team for almost four months without making a single move to strengthen the roster. That didn't bother me, but I did mention to Chicken that I thought we should do something just to show the fans that we were serious about improving the team. Chicken agreed to do some "casting," throwing out some bait to see who responded. We decided to put Jesse Barfield in play and see who took the bait.

I'd learned a lot in a short time. In baseball, "in play" means that the baseball is alive and the runners can advance; in the business of baseball, "in play" means that a player is available. So I called Mike Martinez of the *Times* and casually mentioned that we were thinking about moving Barfield.

The first response came from Bill Lajoie of the Tigers, who called to find out how I was feeling, then said, "Not that we'd be interested, but if you'd consider trading Jesse Barfield, which of course I know you wouldn't, what would you want for him?"

"Trade Barfield?" I laughed. "I really believe Jesse is on the verge of the greatest season of his career. And can you just imagine how many home runs he'd hit in Tiger stadium with that overhanging deck?"

"Not as many as you might think," Lajoie said quickly. "Not with that new wind that we just discovered blowing in. In fact, and we haven't told anybody yet, we're even considering taking the upper deck off the stadium. I think Barfield would have a pretty tough time here. Besides, we'd just be interested in him as a late-inning defensive replacement."

"It doesn't matter anyway. I couldn't trade Jesse. He's such a good guy and we really believe he's going to hit for us. I couldn't do it."

"No, 'course not."

"And even if I'd consider it, I don't think I could take anything less than the Wolfe twins, and I know you'd never even think about trading them."

Now Lajoie laughed. It was obvious we were making progress on the deal. "That's a joke, right? Those kids are the cornerstone of our future. We're building the team around them. I couldn't trade them. And certainly not even up for Barfield."

"All right, okay," I said, "and not that I'm actually saying this, but if I would, you know, hypothetically, consider trading Barfield, suppose I'd be willing to throw in a minor leaguer. Somebody from the Columbus roster?"

"I suppose if you gave me three prospects to choose from, if you were thinking about making the deal, then I'd have to think about it."

We agreed that I would talk to Chicken to see if we were interested in discussing the possibility of the deal, while he would talk to his people. But both of us agreed to keep our conversation completely confidential.

As soon as I hung up on Lajoie, I called Atlanta Braves general manager Louis Aronica to find out what he thought about the Wolfe twins. But before I could get him on the phone Al Rosen of the Giants called. "I understand you're thinking about trading Barfield for the Wolfe twins," he said.

"C'mon, Al," I said, "that's just a silly rumor." Rosen had been a Yankee executive when I was playing, and I'd always respected him. "Believe me, if I was even thinking about moving Barfield, you'd be the first person I called."

"Well, good. But as long as I've got you, let me ask you a question. What would you say if I said Barfield for Riles and Sheridan?"

"Hello?" I said, tapping the receiver, then I shouted, "HELLO, AL? Are you there? We must have a bad connection. I thought you said Barfield for Riles and Sheridan."

We both laughed at that. "Are you kidding?" he finally said, "I don't know where you heard that. What I said was Barfield for Shelley and Washington."

"Oh c'mon now, Al, whattya think, I just got off the pitcher's mound? You know I couldn't do anything like that; but I'll tell you what, if I was going to talk about a deal, I wouldn't mind talking about Shelley. What's he signed for?"

"Let me check." I held for a minute and listened while he rustled some papers. "One year at $475,000."

I thought about that. "All right, let me throw two words at you. Don Slaught. He'd be great in your new ballpark."

Rosen considered it. The Giants needed somebody capable of catching thirty or forty games and Slaught was a tough out and a pretty good defensive catcher. "What's his status?"

"Two years at six."

"All right," Rosen continued. "Not that I'm saying I'd do this . . ."

"Me neither. I'm not saying I'd do this first."

". . . but that's a $125,000 a year difference." He started to do some figuring. "All right, listen. I've got a good kid named Brian Gibson who's at $150,000. So that means we'd be trading you two one-years at $625,000 for one two-year at $600,000. Right?"

I added it up. I was a little confused, but that sounded right. "I think that's right. Just one thing though, what position does Gibson play?"

I heard Rosen rustling some more papers. "He's a good middle infielder."

I spoke to Chicken, and he called Joe Donnally of *Newsday*, who liked the deal, so we made it. I told the reporters that this trade was just the beginning of our new rebuilding program, and we intended to win with good young players like Shelley and Gibson. And that's how I made my first deal.

FEBRUARY 1 ★

Twenty-two days until pitchers and catchers report to spring training and we start playing baseball. I can hardly wait. Things have been pretty quiet around the office. Chicken has been doing a good job getting everybody signed, and the arbitration process begins next week. The only real problem we have is with Dave Winfield. His ten-year, $25-million contract has expired and we can't seem to make a deal with him. Actually, we're not that close. He wants $2.25 million for one year, and we're offering $750,000.

Lou Piniella came in last week to talk about his coaching staff. Besides Yogi at first base, he's hired Graig Nettles to coach third, Jon Boswell as his batting coach, and Bill Lee as his pitching coach. I think a lot of people were surprised when he hired Boswell as the batting instructor. Boswell hit only .211 in parts of five big-league seasons, but Lou says his "woodman's ax" theory is absolutely correct, and he wants our hitters chopping through the ball. The choice that surprised me most, though, was Bill Lee. I always thought that Lee was even crazier than I was, but Lou pointed out that Lee was rarely hurt during his career and he knew as much about conditioning as anyone in the game. So I agreed.

I've gotten some very interesting telephone calls in the last week. Tommy John called to tell me he'd had another operation on his left arm. Apparently the tendon that had been transplanted from his right leg to his left arm, which had allowed him to pitch in the big leagues for thirteen more seasons, had finally snapped and rolled up like a snake's tongue. He then started to tell me about his recent operation. I couldn't understand exactly what he was saying, but it sounded like some doctor had invented a Teflon spring that performed very much like a human tendon, although it's supposedly more resilient, and they'd put it in his arm. He said that his arm felt better than it had in years, and he's been playing catch with his sons, and wanted to come in to spring training.

How could I say no to him? So he's coming in voluntarily. We agreed that I'd pay him $225,000 if he made the squad. Look, I have to admire his determination. It's so tough to admit you just can't do it anymore, particularly when you love the game as much as TJ does. And what's the worst that could happen?

The day after that Reggie Jackson called to tell me he wanted to get back in baseball. Now, as I've said, I had some problems with Reggie, but the man was a winner. Wherever he played, the teams won. Reggie was one of the most confident players I've ever known. He believed in himself. I think we've been lacking that sort of confidence around here for a while, so I had a great idea: I invited Reggie to come to spring training as our confidence coach. Our ego coach. His job is to instill confidence in players. What's the worst that could happen?

But the most surprising call came from George Steinbrenner. He spoke very slowly, and he told me that they would let him out weekends if he had a guaranteed job. He wanted to go back to work as owner of the Yankees. "Bossman," I told him, "that's just not possible."

He asked if there was something else he might do around the ballpark, but I told him there just wasn't anything for him to do. "You'll be sorry!" he threatened, then slammed down the phone. Sorry? What's the worst that could happen?

FEBRUARY 5 ★

I met with Duke Schneider for almost an hour today, and I have to admit that she's doing an excellent job. She's put together a plan for reducing transportation costs by taking advantage of the airlines' "hub city" concept. She explained that by flying to our destinations through these hubs, which would mean only a very brief layover, we could cut our travel costs almost in half. Then she handed me some computer printouts, which I didn't understand at all. They apparently showed how we could use the frequent flyer miles we accumulate to cut down our costs even more, while earning bonus awards like GE appliances and discounts on car rentals and hotel lodgings. "The beauty of the program," she told me, "is that by flying through hub cities we not only save money, but we also get extra mileage for our frequent flyer program." If she's right, her concept could revolutionize the way teams travel in the future.

The second idea she presented was also very interesting. Like most teams in the pro sports, the Yankees have installed a no-alcohol section. Beer isn't sold in that section and people who sit there can't bring liquor. Actually, it works very well. By filling that section even when other sections of the Stadium are empty, we've been able to cut down our security costs. The Duke's idea was to extend the concept into other areas: She suggested that we create a no-sodium section in which we would sell only unsalted peanuts and popcorn; a low-cholesterol section in which we'd sell only popcorn without butter, and skim milk; a large low-calorie section or sections in which we'd sell things like yogurt and diet drinks; and even a Kosher for Passover section where you could only buy kosher hot dogs, blintzes, and soda.

As I sat there, listening to her outline these proposals, I realized she had the best legs of any businessman I'd ever known.

FEBRUARY 11 ★

Even though Chicken has been in charge of all contract negotiations, I decided to sit in on the Tums Taft arbitration. I never went to arbitration as a player, so I wanted to see exactly how these hearings are conducted.

Arbitration is the shotgun wedding of contracts. After a player has six seasons of service in the big leagues he can become a free agent, meaning he can sign with any team he wants to. After three seasons he has to stay with the team that owns his contract; but if he can't agree on a fair deal, he is eligible to go to arbitration. In the arbitration process the player names the figure he feels he should be paid, and the team counters with a fair offer. Both sides argue their case in front of a neutral arbitrator, showing him how they reached their figure. The arbitrator then decides between the two figures. He can't compromise; he has to pick one of the two figures.

It's become a highly professional process. The player usually has his agent, an attorney, or a firm that specializes in these cases present his argument for him. Some general managers prefer to represent the club, but more and more teams are hiring a specialist to make their case. Because Chicken and I were both new to the process, we took Dick Woodley's recommendation and hired the arbitration firm of Stein and Company to argue our side.

Taft had a pretty good season last year. His record was 6–2 with 24 saves and a 2.74 earned run average. When I was playing, the only statistic that interested relief pitchers was how many games we saved, but today relievers are judged on all kinds of different stats. For example, Taft pitched in 44 games. Of the 72 baserunners he inherited, 21 scored, the fifth best percentage in the league. The league batted a cumulative .211 against him, third best, with left-handers hitting .174, also third best, while right-handers hit .245, only ninth best. In addition, he had five blown saves, ranking sixth in the league, but third in the Eastern Division. We wanted to give him a slight raise, and we offered him $835,000. He submitted an offer sheet for $1 million.

We met in a conference room at the American Arbitration Association on West 51st Street. On our side of the table were David Stein, who was going to make our presentation, me, Chicken, Woodley, and

Stein's two assistants, one of them a statistician. Speaking for Taft was his agent, Pat Schulman, who had his own statistician with him. The arbitrator was a large man with a full-length white beard named Richard Hodgeman.

The arbitration process can be tough on a team. The real problem in these hearings is that the team has to emphasize the negative aspects of a player's performance, while trying not to alienate the player. Before the hearing Stein told me he was going to use comparative statistics to show that relief pitchers with statistics roughly equivalent to Taft's were being paid about what we were offering. "It's all very professional," he explained. "We stay away from anything personal. That way there won't be any bruised egos."

"Gentlemen," Hodgeman began the hearing, "what we're going to do here is allow each side to present its case, and then I'll ask a few questions. There'll be no cursing, no kicking, no bellyaching. When I call on you, begin speaking. Please don't interrupt another speaker; everyone who has something to say will get a chance to say it." He turned to Stein. "Mr. Stein, please begin."

David Stein, a professorial-looking man dressed neatly in a gray pin-striped suit, gathered his papers in front of him. "Thank you," he said to Hodgeman. "Now, as you know, we're here to consider the case of Alfred Taft. I've analyzed all the relevant statistics; I've made in-depth comparisons to players performing equivalent duties and have computed percentage formulations based on the current Yankees salary structure. Before going into details, I would like to state for the record that we have offered Mr. Taft $835,000 for one season, while he is requesting one million dollars.

"Now. In view of my analysis, I feel I must say to Mr. Taft . . . What are you, kidding? That's a joke, right? You're asking for a million bucks? Ha! My mother had a better season than you did and she's . . .'"

"Just a minute here," Schulman protested. "This is highly irregular."

Stein pointed at Taft and laughed. "You? Pay you a million bucks? I've seen you pitch. You stink!"

"He does not!" Schulman shouted right back. "Does not!"

"Does too! Does too!" Then Stein stuck out his tongue, put his thumbs in his ears, and wiggled his fingers.

"Gentlemen, gentlemen," Hodgeman warned. "I won't stand for tongue sticking."

"But my client had a fine season," Schulman argued.

"Says you," Stein retorted. "I guess he had a fine season when he gave up a home run to Walt Weiss in the ninth inning on May 3 to cost us the game, huh? You know how many home runs Weiss hit all year? Two. Count 'em: One. Two. And I guess he had a great year when he walked in the tying and the winning runs in the ninth inning on July 15 against Detroit, right? And Detroit finished last. Yeah, sure, he's worth a million dollars." He waved his hand in frustration. "This bum is lucky the Yankees are nice enough to give him a uniform, much less a million dollars. I mean, just who does he think he is? Where does he get off asking for that kind of money? That's five times what the President of the United States makes and, believe me, Walt Weiss never hit a home run off George Bush. I'm sorry, Mr. Arbitrator, but this is just nuts"—he looked at Hodgeman—"and you'd have to be nuts to give it to him. And I don't think you're nuts."

I stood up and applauded.

Stein was just great. After this opening argument he went through Taft's entire season, mistake by mistake. By the time he finished I couldn't believe we were even offering Taft $850,000. Stein ended his presentation by giving Hodgman a folder containing the statistical evidence, which Hodgman said he'd consider before reaching his decision.

After Stein sat down Hodgeman turned to Schulman and told him to begin. Schulman cleared his throat. "Mr. Arbitrator," he began, "I could sit here and scream some silly arguments like my adversary. I could do that. Or we could talk about numbers, and I could prove to you that Tums was the sixth most successful relief pitcher in baseball last year. But is that all we want to consider here? Cold, hard numbers? Open to any interpretation? Mr. Arbitrator, my client—my friend—is a human being. Flesh and blood. When you cut him, he bleeds. So if you don't mind, I'd like to bring in someone to assist me in the proper presentation of our case." Hodgeman looked at Stein, who nodded agreement. Then Schulman went to the door and asked someone waiting outside to come in. He stood at the door waiting . . . waiting . . . waiting, and finally a tiny old woman, breathing heavily, supported by a walker, sort of hobbled into the room. "Let me help you, Mrs. Taft," Schulman said.

We all stood up until she managed to reach the closest chair and collapsed into it. "I'll be all right," she said. "Just give me a minute to catch my breath. You know, since that third heart operation I just haven't been myself, and with all those doctors and nurses . . . well, they're wrong. I'm going to live more than a few more weeks even if it does cost thousands of dollars a week to keep me alive, thanks to my loving, wonderful son. . . ."

When she paused to take a whiff of oxygen from the tank attached to the side of her walker, Schulman said, "I'd like to introduce Mrs. Violet 'Ma' Taft."

"Mrs. Taft," Hodgeman said politely, "if you'll just stick to the facts, please."

"Oh, of course dear," she said. She looked at him a bit strangely. "Say, aren't you Matilda Hodgeman's boy? Well, of course you are." She sighed. "Oh, I knew your sainted mother years ago, years ago. What a lovely woman."

"I object," Stein said.

Hodgeman glared at him. "To what?" Stein apologized, and Hodgeman allowed Mrs. Taft to continue.

"I don't have very much to say, your honor," she said. "Mr. Schulman told me I wasn't supposed to say anything about all of those poor crippled children my son supports and the home for aging abandoned animals that he set up all by himself, and the . . ." She started crying softly. "Excuse me, since his tiny little sister went into that coma it hasn't been easy on any of us." She took a wrinkled handkerchief out of her fist and blew her nose. "So, I'd just like to say one thing. Please give him the money. Please. Pleeeeeeease." She paused. "Oh," she continued, "my heart. My heart." She grabbed at her chest and slid out of her chair onto the floor.

"Mom!" Tums shouted—the only word he said during the entire hearing.

She collapsed. Out cold. Colder than The Boss's heart, as we used to say. The paramedics arrived in eight minutes and managed to revive her. As they wheeled her out of the room on a stretcher, Schulman put all his papers in a folder and handed it to Hodgeman. "Gentlemen," he said confidently, "thank you very much for your kind attention."

I stood up and applauded again.

FEBRUARY 18 ★

I finished packing for spring training today. Being there on the first day is going to be a new experience for me. When I was playing I always believed that spring training lasted too long. I'll tell you the truth, I thought the real reason we played six weeks of Grapefruit League games was to generate extra income to cover spring training expenses. Boy, was I naive.

It's amazing how different things look from behind the big desk than they did from the top of the pitcher's mound. Now that I'm a little older, a little more mature, I see that I was just being selfish, that six weeks is barely enough time to mold the personality of the team. I finally understand how important each of those games are. In fact, with so many young players coming to the big leagues directly out of college, or after only one or two seasons in the minors, I'm beginning to believe that six weeks isn't really enough time to do all the conditioning necessary, as well as teach the fundamentals that have to be mastered. If anything, we need more games. Believe me, the fact that we can draw more than 6,000 paying fans to each game really doesn't mean anything at all to me. Really.

FEBRUARY 20 ★

Spring training opened today for pitchers and catchers. Actually, spring training doesn't so much start as it unfolds. Sort of like a flower. It begins with the most basic aspect of the game, two men standing a few feet apart tossing a ball back and forth. It ends six weeks later with players fighting for jobs in major-league caliber games. There are a hundred different stories written every spring training; it really is the place where some dreams come true and some dreams end. Chicken and Lou and I and the coaching staff have a lot of work to do in the next few weeks. We've got to get to know what each player can do in different situations, fill the few open slots on the roster, rebuild the pitching staff, and instill some confidence in the team. We have to learn how to win.

I had two very big surprises today, Tommy John and Herbie Abramowitz. Tommy John is almost fifty years old but, as he reminded me this morning, "My arm was born just a few months ago." He has a long, nasty scar running from the top of his left shoulder to his wrist, but before I could start feeling sorry for him he picked up a baseball and tossed it easily to Chuck Cary—and almost knocked Cary over. It was absolutely incredible. He brought his arm back over his head in stages, almost like a ratchet clicking from position to position; when his arm was all the way back he stopped, then let it go—and tossed a rocket at Cary. I'd never seen anything like it; it sort of reminded me of one of those old-fashioned pitching machines with the metal scoop that bounced up and down after releasing the ball.

Everybody stopped what they were doing to watch him. Tommy is an old pro; he just ignored them. He caught Cary's throw and did it again. Whoosh! It was like he had a tension spring in his arm. He threw harder today, the first day of spring training, than at any time in his last ten seasons in the big leagues. I casually walked over to him. "Take it easy, Tommy," I said as nonchalantly as I could. "You don't have to prove anything today."

"It's nothing," he said. "I'm just flipping it easy."

"Yeah," I said, as I walked away, "that's what I thought." I practically ran inside to call Chicken.

Herbie Abramowitz is a dentist from Great Neck, New York, whose friends gave him a trip to the Yankees Fantasy Camp for his forty-sixth birthday. Among the former Yankees in the camp were Roy White, Hoss Clarke, Joe Pepitone, and Hector Lopez. White called me after the camp ended and told me that Abramowitz threw the strangest knuckleball he'd ever seen, and suggested I take a look at him. So I called Abramowitz and invited him down for a few days, figuring that would give the media something fun to write about until the full squad checked in. I knew it would be a great story. But let me tell you something, Abramowitz can pitch. He told me he can control his knuckleball so well he can spell words with it. "In script, I mean I can't print with it." He said it has something to do with the way he's strengthened his fingers filling cavities over two decades of dental work. I don't know about that, but I know I've never seen anything like his knuckleball. I'll be very interested in seeing what happens when he faces some batters.

I know I've said that I'm committed to developing our young players, and I refused to sign any of the players from the senior league in Florida, but wouldn't it be great if Abramowitz really can pitch?

FEBRUARY 25 ★

Bill Lee is the most unusual pitching coach I've ever seen. Today he had the whole pitching staff doing strenuous mental workouts. He's a firm believer in psychocybernetics. The way he explained it to me, if you imagine yourself doing something correctly, over and over, the brain sends electrical impulses to the proper muscles while you're thinking about it. That way, when you actually do it, the right muscles are stimulated causing you to do it correctly. So instead of actually working out, the whole pitching staff was sitting in the outfield, eyes closed, imagining they were pitching. When they came in I asked Chris Heller, a prospect who had a solid year at Double-A Albany last year, how he did. He shook his head. "Not so good," he said. "I just couldn't think my curveball over the plate."

That wasn't the worst thing. One pitcher, I don't want to mention his name, went into the clubhouse and asked trainer Gene Monahan for a head rub, complaining, "I hate the first few days of spring training, when you have to use those muscles you haven't used all winter."

FEBRUARY 27 ★

The entire squad is due to report in two days, and the only player not signed is Dave Winfield. Chicken and I have spent a lot of time trying to decide what to do about Winfield, and it was a tough decision to make. Winfield has been one of the most productive players in the major leagues for more than a decade, but he is starting to get old. He did hit 21 home runs last year, but he only batted 308 times. Of course he's still one of the top defensive outfielders in the league, but he did spend almost five weeks on the disabled list. Obviously he's a team leader, but his batting average has gone down two straight seasons. He's a 10-and-5 man, ten years in the big leagues and five straight with the same team, so we can't trade him without his permission, but he worked out all winter and he looks like he's in terrific condition. He came back strong after missing the entire '89 season with a bad back that hasn't bothered him since, but who knows when his back might go out again? He's certainly slowed down; he stole only 15 bases last year. But he did hit .360 with runners in scoring position. And he's asking for a two-year deal at $3 million, while we've offered one year at $1 million.

It's a real dilemma. With Barfield, Kelly, Suarez, and Verola, can we afford to pay him $1 million to be our fifth outfielder and right-handed designated hitter? Can we afford to let another team in our division sign him?

Do we sign him or let him go? He could be the difference between winning the pennant and losing it. He could also cost us a couple of million dollars and spend most of the season on the disabled list. I had Duke run a computer check on him, and that just proved that he is still one of the most productive players in the American League. But a computer doesn't know how forty-year-old bones stand up over a whole season. I admit there've been some times when I've wondered what The Boss would do, and this is one of them.

Finally, Chicken and I had to make a decision. So we went into my office and closed the door. We discussed it for more than an hour. We made probably a dozen different lists of all the positive and negative elements, and then we did the only sensible thing: We flipped a coin. I mean, in the end it's all guesswork anyway. Winfield could be fine or he could step in a hole on opening day and miss the entire season.

Nobody really knows. If there was one thing I learned during my career, it's that even with total preparation, even when you make the right decision, even when you make the perfect play, it all comes to luck anyway.

When somebody figures out how to sign luck, they'll really dominate the game.

Heads we would sign him, tails we'd let him go. Two out of three. It came up heads, twice in a row. We were going to sign him. Chicken called his agent and they agreed to terms, two years at $2 million. "After considering the situation," Chicken told reporters this afternoon, "we decided that Dave Winfield was simply too valuable to the New York Yankees to let him go, and we worked out a very amicable agreement with Dave. We're very pleased he's going to finish his career in the Yankee pinstripes, and we're determined he won't retire without playing in another World Series."

MARCH 1 ★

"Regg-gie! Regg-gie!" I could hear that old familiar cheer from my office in the parking lot trailer. I went over to the window to see what it was all about: "Regg-gie! Regg-gie!" But all I saw was Reggie Jackson pulling into the parking lot in his sunburst-yellow 1968 Avanti convertible. I couldn't figure out where the cheers were coming from until a car started backing out of a parking spot and Reggie slapped his horn: "Regg-gie! Regg-gie!" That was when I realized that the cheer was the sound his car horn makes.

Our ego coach had arrived. Ego intact.

MARCH 5 ★

Lou and I spoke to the entire squad for the first time today. I told them, "This is an entire new ballgame. The old way of doing things around here is now officially over."

"The Boss is dead," someone, I think it was Mattingly, shouted, "long live The Boss!" The rest of the squad joined in the chant. Naturally, I immediately quieted them down, after three or four minutes.

Then I continued, telling them that the whole purpose of spring training this year was going to be to put together a team that would stay together for the entire season. "I don't intend to make changes just for the sake of making changes," I explained. I told them that my goal was to create a sense of harmony and security, that nobody had to be looking over his shoulder. And I told them that Lou and I intended to stress fundamentals during spring training and, while I wanted to create a winning atmosphere, winning spring training games just wasn't as important as getting prepared for the long season.

Then we broke up the squad and played our first intersquad game. It was the first time I'd been on the playing field during a game since the day I retired. It was really a strange feeling; it felt both brand-new and comfortably old at the same time. For a few minutes I thought about putting on a uniform and just working out a little. I caught myself. I'm the owner of the team now, not just another player.

I liked the spirit we showed. In the game the Nettles beat the Berras, 7–5. Abramowitz pitched two innings, striking out two batters and giving up a bloop single. After the game Reggie led the whole team in the repetitive cheer, "I am the greatest, I am the greatest."

MARCH 10 ★

We lost the first game of spring training today, 6–1 to the Phillies. As usual at this time of the spring, the pitchers are way ahead of the hitters. At least the Phillies pitchers were way ahead of our hitters. Unfortunately, it also looked like the Phillies hitters were ahead of our pitchers. I did see a few things that really impressed me. First, Tommy John. He wasn't originally scheduled to pitch, but I just couldn't wait to see him throw in a real game, so I asked Lou to push up his turn a few days. But it was entirely Lou's decision whether to do it or not. Lou was free to do whatever he felt was best; I've promised him that I wasn't going to interfere unless it was absolutely unavoidable, and I just can't imagine that happening. So Lou, on his own, decided to pitch Tommy for two innings or forty pitches, whichever came first.

He completed two innings in twenty-eight pitches. This is really starting to get exciting. He threw very easily and his fastball was in the mid-80s. Tommy never even had a fastball before, much less one in the mid-80s, and afterwards he told me he wasn't even close to airing it out. Every spring training camp has at least one phenom who comes out of nowhere to fight for a spot on the roster; it's just hard to believe that our phenom is almost fifty years old.

The other player who impressed me was "Neon" Deion Sanders. With Roberto Kelly set in center field, Piniella has been working the kid in left field, and he looked very comfortable out there. I've asked Reggie to give Sanders extra attention because I think he can be an impact player, but his confidence really got shattered in Triple-A last year. At one point things got so bad he was only wearing two gold chains around his neck. I think Reggie's making progress: I remember when Reggie first arrived in New York, he told the sportswriters, "I'm the straw that stirs the drink!" Well, two days ago Sanders told the writers, "With a little more experience, I can be the straw that breaks the camel's back!" He's inexperienced, but he's going to be a good one.

We also experimented with the cellular glove in a game for the first time today. We had Barfield using it, and I think it worked out very well. Normally, our "spy in the sky," the coach who positions the outfielders, would have contacted a coach on the bench, who then would have signaled Barfield to move by waving a white towel. Instead the spy called Jesse directly and told him to move over.

Duke volunteered to keep defensive tendency charts for us on her computer. By keeping track of the way opposing batters hit specific pitches, she can create defensive alignments for us.

I guess the only thing that bothered me today, besides losing, was hearing that Don Mattingly had signed with Bantam Publishing to write a book about this season. There's nothing I can do about it, of course. The main reason I don't like it is that now that everyone knows that Don is writing a book they're going to be very careful about what they say to him. I don't like the idea that my players have to think during the season; they have enough to worry about. When I wrote *The Bronx Zoo* the situation was very different—I didn't tell anybody I was doing it, so they could be relaxed around me. At night I'd just go up to my room and make some notes or call my coauthor and tell him exactly what had happened during the day. It seems to me that that's the right way to write a book.

MARCH 12 ★

I don't mind losing games in spring training. I don't mind losing games in spring training. I don't mind losing games in spring training. I don't mind losing games in spring training. I don't mind losing games in spring training.

But I would like to win one game. I mean, how hard is it to win one game?

We're now 0–5 in "A" games, although we have won two "B" games. Either we're going to have to start playing better in the "A" games or schedule more "B" games. Some players are doing well, but I'm very upset by the lack of fundamentals I see on the field. I know that I promised Lou I wouldn't interfere, but as the owner of the team I have a duty to Yankee fans to remind him that the word "fundamental" consists of "fun" and "damental." To me, that always meant you could have fun on the field as long as you paid attention to "da mental" part of the game. We lost to the Cardinals today because Keith Reich couldn't lay down a sacrifice bunt to move the tying run into scoring position, and because outfielder Felipe Suarez threw to second base behind a baserunner, allowing him to go to third and score on a sacrifice fly. Like I told Lou, I don't mind losing games in spring training, but I don't want to give them away by playing dumb baseball. I suggested he schedule extra bunting practice tomorrow morning. I suggested it very, very strongly. I certainly don't want to be like The Boss; I don't want to interfere. But I also don't want to be embarrassed anymore. Before spring training ends we're going to find out who really wants to play here. Lou promised me he would turn this team into a group of bunting madmen before the season begins. We'll see.

At a press conference after the game I introduced the new Yankee logo to the media. Nothing is more representative of a corporation, or a team, than its logo, so I decided that creating a new Yankee logo would clearly mark the end of the Steinbrenner era and the beginning of the Lyle era. To design the new logo I hired Sean Dennis Callahan, who is best known for his Bronx Zoo "Z" and Nell's Microwave Dinners "N." I told him I wanted something modern, yet classic; something bold, yet subtle; something striking, yet reassuring. In other words, I told him I had no idea what I wanted.

His design is beautiful in its simplicity. He's eliminated the old NY, which stood for New York, and replaced it with a "Y," for Yankees. "I did this to indicate that the Yankees are no longer bounded by the artificial borders of New York City," he explained, "that they are a team that the entire world can embrace as their own." I suspect that'll make a good impression on our cable network. The "Y" itself is very different than the old Yankee "Y". Callahan describes it as "Rounder, wider, more graceful, yet demanding of attention. A logo to march into the 21st century with."

I think it accomplishes everything I wanted it to do. By making the old NY outdated, we're going to sell a lot of caps and T-shirts.

MARCH 14 ★

We finally won a Grapefruit League game, beating the Orioles 11–2. I knew that all that extra bunting practice would prove worthwhile. The stars of the game were a big power-hitting first baseman named Kevin Walton, who played at Prince William (A) last year, and Herbie Abramowitz. Walton is just a baby, but he looks like he has all the tools to be a useful player in the future. Abramowitz threw two more scoreless innings; that's four complete innings without one ball being hit hard. He threw a knuckleball to Phil Bradley that moved so much that Bradley actually took two complete swings at it before it picked up speed and crossed the plate. The other players seem to really like "Doc," as they've started to call him, and the writers have named his knuckleball the "Terrible Toothache." It's fun. I don't think either of these players will go north with us to start the season, but this kind of competition is great for the team.

We did have a small problem with Hanko Tsumi. He's still having difficulties understanding English. When his translator told him that the *Post* had written he was "going to have to fight it out with Clay Parker for his baseball life," he challenged Parker to finish the duel with long swords.

MARCH 15 ★

Both the "A" and "B" squads won today, the first time that's happened. Lou has the whole squad playing aggressive baseball. Today was also baseball-card photo day, the day the photographers take all the pictures for baseball cards. It used to be a very simple process— the photographer would grab the players as they finished their workout and take a few snaps. Today there are nine different companies selling cards, and each one of them wants some sort of special pose. What used to take five minutes now takes two hours.

And today the photographers have to be baseball experts as well as cameramen. A few years ago the players realized that anything that made their card a little different would make it much more valuable, and since then they've tried everything they could think of to fool the photographer. At first they did all the obvious things: wore somebody else's uniform, posed throwing with the wrong hand, wrote dirty words in very small letters on their equipment, kept their middle finger off their bat or out of their glove. Several people have posed with their zippers open. One player even had a batboy wear his uniform and stand in for him. The photographers know what to look for now, but the players keep trying to fool them. This morning Joe Verola posed with charcoal under his eyes—and mascara on his eyelids. And Big John Nicholson had a tiny ring in his nose.

I am now going to reveal something that I've never admitted before. If anyone takes the time to examine my 1977 Topps card very carefully, they'll discover that I'm wearing two left spikes, and written in very small letters on the flap of the tongue of the left spike on my right foot are the words . . . well, I'll let you find out what those words are.

MARCH 17 ★

We completed our twenty-four-man broadcasting roster today when we signed Reggie Jackson as colorman on our cable broadcasts. Of course, Reggie is very sensitive about being called a colorman, so officially he's our cable TV highlight commentator. Whatever. The fact is that he's done a really good job for us this spring building everybody's self-confidence, convincing them that if they really work hard, someday they might be half as good as he was. I really think that he'll be a terrific highlight commentator, and work well with his partners, Gary Thorne and Mickey Rivers. Besides, we had to hire him. We were running out of ex-ballplayers for our broadcasting team.

When I was playing, each team had two or three men who did the local television broadcasts and two more who did the games on local radio. Usually three of the five men, sometimes two, were not ex–major-league players. These people were known as "professional broadcasters," and they usually did the play-by-play. They were supposed to describe what happened, while the ex-ballplayers, the colormen, were supposed to explain why it happened, based on their own deep knowledge of the game, as well as their experiences on the field. Here in New York, for example, professional broadcaster Frank Messer would say, "There's a line drive up the middle into center field for a base hit," and ex–major-leaguer Phil Rizzuto would explain, "Holy cow!"

The baseball broadcasting business has changed as much as the baseball-card industry. Now the Yankees have exactly as many broadcasters as we do active players. In addition to the three men working local TV and the two men on radio, we have a three-man team on SportsChannel, our cable station; we have two men broadcasting the games in Spanish for our TV satellite transmission to South and Central America, and two other people doing Spanish radio. After the games Tony Kubek is doing "Kubek's Korner" on free TV, Jim Kaat is hosting "Kaat's Korner" on cable TV, and Bert Campaneris is doing "La Korner di Campaneris" on Spanish TV. Stick Michael does the postgame scoreboard show on radio. In addition, Mel Allen is hosting the weekly show on which fans can speak directly to the manager, "Piniella's Korner"; Mickey Lolich and Denny AuClair are hosting the daily talk show "Yankee Fans Korner" from Mickey Mantle's restaurant on Central Park South; Joe Pepitone and Dooley Womack are doing the *Yankee Game of the Week* on European TV; Susan Waldren is traveling with the team doing live pieces for all-sports radio WFAN in New York; and this year, for the first time, we're even broadcasting to the Far East. Probably because Tsumi's on our roster a Japanese television station wanted to broadcast our games, so they've parked a satellite in stationary orbit directly above Yankee Stadium and have assigned two Japanese announcers to do the games. Somebody in the clubhouse said they were going to turn baseball into a religious experience. "It's the first baseball game that's going to be broadcast pray-by-pray."

Maybe the most interesting thing about this announcing team is that, with the exception of the cable TV crew, they were all hired without our approval. We had absolutely no control over who these stations hire or fire. Just like The Boss. Oh, we may have offered a suggestion or two, but believe me, they didn't have to listen to us. It was completely their decision. In this regard, we're no different than The Boss himself.

MARCH 19 ★

We won our fourth straight game today, beating the White Sox 2–1 on Raoul Rojas's suicide squeeze. Of course it doesn't matter if we win or lose in the Grapefruit League, but winning does get the fans at home excited and sells tickets. Getting our players in shape is much more important than winning the Grapefruit League championship, but I've always believed a winning attitude develops in spring training.

The most exciting thing about this winning streak is the quality of our pitching. This team is going to go as far as our pitchers can carry us with their arms, and Lee has done a great job with the staff so far. Maybe he has his own way of doing things, but as long as he gets results, that's fine. Whenever I try to talk to him about the pitching staff he tells me, "Pitching is a science and we are all scientists."

He's sort of isolated the pitching staff from the rest of the squad. He's actually founded a semisecret organization that only pitchers can belong to. Nobody is allowed to talk about it out loud, but it's called Leeism. When I asked him about it he shrugged it off and said, "It's kind of a disorganized religion, based on the belief that the ball goes where it is thrown, and each pitcher is solely responsible for his own baserunners. And that he who shall error behind us shall error in vain."

It's a method of building pride, he explained. He's given each pitcher a secret word, a "mantra" he calls it, and whenever a pitcher is having trouble during a game he's supposed to walk behind the mound and repeat this mantra over and over. Supposedly, this will calm him down. "It's based on an old Eastern Division philosophy I discovered when I was with the Red Sox," Lee explained. "I've just extended it." He makes up all the mantras himself, he said, using mostly nonsense words, words that make no sense at all, like "valdivielso," "portocarrero," "regalado," "minoso," "podbielan," and "klimkowski."

I don't know if it'll work. The times I used to get into trouble on the mound were the times I started thinking. When I just kept my mind closed and threw sliders I was fine. Besides, when I was out there it was as if I was already in a trance. I wasn't really aware of the people in the ballpark. Sometimes I didn't even know who the batter was. I just threw sliders.

The only problem we had today was that some of the players are complaining that Yogi's hands are too hard. When they reach first base and he slaps them on the rump, he's hurting them. Piniella told them that it's still early in the season and Yogi's hands are ahead of their behinds. He suggested they spend a little more time sitting on the bench toughening up.

MARCH 21 ★

Believe it or not, I think Tommy John is going to make the team. He got his fastball up to 94-mph on the Jugs gun today, and by mixing that with his 26-mph change-up, he's been absolutely devastating. He threw four more shutout innings today, as we beat the Rangers 6–3 down in Port Charlotte. In the third inning TJ set up Pete Incaviglia for the fastball then threw him a change-up. Incaviglia actually wrenched his back trying to hold up on his swing and had to leave the game. Bobby Valentine sent up a kid named Lyndon Johnson Healy to finish Incaviglia's at bat and Johnson was in the batter's box when TJ's last pitch to Incaviglia finally crossed the plate.

Maybe I'm exaggerating, but it was a beautiful pitch.

Herbie Abramowitz followed Tommy with three more good innings, although he gave up his first earned runs this spring. Abramowitz has a chance to make the team, and if he did, it would be the sports story of the decade—a 46-year-old Jewish dentist comes out of suburbia to pitch for the New York Yankees! Imagine what the movie rights to that story would be worth. I know some people are laughing at the idea, but they haven't seen him pitch yet. Abramowitz did make his first big mistake in the game today. He tried to throw his fastball past Ruben Sierra. Abramowitz doesn't have a fastball. NASA is still tracking the ball. On the other hand, I know Piniella was very impressed when Abramowitz spelled "Lou" in mid-air on a pitch he threw to Jeff Kunkel.

MARCH 23 ★

American League umpire Ken Kaiser came into camp today to go over the new rules or changes in the rules with the players. After that he took the first- and second-year prospects aside and taught them the correct way to argue with an umpire. A lot of fans aren't aware that this meeting takes place, but it's actually one of baseball's oldest traditions. Fans have a real misconception about the relationship between umpires and players and managers. They think we don't get along with the umpires, and that's not true at all. Actually, we all get along very well. Umpire Bill Haller and catcher Tom Haller were even brothers. In fact, although I'm sure you'd never get an umpire to admit it, umpires really like it when a manager or a player argues with them. Arguments give them a chance to relieve some of the tension, get them some of the attention they really deserve, help keep them awake during boring games, and allow them to demonstrate their wisdom to the fans. And managers enjoy these friendly arguments too, because it's really the only time fans get to see them do anything positive. Usually the only time fans see a manager during a game is when he's sitting on the dugout steps tossing pebbles onto the field or coming out to talk to a pitcher in trouble. And players like these arguments too, because everybody knows they're all in good fun.

But there are rules, and they have to be respected: No cursing about members of each other's family. No spitting. No throwing objects. And keep moving to the right so that everybody gets equal time facing the camera. Some umpires object to managers and players kicking dirt on them, but they realize that the fans love it, so as long as managers and players continue paying the umpire's dry-cleaning bills it'll remain an acceptable action.

Today's meeting got off to a rocky start. Piniella introduced Ken Kaiser to our young players, warning them that he never wanted to hear any of them calling an umpire "a rat, a pig, scum, jerk, asshole, motherblanker, dumb blank . . ."

Kaiser started getting angry.

". . . blankhead, blankety-blanker, no good lousy blank . . ."

Piniella told them every name not to call an umpire, while Kaiser stood right next to him. Kenny knew exactly what Piniella was doing, and his face got bright red with anger, but there was nothing he could do about it. Meanwhile, the players were hysterical. Finally, Kaiser couldn't take it anymore. He picked up Piniella in a bear hug and body-slammed him, softly, on the grass. Those two should take that act on the road.

After Kaiser had explained the "Rules of Engagement," as they're known, to the kids, he and Piniella staged a demonstration argument. It was actually sort of tame, proving, I guess, that umpires need spring training too. Finally Lou had a couple of kids come up and argue with Kaiser. And even Kenny couldn't keep a straight face when a really nice young kid who played at Ft. Lauderdale last year, an outfielder named Reg Bragoni, got up and screamed as loud and angrily as he could, "Golly, I really think that was a bad call, Mr. Kaiser."

"Son," Lou told him, "you don't *think* in an argument. You *know*. And Kaiser here may be a lot of things, but none of them is Mister."

When I was playing I always got along pretty well with the umpires. I knew that they were trying to do the best job they could, that they just couldn't help themselves. Besides, I didn't depend on umpires calling strikes and balls. I wasn't a strikeout pitcher. When I got a lot of strikeouts I was usually in trouble. If batters weren't banging my slider into the ground, no umpire could help me anyway.

After the meeting Kaiser came into my office for a cold drink, and we started talking about old times. He admitted something to me that he swore he'd never told anybody before. He told me that every once in a while, on a really warm, humid night, during a bad game, he begins to get bored, and when that happens, he actually misses Billy. "I could always handle Billy," he said, "and with all the yelling he did he used to keep the umpires in the game. And we appreciated that. Besides that, you know how much the fans loved him, and most umpires understand that we owe our jobs to the fans and really like to see them entertained."

Kaiser told me that his new line of umpire merchandise, especially the men's clothing label, Umpire Fashions, is doing very well, and that he was coming out with a video, produced by Sports Illustrated Films, called *Kaiser's Greatest Arguments*. He offered to sell me a copy at a discount. So I threw him out of my office.

MARCH 24 ★

I met with the coaching staff to talk about the cuts they wanted to make this morning. Mostly I just listened, because this is their decision. Occasionally I did make a small suggestion, but that was all. The roster is going to be pretty close to what Woodley predicted last winter. Bob Geren has had a good spring so he'll be the starting catcher. Jim Sundberg, whom we bought at auction, will back him up. Lou intended to carry only two catchers, but Jorge Burns, a left-handed hitter who had 16 home runs at Columbus last year, is having a great spring and Lou could decide to bring him north if we can't pick up another left-handed bat. Mattingly is the first baseman. Rosey Rogers will be the backup unless Chicken can make a deal. He's waiting until everybody makes their final cuts to see who's available. Steve Sax and Alvaro Espinoza are the double-play combination. Keith Reich has surprised everybody by coming back so quickly from his foot injury, so he and Raoul Rojas will probably be the reserve infielders, but Rafael Santana may make the roster. Nobody has really won the job at third base, so I'm guessing that Lou'll carry Randy Velarde and Bam Bam Meulens. Meulens may not really be ready, but Lou likes him. "This kid is going to be our hot cornerstone for a long time," he said. Besides, we all want to carry as many players from our farm system as we can, to prove to our minor leaguers that we're through trading away young players for a quick fix, and that every one of them now has a chance of playing for the big club someday.

Suarez, Kelly, and Barfield will probably be our starting outfield, with Verola, Deion Sanders, and Winfield backing them up. Winfield will start this season as the full-time DH. Both Kevin Maas and George Cole really played well this spring, but there just isn't room for them on the roster. Lou is going to tell them that we're watching them carefully and that they should go down to Columbus and bust their humps and if we have an injury or any problem, they'll be right back up here.

The pitching staff still isn't settled. I think that Plunk and Cadaret are set in the rotation. Tommy John has earned a starting spot. The final two spots will be filled by either Hawkins or Cary or Parker or Tsumi. Taft is our stopper coming out of the bullpen. Frank Biondo will be the long man, unless Hawkins doesn't make the rotation. Big

John Nicholson is devastating against left-handers and I still think Bob Forsch can hang on. But with a couple more good outings, Abramowitz can force his way onto the staff and change all our plans. And I still think we need a strong number one starter, a horse who can give us 40 starts and keep us in every game.

Without question the biggest disappointment of the spring has been Roger Shelley, who we got in the Slaught deal. I thought he had a good shot at winning a spot in the rotation, but he has a real problem mixing up his fastball and change up. We tell him to throw a fastball and he gets confused and throws a change up. So unless Lou needs a pitcher who specializes in giving up long home runs, I think Shelley'll start the season at Columbus.

I'd hoped Forsch had one more season left in his arm, but it looks like all those innings he's pitched have finally taken their toll. I think TJ has won his spot on the pitching staff. The truth is that Forsch has had a bad spring, while TJ has a new spring.

I like this team. It's a good mix of veterans and talented youngsters. Our big need is still a left-handed bat. Maybe Reggie wants to come out of retirement. Gee, I'd better not even think that, it might give him an idea.

We lost to the Dodgers in a rain-shortened game at Vero Beach, 5–3. I think we've had more rain this spring than ever before in history. The really bad news is that Verola announced that he also has a contract to do a book about this season. That's two, not counting this one, and I'm not counting this one because nobody knows about it.

MARCH 27 ★

The most unbelievable thing happened today. Besides the fact that we beat the Reds 1–0, with Chuck Cary, Herbie Abramowitz, and Tums Taft combining on a one-hitter. Police in Los Angeles announced the arrest of a notorious three-man elevator holdup gang, and one of them was wearing George Steinbrenner's 1977 World Series ring. Incredible as it seems, the police have finally found the guys who beat up George Steinbrenner in an elevator during the 1978 World Series. I have to confess that I was one of the many people who doubted that fight ever really took place. Apparently I was wrong. And listen to this: Not only did they find The Boss's World Series ring, in one of the perpetrators' car they found a diagram of the San Francisco International Airport, a copy of Morton Downey, Jr.'s travel schedule, and a newspaper story telling how Downey claimed he was attacked and beaten up in the men's room of that airport by "a gang of unknown assailants"! The police think that these people might have been involved in that crime, too.

There's more. After arresting these men the police searched their homes. In one of them, way up in the attic, in an old trunk that one of the perps claims belonged to his grandfather, they found a fading photograph and several yellowing newspaper articles about the disappearance of New York judge Joseph Crater. Now, the LAPD aren't claiming that there's a connection between that crime and the Steinbrenner mugging, but they are continuing to investigate.

The strange thing is that I'm beginning to feel a little sorry for The Boss. I think, sometimes, he might have been misunderstood. All he tried to do was put together a winning team for New York. Maybe he went about it in the wrong way—Chicken described it as killing mosquitoes with a nuclear weapon—but his only desire was to win for the people of New York City. To make them proud of the Yankees. Nettles is always reminding me how good The Boss was to so many people. Every time he fired somebody he gave them a bonus. And let's give him some credit: He never fired anybody he didn't know.

If I knew where he was right this second I would call him up and apologize to him for doubting his elevator story. The problem is that nobody seems to know where he is. Since he sold American Ship Building he seems to have disappeared. I've heard rumors about him wandering the streets at night, stopping people and telling them, "I'm The Boss. I am The Boss." Reggie said he heard that The Boss was meeting secretly with Donald Trump. Who knows? I'll tell you something though; not knowing makes me a little nervous. I feel like I'm at the movies and the scary music is playing and the door is opening slowly. I'd feel a lot better if I knew The Boss was okay—and where he was.

MARCH 28 ★

We discovered today that Hanko Tsumi can read minds. He was out in the bullpen this afternoon. Everybody was talking about the season, and he said suddenly, in perfect English, "If we can stay close to Toronto until we get our pitching rotation settled, I think we're gonna win this thing." Everybody was shocked—Tsumi speaks almost no English. But the really incredible thing about it was that Clay Parker drawled, "Gee, that's exactly what I was thinkin'. I mean, word for word, that's what I was thinkin'. That boy read my mind."

They decided to try an experiment. They had somebody stand a few feet away and think of something to see if Tsumi could read his mind. Frankie Biondo went first, and when Tsumi didn't say anything everybody assumed the Parker thing was just a strange coincidence. Until Biondo admitted he couldn't think of anything to think of. But when they tried the experiment with several other people, most of the time—not every time—Tsumi was able to repeat whatever they were thinking. Then Jim Sundberg tried thinking of specific pitches, as if he were calling them, and Tsumi was able to tell him what pitch he was thinking of. If this isn't a trick it could be one of the greatest discoveries in baseball history. Can you imagine the advantage we'd have if we knew what pitch the other team's catcher was calling? Or if we knew what the opposing manager was thinking?

When the bullpen guys told Piniella about this, he said, "I don't believe in that kind of mumbo jumbo. I'll tell you what I do believe in,

I believe in playing for a tie at home and a win on the road, getting a right-handed batter up there against a left-handed pitcher, never sacrificing with your number three, four, or five hitters and not letting their big guy beat you."

I decided to keep this thing very quiet for a while, and I asked everybody not to think about it.

Later in the afternoon Duke Schneider came into my office with our travel arrangements for the whole season. She's done a tremendous job, compiling over 4 million frequent flyer miles for the team, which includes a traveling party of twenty-six people for eighty-one road games. That means, she explained, that we're entitled to almost 80,000 upgrades to business class and 50,000 upgrades to first class, if we want to spend our mileage that way. We can also make 12,500 round trips to Hawaii or 8,600 trips to Europe during nonholiday periods. I asked her to call the airline and find out if we can apply these miles toward our travel next season, reminding her that it will only work if we can get confirmed reservations. Obviously I can't expect the New York Yankees to travel standby.

While she was in the office I asked her how she was getting along with the team. So far, she said, everything was going very well, although she hadn't been in the clubhouse yet. I noticed she was wearing a wedding ring. She told me it was actually a warning ring—her way of avoiding conflicts with the players. Just before she left she mentioned that she had started charting batting and pitching tendencies with a new computer program she'd worked out. "It gives me something to do while I'm watching the game," she said. "You know, if this works out like I think it might, it'd be like we could read their minds."

I didn't say a word to her about Tsumi.

MARCH 29 ★

These are the toughest few days of spring. Everybody is in shape and ready to get the season started and we still have three days of spring training left. This was right about the time I liked to report.

By this time of the spring the reporters have just about run out of things to write about, and they're forced to print the annual quotes and predictions. In the papers the last few days, for example, Darryl Strawberry promised, "This time I really am going to have a monster year. And I *really* mean it now." And Whitey Herzog said, "The truth is that we just don't have enough pitching to be in it this year. We've been hit by some of the most unbelievable injuries I've seen in all my years in this game." In Texas, Bobby Valentine said, "This is the year our young kids are going to finally come of age." And naturally, Wilt Chamberlain told a reporter, "I could still be a dominant force in major league baseball if I wanted to. But I'd rather stay here in Los Angeles and play volleyball."

Our writers told me they felt a little cheated that George wasn't around to guarantee that Piniella was going to be the manager all season no matter what happened, "and you can take that to the bank." I tried to help out, telling them, "Lou Piniella is the best manager we've had since I've owned the team, and I see no reason to anticipate making a change." They asked me if that meant I guaranteed Piniella would be the manager all year, and I told them that there were no guarantees in baseball. That proved to me how tough the New York writers are. A story in the *Post* the next day was headlined, "Sparky Greasing Skids for Lou? Bucky III?"

The writers also made their predictions. Almost nobody thinks we can win. In fact, most writers are picking us to finish third or fourth. They feel we don't have enough starting pitching to go with not enough relief pitching, and they believe no Yankee team in recent memory has gone into the season with less left-handed power than we have. They're probably right about that. Chicken and I talk about it every day, and he is talking to a few people. If we can make a deal, we will.

I think the writers are wrong. I think the pitching is going to be much better than they do, and if we can get that left-handed bat . . . we're only a player or two away from really being a contender.

Rosey Rogers came into my office this afternoon with a serious problem. "My girlfriend wants to come to Opening Day," he told me. I asked him what was wrong with that. "So does my wife."

Ah, women. Baseball's oldest problem. A lot of general managers believe that the toughest part of their job is keeping the players' wives and the girlfriends happy—and separate. Listen, players are men, and women are women. How can there not be some problems?

I asked Rosey what he wanted me to do. "Maybe you can tell my wife you've traded me for a few days. She's not too smart."

We decided to give them tickets in separate sections, although he was really hoping for separate ballparks. But these are the kind of crises a compassionate owner has to deal with.

APRIL 1 ★

We broke camp today, flying to Port St. Lucie to play the Mets in a game that was being broadcast back to New York. I sat next to Lou on the plane and told him, "I really want to win this game."

"Me too," he agreed. "I want to win them all. But with opening day . . ."

"I don't think you understand, Lou," I said, keeping my voice down. "I think it's very important that we win this game. No matter who we have to pitch." I reminded him that when we were playing, the Yankees owned New York, but that that had changed. The Boss had alienated tens of thousands of Yankee fans and we had to win them back. "We're in a battle for the hearts and wallets of New York, Lou," were my exact words, "and the best way to win that battle is to prove we're competitive with the Mets." That meant beating them head-to-head. "This is a new beginning," I pointed out. "You understand what I mean?"

"New beginning is redundant," he said.

"Excuse me?"

"I understand," he said sort of sadly. "You're the boss."

"No!" I practically shouted, "I'm not. Don't call me that."

Lou held up both hands like he was surrendering. "Hey, sorry." So he started Cadaret, who had been scheduled to pitch opening day, and followed him with Tommy John and Nicholson. And we won, 3–1. TJ solidified his spot in the starting rotation with four more solid innings, cranking it up to 96-mph with his new arm. The only problem he had took place at the airport when he tried to go through a security gate and the alarm kept going off. Apparently some metal device in his new arm activates the system. The head of security told us to get a note from Tommy's doctor detailing what is in his arm, as well as a copy of his X ray, in order to bypass security gates in the future. But they let Tommy go after a hand search.

The most disappointing moment of the whole spring took place this morning. I called Herbie Abramowitz into my office to tell him the wonderful news—he'd made the team. Lou had decided to take him north with us. "Congratulations, Herbie," I said. "What you've done is even tougher than winning Ed McMahon's sweepstakes. You've made the team." I handed him a contract. "Here, just sign this and you're a member of the New York Yankees." I stuck out my hand.

Herbie just looked at it. "I can't," he said.

I figured anybody could shake hands. "You can't what?"

"I can't play for the Yankees." He handed the contract back to me. "Sparky," he said, "I didn't think . . . I didn't know . . . believe me, if I ever, for one minute, thought that this was really going to happen, I never would have put you through it."

"What are you talking about?"

"I just don't know how to tell you this. I mean, I'd love to pitch for the Yankees. Who wouldn't? Besides Ed Whitson, of course." We both chuckled a little at that. "It would be a dream come true. But Sparky, dentistry is my life. It's what I live for. And I couldn't give it up. See, when I was a little kid, while the other kids wanted to play baseball or football, or fly airplanes, all I ever wanted to do was fix teeth. Like, one night, when I was no more than five years old, my grandmother left her false teeth in a glass next to her bed, and while she was asleep I'd sneak in and take her teeth and make clay molds to play with. Asking me to give up orthodontics is like asking Deion Sanders to give up pro football. I just can't do it."

"Bill Lee put you up to this, didn't he?"

"I'm not kidding, Sparky. If you could . . . just for one minute, look into the mouth of some trusting little kid, knowing that you can make a difference in that child's life, I think you'd give all this up in a minute. I'm a dentist," he said proudly. "Maybe I'm not the best dentist who ever lived, but I'm damn good. So I'm very sorry, but I can't pitch for the New York Yankees this year."

"Bill Lee put you up to this, didn't he?" I repeated. "This is a joke, right?"

He smiled. "I wish it was. Believe me, there are some things worth giving up your passion for, but pitching for the Yankees isn't one of them."

I didn't know that. I just sat there silently. Stunned. It was the most incredible thing I'd heard since George had called me into his office after I'd won the Cy Young Award to tell me he was giving me a bonus. Abramowitz and I spoke for a few more minutes, but he was serious; he wouldn't give up his dental practice to pitch for us. I knew the team would survive without him. I knew the world of baseball would never even know what it had missed. But somehow, I also knew that I was going to be just a little bit changed forever. And I knew that I'd never be able to look at my dentist the same way again.

APRIL 2 ★

We traded Bam Bam Meulens to the Padres this morning for Ken Davis, the left-handed power hitter we desperately needed. We hated to give up Meulens, but we think we can win this year, and we have to have more left-handed power to do it. Davis has been in the big leagues for eight years, so he isn't going to be affected by the pressure of playing in New York. He certainly has enough power. As a pinch-hitter last year he had 8 home runs in 75 at bats, a tremendous ratio. Since they replaced his kneecap he doesn't run very well, but he can still back up Mattingly at first base if we need him.

I know, I know, a lot of people are going to start thinking, there go the Yankees again, trading away their future for a quick fix. But if we're going to be competitive this year we had to make this move. And every other team knew we needed a left-handed power hitter, so they were going to hold us up. We had no choice.

The sportswriters are all going to call this "Sparky's deal," but it wasn't my decision. When the Padres told us Davis was available and what they wanted for him, Chicken and Woodley and Piniella and our superscout, Alex Stein, and I sat down to hash it out. I can tell you that Stein was against the deal. But eventually we agreed, all of us together, the entire group as a whole, including me with my one vote, only one vote, that we had to make the deal. I'm not afraid of taking the responsibility, I'm not afraid of taking the heat, but this was a decision made by my baseball committee.

I happen to like the deal. Davis is a real pro and if Lou can get him enough at bats he's going to be a huge help. Just his presence on the bench in late innings is going to be enough to make the opposition manager think twice before bringing in a right-handed reliever. And the truth is that Meulens hadn't developed as quickly as we'd hoped. He does have great power, and he looked like he might hit .270, and his defense has improved, but he struck out twice yesterday against the Mets' Dwight Gooden, and did not look good.

With the addition of Davis I really believe we're a serious contender. But that's really the last time we're going to be trading youth for experience this year.

APRIL 3 ★

We had our first workout at the Stadium today, and the players got their first look at our completely redone clubhouse. I hadn't told anybody except Chicken about my plans, but while we were in Florida I had the entire locker room redone. I tried to create the kind of clubhouse I would have liked to have had when I was a player. The first thing I did was get big, comfortable chairs for everybody. I always hated those silly metal stools that most teams provide. When I was playing in Texas, in fact, the stools they gave us had thick bolts sticking up out of the seat, so it was impossible to sit in one position for more than a few seconds. In that clubhouse we looked like the most nervous team in history. So on the last day of the season we decided to execute one of those stools for the crime of being a real pain in the ass. Jim Kern brought in his .20-gauge shotgun. We took the stool out to the bullpen before the game, put a white sanitary sock around it like a blindfold, then started blasting it. Blam! Blam! The

Orioles were trying to take batting practice, and we were blasting away at that stool in the bullpen. Blam! I guarantee you, by the time we were finished, that stool was never going to make anybody else uncomfortable again. Finally, somebody told one of the executives what we were doing and they made us stop. I guess you could call the person who told on us a stool pigeon.

So that's why the first thing I did was install comfortable chairs in our locker room.

Then I added a mood room, an isolation tank room, and an exercise room, just like we'd had when I was with the Phillies. From the outside my mood room looks just like a sauna, with a big wooden door. I had it installed where the umpires' room used to be, between the two clubhouses, and moved the umpires to a former storeroom, down the right-field line. Three walls inside the mood room are painted a soothing sky blue, while the entire fourth wall is a screen. Facing the screen is the mood chair, which is a combination massager and sound system. When someone sits in it, it vibrates slightly, and rollers put pressure on their muscles. It has four speakers built into it, so whoever is sitting in it can listen to anything he wants to. The difference between my mood room and the one we had in Philadelphia is that in my room we can play a video on the screen, while in Philly we just had to stare at a still photograph of the ocean with waves rolling in. Now we can play a tape of the ocean with the waves rolling in.

The purpose of the room is to allow a player to put himself in any mood he wants to simply by playing the right audio and videotapes. In Philadelphia, for example, Dave Bristol would only listen to Willie Nelson tapes, which would relax him. I've stocked the library with a lot of inspirational tapes, highlights-of-Yankee-history tapes, and specially prepared tapes of our players being successful and opponents failing. I mean, before a game Don Mattingly can go into the room and watch fifteen minutes of himself hitting home runs and making great plays in the field. If Roger Clemens is pitching against us, he can put on the Clemens tape and watch Clemens being knocked around. So much of this game is confidence, and I intend to do everything possible to build my players' confidence.

The isolation tank, or flotation tank, is a long metal tank half filled with salt water. Because of the salt, when someone lies in the tank he floats on top of the water without any effort. When the lid is closed the tank is pitch black and soundproof inside, although it does have a built-in sound system. Think of it as Dracula's swimming pool. Tug McGraw had the first one in Philadelphia, and I liked using it so much I bought one myself. But because I had no place to keep it at home, I left it at Veterans Stadium when I retired. One of the first things I did when I bought the Yankees was have it shipped to the Stadium. The other thing I did was get one of New York's top jingle houses, the people who write music for commercials, John Hill Music, to create special tapes for each player, to provide positive reinforcement.

I used to love lying in that tank, letting my mind wander. But the main thing I used to think about was how long I'd been in that tank.

I called the third room an exercise room, but it's really the frustration room. In Philadelphia we had a completely padded room, floor and walls. Steve Carlton would do his martial arts exercises there. He also kept a barrel filled with rice in that room, and would strengthen his arm by trying to punch his fist into the rice. It's very difficult to punch your arm into a barrel of rice, but Carlton could make it halfway down the barrel. I tried it; I punched oh, three or four kernels deep. But my frustration room is very different. When I was playing it was so obvious to me that players needed someplace where they could be by themselves and release all the tension and anger that built up during a game. Unlike football, basketball, or hockey, baseball is not supposed to be a contact sport. Players and managers aren't supposed to hit other players, so instead they smash water coolers, bat racks, and lightbulbs and turn over tables full of the post game meal. I'll tell you who had the worst temper I've ever seen: my manager, Mr. Piniella. Lou expected so much of himself that when he failed he just had to clobber something. Once, I remember, I personally bought a twenty-cup coffee maker for the clubhouse. In the seventh inning of that coffee maker's very first game, Lou struck out with one out and a runner on third base. A few minutes later somebody called me in the bullpen and told me my coffee maker had been murdered. On another occasion Lou stomped back to the dugout after striking out and went after the water cooler. Everybody in the dugout knew what was going to happen and started moving in the other direction. Everybody except Jay Johnstone. Johnstone had been in such a terrible batting slump for about a month that he just didn't care. When Piniella got to the water cooler he lifted his bat, then stopped. He looked at Johnstone. "Here," he said, handing him the bat. "You do it. You haven't hit a damn thing in a month."

So Johnstone stood up and smashed that water cooler to a drizzle.

There was a series of lightbulbs on the ramp leading from the dugout to the clubhouse and somebody was always smashing them, so The Boss decided to put protective metal cages around them. Piniella didn't realize that, and the first time he took his regular swing at the bulbs his bat bounced off the metal frame and hit him in the head. Then he *really* got mad.

Of course, Piniella wasn't the only one. So I decided we should have a room where players can really let out their frustration. I covered the walls and floor with protective padding, and installed a wooden table, two punching bags, a big hanging heavy bag, boxes of plates and glasses, a plastic water cooler, and lots of bats and balls. Any player who wants to can go in there and hit the bags with his fist or a bat, break plates and glasses on the table, even kick the water cooler around. Then he can come out, and very calmly go into the mood room to get into a good mood.

And fans think running a team is simply a matter of providing bats and balls and a ballpark and uniforms and 30,000 fans and hot dogs. But major-league baseball players are human beings too. Well, at least most of them are. I'm still not so sure about Nettles. And to be successful management must be concerned about the way a player thinks and lives, as well as how he performs on the ballfield.

I really couldn't wait to see how the players would react to the new additions. I was hoping they'd understand what I was trying to do. I'm not sure they do, though. As I walked by the flotation tank room I overheard Rosey Rogers asking somebody, "You think two people could do it in there?" Then I saw Raoul Rojas walking into the mood room with a handful of Twisted Sister tapes. Everybody liked the chairs, though. As Steve Sax sad, "This is so comfortable I think I'm just going to sit here all season."

It's nice to be appreciated.

APRIL 4 ★

Opening Day. I don't think there is anything in the world filled with as much promise as an empty baseball field in spring. I got to the Stadium very early this morning, by myself, just to spend a little time here before the gates were opened. I wanted to feel the anticipation. The morning was cool, about 55°, but the sky was a beautiful clear blue. It was a beautiful day to play baseball.

There were a few people moving around the ballpark, getting ready for the crowd. Somebody was testing the scoreboard lights; in the National League the Pirates were beating the Mets 1,285–1. Somebody else was working on the sound system, and every few minutes the first four or five notes of "New York, New York" would blast through the empty ballpark. I just sat in a seat behind first base, looking out at the newly sodded field, and loving the moment.

It's funny. Sitting there, staring at my old office, the pitcher's mound, where I'd had some of the most exciting moments of my life, I didn't think about the past. I wondered about the future.

Opening Day is always special. No game has as little real meaning in the standings—there are 161 games after this one to make up for whatever happens—but few other games have as much meaning. Everybody believes it's an omen for the rest of the season—if the first pitch you throw is a strike you're going to have a good season; if you get a hit your first time at bat you're going to have a good season. I'll tell you how much it really means: At the end of the first day, Cleveland can be in first place!

I never got nervous on Opening Day. Maybe because I never knew if I was going to get into the game, and by the time I got the call to warm up it was too late to be nervous. Besides, I never really got nervous when I was playing. Some people thought, because I had such an even temperament, that I didn't care. That was never true. I cared. I really cared, but I knew I could never let myself get too high or too low about one game, because there was a good chance I was going to be in the game the next day. Like we used to say in the bullpen, for relief pitchers, there's no tomorrow today!

I think it's going to be a great season. Of course, on Opening Day I always thought it was going to be a great season. That's what Opening

Days are for. But the addition of Davis makes us a legitimate contender. If we get some starting pitching . . . It won't be easy, though. Toronto is still young, they've won, they're confident and they've got Dave Steib, Jimmy Key, and Fred McGriff. Boston can repeat if Clemens continues his comeback and Pete Runnels III can put up the same kind of numbers he put up last year. The Tigers look like they're going to be very tough, with the addition of rookies Freaky Thompson and Asher Berns to a veteran team including Lou Whitaker, Alan Trammel, and Jack Morris. The Indians' rookie pitcher, Lefty Wright, can be a dominating force, and combined with Tom Candiotti and Richard Yett could make them a legitimate contender. As long as Baltimore has Cal Ripken, Jr., Mickey Tettleton, and William Powell, and a manager like Frank Robinson . . . And Milwaukee has a bunch of good kids to complement Robin Yount, Paul Molitor, and Teddy Higuera.

There is one question that I finally had to answer today: Does the owner belong in the clubhouse? Should I go in there before the game? If I have something to say should I go in there after the game? I mean, there are times when an owner has to be there—for example when his team clinches a division or league championship, or wins the World Series. But what about the other times? I remember being told about Walter O'Malley, who went into his Brooklyn Dodgers locker room after the third and final game of the 1951 playoffs against the Giants—minutes after the Giants' Bobby Thomson had hit a three-run homer in the bottom of the ninth inning to cap the greatest comeback in baseball history. The Dodger players were sitting there in silent shock when O'Malley told them, "Fellows, these things happen."

And somebody, I think it was Wayne Terwilliger, said, "Jeez, not too often, I hope."

Every owner I played for was different. In Philadelphia Ruly Carpenter would come into the clubhouse hours before the game; he liked being around the players and most of us liked having him around. But when the clubhouse started filling up, he always left. We didn't see Brad Corbett too much in the clubhouse in Texas, but he often invited players he liked to his house for a barbecue. And in New York? People have accused The Boss of almost everything, but nobody ever claimed he was shy. The Boss would usually come down to lecture us after we'd lost at least three games in a row, because we were so good that chances of us losing four or five in a row were slim. He'd come down and make his speech, we'd win the next day, and he would feel responsible. He'd always begin his speeches by telling us, "You know, down on the docks if this was going on . . ." Whatever was happening: "Down on the docks . . ." And he would usually finish by reminding us that he signed our paychecks.

I'll tell you one thing for sure: During my big league career I heard a lot of speeches in the clubhouse, and not once, never, did I hear a player say after the speaker was finished, "You know, he's absolutely right. We haven't been trying to win. Why didn't we think of that? From now on, let's go out there and try to win!"

So I decided I didn't belong in the clubhouse. Then, after I'd thought about it a little longer, I realized—it's my clubhouse! I can go there anytime I want to. I can swing from the ceiling if I want to. I can get naked and sit on a birthday cake if I want to. Because it's my clubhouse. I own it. Mine, mine, mine.

The first person I ran into on the way down to the clubhouse was Mickey Rivers, who was talking to reporters about his new broadcasting partner, our spring training ego coach, Reggie Jackson. Mick and Reggie have had a friendly feud going since we all played together. Reggie was always trying to impress everyone with his intelligence, and Mickey was always able to find his weak spot. Once, I remember, on a bus trip, Reggie claimed loudly that he had an IQ of something like 140. And Mickey asked him, "Is that out of a thousand?" But this morning, as I walked past him, Mick winked at me and I heard him tell the writers, "Oh, I like Reggie well enough, but you know, it's like Reggie says, 'Reggie Jackson is the man who put the "I" in "team." ' "

There was a tremendous feeling of anticipation inside the clubhouse. In the big corner locker that the great clubhouse man Pete Sheehy had handed down from Thurman to Gator to Rags, Don Mattingly was swinging a lead bat, working on his stroke. A few lockers over, Tommy John was lying on his back, pumping five-pound weights with his left arm, trying to loosen up his spring. Tums Taft, dressed in bright red long johns—he wears something bright red every game to remind himself that he's faced the bulls, so batters can't really hurt him— walked by me and whispered, "Olé today, José."

"Know what you mean," I lied.

I stopped by Frank Biondo's locker and wished him luck for the season. "Luck is what happens when opportunity meets preparation," he told me, "and I think we've got a great opportunity to be prepared this season!"

"Right," I agreed. Whatever. I saw Hanko Tsumi sitting by himself, so I thought I would go over and wish him luck for the season. But before I could say a word to him, he stood up and bowed to me, then said, "I thank you very much for your nice thoughts to me."

I bowed back. A few feet away from Tsumi, Dave Winfield was surrounded by a large group of reporters. "Sure I'll miss The Boss," I heard him say. "Whatever differences we had, I knew that he was always there. And let's be frank, The Boss and I got some great press together, didn't we? But I'll tell you, I think that most of all, I'll miss his sense of humor. Believe me, that man could make me laugh."

Before going back upstairs, I made a point of stopping at Raoul Rojas's locker to try to calm him down before his first major-league game. Until you've played in that first major-league game, thrown that first pitch, gotten that first hit, the pressure is tremendous. I really wish I could remember the first hitter I faced; if I could I'd never forget it again. I've seen players forget their equipment before their first game. I've seen them get sick from nervousness in the dugout. I've seen them be so scared they couldn't speak. Rojas is a very confident kid, and I knew he'd be all right. I just wanted to pat him on the back and remind him that he wouldn't be here if we didn't think he was ready for the big leagues. Unfortunately, I found him curled up on the floor of his locker fast asleep, and I didn't want to wake him up.

At exactly 1:05 P.M., after a brief ceremony unveiling the Perez Memorial in centerfield, Robert Merrill sang "The Star Spangled Banner," Joe DiMaggio and Mickey Mantle threw out the first balls, umpire Steve Palermo screamed "Play ball!" and the season began.

It would have been a perfect day, except for the game. The Tigers beat Tums Taft in relief of Chuck Cary, 4–3. I know it's only one game, but it is Opening Day, and I really wanted to win. Just in case it really is an omen.

I don't mind losing one game, I just wasn't happy about the way we lost it. I'm certainly not going to start second-guessing Lou Piniella, but with the score tied 3–3 in the eighth, we had Geren on first base with no outs and Espinoza at bat. Instead of sacrificing, Piniella tried to hit and run. I'm really not second-guessing, but what in the world was he thinking? Espinoza is the best bunter on the team, the game was tied in the bottom of the eighth inning, and he doesn't sacrifice! Then in the bottom of the ninth, after Taft had given up the home run to Alan Trammel that put the Tigers in front, Lou didn't pinch-hit Davis against Jack Morris. If I were second-guessing, which I'm not, that's the move I'd really second-guess. But I'm not. It just seems to me that we got Davis to provide left-handed power against right-handed pitchers in late innings, and we were facing a right-handed pitcher in the ninth inning. There is no later inning than that. So? It was a perfect situation. I suppose it's a good thing I'm not The Boss, because right now he'd be on the telephone asking Piniella some serious questions. Not me; I don't do that sort of thing. Even if it is my clubhouse.

APRIL 5 ★

Two losses in a row to the Tigers do not make me a happy owner. This time Taft couldn't hold a one-run lead for an inning, letting the Tigers score two runs in the top of the ninth to win 6–5. Maybe I could understand losing two straight games if we were playing the Blue Jays or Orioles, but Detroit? This is an old team. Trammel. Whitaker. Darrel Evans has to be close to fifty. Yet we let them beat us twice. I know it's a long season, but it's two games shorter than it was yesterday morning, and Toronto is already two games ahead of us.

The thing that bothered me most is that Keith Reich bobbled a perfect double-play ball in the ninth inning to give the Tigers an extra out, and they took advantage of that. I don't know, maybe Reich is finished, maybe it's time to let him sit on the bench for a while and think about things. Besides, I'd like to see the kids like Velarde play a little. We have to find out early if our young players are going to be able to help us or not, and if they can't we have to make some changes before it's too late.

I'm not panicking; I'm just a little nervous.

Before the game I got some disturbing news from Dave Dunn, chief of Stadium Security. Apparently a man who looked suspiciously like The Boss, wearing a mustache and a wig, tried to sneak into the Stadium using forged press credentials. Fortunately, one of our security people realized that *Psychology Today* was not an accredited sports publication, at least not yet, and challenged him. When he did, this guy ran dropping the false mustache in his getaway. Could it really have been The Boss? Why would he try to sneak in instead of just buying a ticket? He must have known that if we knew it was him we would have sold him the best available seat. I've sent a memo to the security staff alerting them to this incident and reminding them to be vigilant in the future.

APRIL 6 ★

Before the game today Duke Schneider handed me a folder filled with computer-produced charts and said, "I think these might be useful to you." Turns out she'd compiled a "Tiger Batters' Tendency Chart," which, she explained, divided the hitting zone, "any place that a pitched ball can be reached by the batter," into sixteen small sections. Then, based on the first two games, she calculated the tendency of every Tiger batter to swing at pitches in each of those areas, as well as the subsequent result. For example, her "Matt Nokes Chart" showed that in nine at bats in two games, Nokes had seen a total of twenty-eight pitches. Of those twenty-eight, five had been in sections 13 and 14, the low inside corner. Of those five, he swung at four, fouling off one and missing the three others. "Therefore," she pointed out, "Nokes has a weakness low and inside. Look, I know this is just preliminary; the sample isn't large enough, and it doesn't even take into account the type of pitch thrown, the velocity, the situation . . ."

"Can you figure all that in?" I asked, still looking at the chart.

"Oh sure, I just need a bigger sample. Want me to?"

I nodded. "Yeah, sure. Meanwhile, I'll just pass these along to Lou."

Lou shook his head and smiled as he examined them. "It took a computer to figure out Nokes doesn't like to be pitched inside, huh?" he chuckled. "You should have saved your money, Sparky. Just check the scouting reports. Everybody's known that about him since the day he came up. What these numbers don't tell you is that that's also where his power is. Maybe he's only gonna hit the low inside pitch once every eight or nine at bats, but when he does . . ." Lou pointed into the distant sky. "Look Spark, she seems like a sweet girl. Just keep her busy taking care of the defensive alignment charts. That's where her fancy computers might actually do us a little good."

"Well, why don't you look them over anyway," I suggested. "You know, it'll make her feel good."

Lou laughed. "What is this? What are you looking for, a manager or a guidance counselor? Make her feel good?" He shook his head again. I think he was a little disgusted.

And then we finally won a ballgame. Tommy John pitched a four-hit shutout, Kelly and Winfield hit home runs off Hank Kleinschmidt, and we won 4–0. TJ was just overpowering. His fastball, which we clocked consistently at 93 mph, was rising, so the Tigers hit a lot of pop-ups and fly-ball outs. As long as they don't pull the ball, this ballpark is big enough to hold most fly balls, and TJ is smart enough to keep them from pulling the ball. Our outfielders had sixteen put-outs. After the game Sparky Anderson said Tommy's arm reminded him of a young Dwight Gooden, although the rest of his body reminded him of an old Casey Stengel.

It feels good to get that first victory, though. If we can just start playing the way I know we're capable of playing, we'll be all right.

APRIL 7 ★

Nettles, Reggie, Chicken, and I sat around last night until much too late talking about the old days. Chicken did his famous Billy-George bit: "You're fired." "You can't fire me, I quit." "You can't quit, I've already fired you." "You can't fire me, I've already quit." "Okay, let's start again; you're hired."

Of all of us, Graig had the longest career, playing in the big leagues until he was forty-four years old, then playing and managing in that Florida Seniors League. "I'll tell you what the real secret was," he whispered. "Playing third base." We all laughed. "No, no really, I figured it out once. I was responsible for covering what, maybe 25 feet from the foul line to the hole. I got maybe three or four balls hit to me a game for which I had to move maybe another 30 feet. Meanwhile, the outfielders had to run a quarter mile just to get to their positions. And then they run probably another quarter mile every game chasing fly balls, or backing up the infield." He looked at Reggie. "Well, maybe not every outfielder . . ." And everybody laughed, even Reggie. "But what I mean is, over a whole season outfielders run about 55 miles more than first basemen or third basemen, and over ten years that's 550 miles. Believe me, 550 miles on artificial turf can take a lot out of your legs. See, I could have been a great outfielder if I'd wanted to, but I was just too smart."

I couldn't believe that he had really figured all that out. "Is that true?" I asked. "You really think that's why you lasted so long?"

"You kidding? Of course not. But I had to have something to tell the writers. Sounds great though, doesn't it?"

"I think I got the real reason," Reggie decided. "Graig was always so slow that nobody even noticed when his legs went." And we all laughed.

"You mean like your batting average?" Graig said to Reggie, and we all laughed, but not as hard. That was when I ordered another drink.

APRIL 8 ★

I did something today I've never done before. I fired somebody. Kansas City's in town for a two-game set, and it happened during the game. At one time all the music in the ballpark was provided by an organist who played songs like "Three Blind Mice" when the umpires came out, or "Swing on a Star" when Mattingly came to bat. But a few years ago The Boss replaced the organist with a disc jockey who played popular records, even some rock and roll, between innings. That was supposed to appeal to younger fans. The DJ at the Stadium has been Jay Bauman, who also works at WTIN, a local rock station. I met with him briefly before the season and told him I wanted him to play contemporary, upbeat, family music. I wanted to feel life inside the ballpark. I guess Bauman didn't really understand what I meant.

Between the third and fourth inning I suddenly heard, blasting through the entire ballpark, somebody named George Michael singing a song called "I Want Your Sex." I just ignored it, hoping that nobody else would notice it. But when he started playing some Bon Jovi songs, "Love for Sale," "Social Disease," and "Lay Your Hands on Me," I started searching for his booth. It took me a few minutes to find him in the auxiliary press box, and by the time I got there he was playing, "If I Say You Have a Wonderful Body, Will You Hold It Against Me?" I pulled the tape out of the machine in the middle of that song. "I want you to put on the Sinatra version of 'New York, New York,'" I said.

He looked at me like I was the crazy one, then brushed his hair out of his eyes. "I can't do that," he said.

"If you don't," I said calmly, "you're fired."

"I wish I was the kind of person who could play a song like that," he said. "Honestly I do. But it's against everything I sit behind a desk for."

"Then you're fired. Clear out your tapes."

He just stared at me for a few seconds, then asked, "Can you really do that? Just fire me like that, in the middle of a game?"

I thought about it. "I guess I can," I told him. "It's my team, right?" I smiled a little. "You know, you're the first person I've ever fired."

He offered his hand. "Congratulations." We shook hands. "You did real well. I've been fired a lot of times. For a first time, you were very good. And you'll get better at it when you have a little more experience."

"Thanks," I said, a little shyly. Then he packed up his tapes and left. But a funny thing happened as he walked out of the booth. I liked the feeling that came over me. I knew I was doing the right thing; because it's my responsibility to make sure nothing that happens at the ballpark offends our fans. But much more than that, I liked the feeling of power. Knowing that made me a little nervous. I suspected this was the way addicts started.

We lost the game to the Royals, 6–1. Seitzer had a home run and three RBIs. The team still hasn't started hitting. But somehow I couldn't get angry. That other feeling was just too strong.

APRIL 9 ★

Before tonight's game I noticed that Bill Lee had the entire pitching staff doing laps around the ballpark. I didn't like that at all. Personally, I never believed that running was all that important to a pitcher. I mean, if it was, Jesse Owens would have been a 20-game winner. But Bill Lee always believed differently. In his playing days he'd go into the outfield before games to shag fly balls, announcing, "I'll take everything from left-center to the foul line." Then he'd spend the next half hour running full speed after fly balls, diving for them, crashing into walls. I think all that running was very important to his pitching success—as long as he didn't lose his fastball. But I didn't think it was so good for our pitching staff. So I went down to the field to talk to him about it. "Gee, Bill," I said, "I was watching the pitchers running in the outfield before the game. Let me ask you a question. You ever think about entering them in the Boston Marathon?"

I thought I was being clever. But when I said that, he looked at me quizzically. "You know," he said, "I never thought of that. That's a great idea." Then he walked away shouting, "Hey, Tums, c'mere a second. . . ."

We also had our first real problem with our broadcasters. I found out that several players are upset about some of the things Reggie is saying on television. Most broadcasters have a personal slogan they become known for. Scooter and Harry Caray are known for saying "Holy cow!" for example. Mel Allen was famous for "That ball is going, going, gone!" Apparently, Reggie's slogan is "I could've done that." Every time a player fails to do something—sacrifice, make a play in the outfield, hit a home run—Reggie says, "Too bad, fans, I could've done that." And the players don't like it at all. So after speaking to Lee, I went and found Reggie in the pressroom. "Believe me, Reggie, I want you to be completely honest; I just don't want you to say anything that'll hurt anybody's feelings."

"I'm just telling it like it is, Sparky," he said. "Besides, I want them to get mad at me, I want them to try to show me up. I've changed a lot since I've retired, and I think I've finally realized that The Boss was absolutely right about one thing: Anger motivates people to reach their greatest potential. I mean, that man knew it would work for me. He got me so angry I took it out on the baseball. I'm just trying to do the same thing for these kids. And I can take the heat better than most people. Remember, Spark, it's me, Reggie, the guy who would do anything to help the team."

Actually, I didn't really remember that. "Sure, Reggie," I told him. "But just try to keep it down a little. Know what I mean?" The fact is that I don't think anybody would care what Reggie said if we were winning. But when a team is losing, every minor irritation becomes a cactus grove. No jokes are funny. No food tastes good. As Rosey Rogers says, "In situations like this, thank God for women." We lost again today, and this time I have to blame Graig Nettles. I guess more than a few feet separate third base and the third base coaching box, because Graig doesn't seem comfortable in the coaching box. With the score tied 2–2 in the seventh, and Geren on second with one out, Raoul Rojas, who started at third base, lined a base hit to left field. Bo Jackson took it on the first hop. For some reason, Nettles waved Geren home. On Bo Jackson's arm! I'll tell you how much he was out by. He was out by so much that up in the second auxiliary pressbox, Reggie told his listeners, "Gee, I'm not really sure even I could've made that one."

I've always tried to be available to reporters, but I didn't want to speak to them after this game because I was afraid I might say something I'd regret. So I told them, "I have absolutely no comment to make, except to say that I'm disappointed in the effort I've seen put forth by some of our players. I just don't want to say anything that might sound like criticism. You all know that that's just not my style. Besides, you all saw the same incredibly stupid thing I did."

I'm going to suggest to Lou that he ask Graig to sit down and watch some of the old highlight films of the great third base coach Frank "The Old Crow" Crosetti at work. I wonder if there's a good instructional video on coaching third base. If there isn't, maybe we should consider producing something like *Coaching Third Base the Yankee Way*. If we do, though, we're certainly not going to use Nettles on it.

APRIL 10 ★

We released the following statement to the newspapers this morning: "New York Yankees sole owner Albert 'Sparky' Lyle today announced the formation of a five-man panel consisting entirely of Yankee fans to meet monthly with team executives to discuss those matters of particular interest and concern to Yankee fans. Members of this panel will be selected from letters received by the Yankees dated prior to midnight, May 1, explaining in 75 words or less 'Why I Should Be on the Yankees Advisory Committee.' Each member of the committee will receive a season box for himself and three friends, to enable him to attend as many Yankee home games as possible. Members of the committee will be selected based on their loyalty to the Yankees and the sport of baseball, and all entries will remain the property of the New York Yankees. The creation of the committee is intended to demonstrate the renewed commitment of Yankee management to be responsive to the needs and desires of our loyal fans. All letters should be addressed to The Yankees Advisory Committee, Yankee Stadium, The Bronx, New York 10451."

We did it on the advice of our public relations/marketing firm, McElnea Associates. When I met with them last January they showed me the results of a very expensive study they'd conducted. This study indicated Yankee fans had become alienated over the last decade, that they no longer thought of the Yankees as "their team," that they had stopped making emotional investments in players because few players remained with the team more than two seasons, and that they did not believe the organization cared about the fan.

They needed to conduct an expensive study to figure that out?

To win back the loyalty of former Yankee fans as well as attract new fans, the firm suggested several options, one of them being an advertising campaign. Among the slogans they suggested for this campaign were, "The Yanks Are Coming Home," "The Home Team Is Home," "The Pride Is Back Again in the Bronx," "The Bombers Are Back," "We've Got a Cheer for You in the Bronx," "Yankee Fans See, Yankee Fans Know," "Bats About the Yankees," "Have a Ball in the Bronx," and "Return of the Tradition!"

I thought about it, then decided we didn't need a slogan. I never played for a team that had a slogan. When I was with the Yankees in our great days our slogan was simple: Game Tonight 7:30. The only thing we needed to do to draw people to the Stadium was play exciting baseball. You can't talk about it; you have to do it. And besides, the Mets already had all the best slogans.

When I rejected that idea Jeff McElnea suggested we form a Yankees Advisory Committee. Chicken and I are supposed to meet with these fans once a month so we can hear, in person, "the voice of the fan." At first, the McElnea people wanted to say, "the voice of Joe and Jane Fan," but I wouldn't let them. At these meetings these fans will have a chance to tell us about the things that concern them: the status of the team, ballpark safety, food, parking conditions, even prices. Then we'll give them a nice lunch and send them home, and give the story to the papers. I thought it was a great idea: It'll make the fans feel we really care about them, it will generate a lot of positive publicity, and it costs almost nothing. The only thing that surprises me is that every other team hasn't done the same thing.

APRIL 11 ★

The first road trip of the season is always exciting. It feels sort of like going on a field trip in elementary school. It means getting away from the routine at home. I certainly don't intend to make every trip with the team, but since we're not playing well, and I haven't been to Cleveland in years, I decided to make this one. On the flight I made a point of moving around the cabin, spending a little time with several different people. Mattingly was sitting up front, gently swinging a bat to strengthen his wrists, while watching a videotape of himself at bat on a personal VCR in his lap. "See," he told me, nodding towards the tape, "I'm just pulling off the ball a little. I really think it's just a minor adjustment, then I'll be okay." One thing I know I'm not going to have to worry about is Mattingly hitting.

Keith Reich—"Plug," as he's known around the league because he's built like a fire hydrant, short and squat—looked at me nervously as I sat down next to him. "You have something to tell me, right?"

I didn't know what he was talking about. "I don't think so," I said, shaking my head. "Should I?"

"I'm in a deal, aren't I?" I shook my head again, and before I could say no, he said, "Then I'm on waivers, right?"

"Plug, I just . . ."

"You're giving me my death certificate?"

He meant his unconditional release. "No, nothing," I told him. "I just wanted to see how you were doing. You know, I wanted to talk owner-to-player."

He looked at me suspiciously. "Really?" I nodded, and his face brightened. "Oh. Well then, how you doin', Spark? It's real good to see ya."

It had taken me only a few seconds to realize that Reich was suffering from an advanced case of "Veteran's Paranoia." That's when a veteran player knows he's near the end of his career, and he's desperately trying to hold on for one more season before he has to enter that dreaded new world: Real Life. This is the time in most ballplayers' careers when they start to read meaning into every word, every gesture; the time when every hello from a general manager can really mean good-bye. And the truth is that Reich is near the end of his career. He's been a useful big-league player for eight seasons, but he's never hit very much. This is a good situation for him here, but if we have to make some changes, he may be expendable. The numbers are against him: his age, his batting average, and the fact we can only keep twenty-four men on the roster. "How's it going with you?"

"Oh, great," he told me. "I really like being here. And I think I'm a good influence on the young kids. In a couple of years they're going to be ready to step in and play every day."

"Keith," I said softly, "don't worry so much. We need a few veterans who've been through a pennant race. I know what you can do for the club." I didn't want to be too honest with him.

"That's me all the way, Sparky, Mr. Stabilizing Influence. And hey, you know what else? I've been meaning to mention this to Lou, but a few years ago, when I was playing winter ball down in the Dominican, I did a little catching. So if Lou ever gets into a spot where he needs somebody to go behind the plate for a few innings . . ."

I promised to mention that to Piniella, and moved back a few rows and found Jesse Barfield reading *USA Today*. "How's it going with you?"

"Good," he said confidently. "Yeah, real good. I'm almost there, I can feel my stroke coming back. I just missed really getting on a couple of pitches off Gubicza the other day."

I told him to keep swinging, that we really needed his power, and moved over next to Rosey Rogers. I knew there was something bothering Rosey—we'd been in the air almost forty-five minutes and he hadn't tried to date a single stewardess. Instead, he was just staring out the window at what looked like an ocean of fluffy white cotton. "How you doing, Rosey?"

"Fine," he said tonelessly.

"Olé!" I heard Taft shout from the back of the plane, where the card game was in full progress.

"What's the matter?" I asked Rogers.

He shifted around in his seat and faced me. "It's nothing. It's silly. I just . . . I don't know, I think my girlfriend's cheating on me."

"How do you know?"

"Little things. Sometimes she's not home when I call; she's wearing a new kind of perfume; when I called this morning to say good-bye a man answered."

Before I could say anything, Joe Verola leaned over the back of the seat and stuck a tape recorder in front of me and Rosey. "You guys mind if I get some of this for my book?"

Rosey took a swipe at the tape recorder, but Joe V was too quick for him. "I don't think this is the time, Joe," I said. "Maybe next season."

Joe mumbled something like, "What am I gonna tell my publisher?" but he sat down. I turned back to Rosey. "Didn't you ask who it was? Maybe it was just a relative, or a friend."

"At 7:30 in the morning? Yeah, it was a friend, all right. Hey, I know what's going on. She thinks that just because I'm married I'm not serious about her." He forced a hollow laugh. "Women. I swear to God, I'll never understand them."

I slapped his leg. "Hey, lemme tell you something. If she is seeing somebody else, that's her loss. You just wait until September, when we're right in the middle of the pennant race and everybody in New

York is talking about us, and your phone is ringing every five minutes and it's somebody you went to school with in second grade calling to say hello and begging for tickets. You won't even be able to take out your garbage without having to sign autographs. You watch and see how interested she'll be in this other guy then."

"You really think so?"

"I *know* it. That's why I'm the owner. Believe me, a pennant race is the best aphrodisiac ever invented. All we got to do is get there, and she'll be over you like clam sauce on linguini. But Rosey, we can't do it without your big bat."

He slapped his chest. "You got it, Spark. Pennant race, here we come."

I kept moving around the plane. A few people were twitching to the beat of their Walkmans, Rojas was fast asleep, the card game was loud and cheerful. I started to sit down next to Tsumi. "I'm fine, thank you very much for thinking," he said, before I could open my mouth, so I just kept moving. Finally I settled in next to Nettles. I knew the rest of the flight would be quiet—after what I'd said about him in the papers, he wasn't talking to me.

My presence on the trip didn't do much good. We dropped the opener to the Indians 9–2, in front of 38,000 fans. That's a big crowd in Cleveland, but if they get good weather at the beginning of the season, while they're still in the pennant race, they draw well. Unfortunately, in Cleveland, April usually is the whole pennant race. I honestly believe if the Indians ever became real contenders they'd draw 3.5 million fans. Who knows? Maybe this year. They've been steadily adding talented young kids to a solid nucleus of veteran ballplayers. Their rookie outfielder, Joey Alou, Jesus Alou's son, looks like a real prospect—he hit a long home run, walked and stole a base, and made a terrific catch to take at least a double away from Winfield. As always, our starting pitcher got us into a jam our middle relievers couldn't get us out of. To go with our bad pitching, we're getting almost no hitting. Mattingly is 2-for-19 with no extra-base hits, so I've got to wonder if his back is bothering him. Winfield is trying to pull everything and the result is weak ground balls to shortstop. Suarez seems completely lost at the plate. Only Sax and Espinoza are doing anything. But all I can do about it is watch and keep my mouth shut. I want to give Lou a real chance to shake things up a little before I step in.

After the game Marty Noble asked me if Lou's job was in jeopardy. I'd forgotten how tough the New York reporters can be. The team's played eight games and already people are wondering about the manager's job. "Why should it be?" I told him. "He's not the one not pitching, he's not the one not hitting. All he can do is send them out there. So why should it be?"

"So you're not denying that you're thinking about it?" Noble asked.

I think tempers are beginning to get just a little short around here.

APRIL 15 ★

I'll tell you how bad things have gotten. The best thing that happened today was that I paid my income taxes. We finally won our second game yesterday, but tonight Tums Taft came out of the bullpen in the ninth inning to try to protect Tommy John's three-run lead. He struck out Scott Jacoby, got Andy Allanson to bounce out to Sax, and then walked the bases loaded on twelve straight pitches. My stomach was really churning—that's why they call him Tums, right?—but I calmed down when he threw two gorgeous breaking pitches for strikes to Cory Snyder. Then he tried to challenge him with a fastball, and Snyder hit it into the center-field bleachers for a game-winning grand slam home run. Tums? They should have called him Arsenic! I know, sometimes the bull, she gores you right in the stomach.

But I'm still not panicking. I've learned from experience that a baseball team is a lot like an engine. In April, it sputters into life. In May, it slowly begins gaining power. By June, it's churning away, occasionally missing a few strokes, but running smoothly. And in September, it goes into top gear; a well-oiled machine producing power.

We're playing like an old lawnmower engine that doesn't want to start.

I really don't know why a team suddenly comes together and starts winning. I know that in baseball it isn't always the team with the best starting lineup that wins. Maybe that's because the season is so long that before it's over every player on the roster has to contribute if a team is going to be successful. If a team has a weakness, over the

162-game schedule that weakness is going to be exposed, and end up costing the team at least a few games. In football, a great quarterback can turn a team into a winner. In basketball, a great center can turn a team around. But baseball really is a team game. Maybe that's the beauty of baseball. Or, maybe not.

Right now the best thing I can say about this team is that we're consistent. We stink every day. I don't want to make changes for the sake of making changes, but why else do you make changes? If we see that certain players aren't contributing, and we have a player in the minor leagues who looks like he can help us, why shouldn't we bring him up? I'd be ready to bring somebody up from Columbus right now, but they haven't even opened their season, so I don't know who can help us.

I'll tell you how upset I was after the game. I walked into the locker room. It was absolutely silent, and before I could say a word Saxy grabbed me and whispered, "Not now. It's not the time."

"I didn't know mind reading was catching," I said.

"Your face is redder than a bottle of Heinz ketchup."

APRIL 16 ★

We just made the longest recorded flight from Cleveland to Detroit in the history of jet travel—probably because we had to make a brief stopover in Atlanta. For all of you who aren't very good in geography, Cleveland and Detroit are on the Great Lakes, while Atlanta is still in Georgia. Fortunately, there wasn't too much complaining on the airplane. Everybody was so deeply involved in killing time that they didn't seem to realize how much time they were killing. Only Tommy John was bothered by the trip. "Hey, Spark," he asked me, "isn't this an unusually long flight between Cleveland and Detroit?"

"Headwinds," I told him. But after checking into the hotel in Detroit I found Duke sitting by herself in the coffee shop. "Did we really have to go to Atlanta?" I asked.

"That's 26,000 frequent flyer miles," she pointed out. "You just qualified for the Chairman's Lounge. In one trip."

She looked so lonely sitting there by herself that I really couldn't get too mad at her. Instead, I sat down and ordered a cup of coffee. "So how's it going?"

"Not bad," she said, looking at the pile of papers she was working on. "I think I'm beginning to see patterns developing on ball and strike counts that . . ."

"Wait a second, I mean with you, how's it going? You getting along okay?"

She faked a tight smile. "Just fine, I guess. Except every time I walk into a room some player starts meowing. And when I try to talk to them about an important statistic they start asking about my statistics. I really don't understand men, sometimes. Can't they ever take a woman seriously? You think that all I am is this body?"

I looked at her body. I was glad that that was a rhetorical question. I also knew that my wife, Mary was going to help me edit this diary. So I really didn't look at her body; I pretended to look at her body. I guess I'm a pretty good actor, because she didn't realize I was faking it. "I know you're not just another pretty girl," I told her, "and I think you're doing a real good job for us. Just keep it up and you're gonna win them over. But there is one thing . . ."

"What's that?"

"No more layovers in Atlanta between Cleveland and Detroit."

APRIL 20 ★

I found out tonight that Big John Nicholson's hobby is collecting a "representative bug or insect" from every ballpark he's played in during his professional baseball career. I found that out when his Detroit specimen, a big, round, green thing with wings and long red antennae, escaped from a jar in Nicholson's locker and hid in one of Eric Plunk's slippers. Nicholson is going to have to find another specimen. The doctor said the bite didn't look infectious, and the fight ended when Nicholson agreed to buy Plunk a new pair of slippers.

After the incident I talked to Nicholson about his collection. "A lot of players, when they retire," he explained, "they've got all these awards and trophies that they can look at to remind them about their career. I don't have any of that stuff. I've never won a goddam thing.

So instead, I've got my bugs. I've got a whole display case of them; they're all mounted on a wall in my garage. All I have to do is look at them and I can remember every goddam place I've ever played.

"See, every bullpen is different. Maybe it's because of climate, maybe it's because of where they put the ballpark—you get a very different kind of bug near water than on a ridge or in a valley, you know—but there's something unique about every goddam bullpen. For example, I see a big moth, immediately I think, Kansas City. I look at my giant mosquito, it's gotta be Texas, right? Anaheim is the cutest little ladybug. When we played the Mayor's Trophy Game at Shea a couple of years back I got a perfect water bug. That goddam thing was so big for a while I thought he was trying to add a relief pitcher to his collection. Tumsie fought him down with his cape, though.

"You know, I pitched six seasons in the minors. I couldn't guess where they came up with some of the creatures I found in minor-league ballparks. They must breed them. I got one from Spartanburg, South Carolina. I swear to God, this thing has two bodies going in different directions, and both of them have antennae. You can't tell if it's coming or going. So I call it my general manager . . ."

To Big John, Fenway Park means spiders, "big brown ones, and fast," and Yankee Stadium is roaches. "They started out as monsters," he explained, "but they outgrew it." I guess his collection isn't all that unusual—for a relief pitcher. I can tell you from experience, one of the toughest parts about being a relief pitcher in the big leagues is finding ways to keep your mind occupied. Life in the bullpen gets really boring sometimes. We're at the ballpark at least seven hours every day and rarely get in the game for more than a couple of innings every few days. The rest of a relief pitcher's time is spent watching the game from the worst seats in the ballpark, seats that are usually so far away from the plate you can't even see what's going on in the game. The Yankee Stadium bullpen is so far away that once, I remember, I asked Dirt Tidrow, "What's going on in the game?"

"What's going on?" he said. "I don't even know who's playing."

So people would do anything to keep awake in the bullpen. In Boston we had a pitcher named Gary Weber. He wasn't much of a pitcher, but he could eat grasshoppers. It's funny the things you remember about people, isn't it? Gary would just catch one and bite off its head, then chew it up and throw it away. Then he'd say something like, "Needs salt." It was awful. People were telling me I was crazy just because I liked to sit on cakes, and this guy was biting the heads off grasshoppers.

Rawley Eastwick would collect things in the bullpen, little scraps of junk, and keep them as mementos. Moe Drabowsky was a legend among relief pitchers: Moe would get an outside line on the bullpen telephone and call all over the world. Once he called Italy to make a date with Sophia Loren; another time he tried to call China to see if he could find a restaurant that would deliver. He also was an expert in the fine art of the hotfoot. He once gave a hotfoot to the commissioner of baseball. The Phillies had a guy named John Boozer who would spit a wad of chewing tobacco into the air and try to catch it in his mouth. Unfortunately, most of the time he'd miss. Another great reliever, I'm not going to tell you who it was, but he was known all around the league for passing the worst gas in baseball. He was a star pitcher, but anybody who ever played with him only remembers the gas. I'll tell you what he did: Everybody liked to crawl into the back seat of the bullpen car and go to sleep for a few innings. When he caught somebody sleeping, he'd open the door, bend over and bomb them. Then the rest of the people in the bullpen would hold the car doors closed to make sure the person inside couldn't get out.

A relief pitcher named Gene Braebender was the strongest player I ever saw. He'd stay out in the bullpen bending things with his hands— like the spikes that held down the bases. Tony deFama decided to take advantage of the time he had to spend out there by learning a language a season. He'd bring a Walkman and language tapes out to the bullpen and sit there repeating phrases over and over. He drove everybody crazy, except a reliever from the Dominican named Charlie Glosa, who spent the year deFama studied Spanish wondering why Tony kept asking him how to get to the library. But deFama learned Spanish, French, and Italian. A sore arm kept him from learning German. Tums Taft used to give bullfighting lessons in the bullpen. I guess by now everybody has seen the great tape they made a couple of seasons ago, when a TV camera caught Clay Parker, with a blanket over his head, using two bat handles as horns, playing bull to Taft's matador. Then there are the word games everybody plays in the bullpen: Trivia, 20 Questions, Ghost, Hangman, crossword puzzles. Once Frank Biondo was playing Hangman and when his turn came he picked the exact same word that someone had just used. When somebody pointed that out, Biondo admitted, "I knew I'd heard it somewhere."

Look, I don't care what people do in the bullpen, as long as they're ready to pitch when Lou needs them, and they can get people out. One lesson I've learned about baseball: You can eat all the grasshoppers you want if you've got a low earned run average. As long as you can pitch effectively you're a character; when the batters start hitting you, you're crazy.

And we won another ballgame tonight. This was a real pitchers' battle, 10–9. We almost blew an eight-run lead, but the Tigers ran out of innings. I really believe they would have caught us if we'd gone one more inning. Sometimes you just feel that, like tonight. Every baseball game has its own rhythm. Sometimes you have a two-run lead and you absolutely know it's going to be enough. Other times, like tonight, you get a big lead but you just feel something is going to happen. Of course, when the wind is blowing out in Tiger Stadium that's a big hint. Mattingly had his first extra-base hits of the season, dropping two doubles into left field, knocking in three runs. But after the game he spent forty-five minutes under the stands hitting a ball off a tee. He says he's not at all happy with his swing.

It's much too early in the season to see anything meaningful developing. The Indians are still in first place. But the Red Sox are 8–2, and the quality of their starting pitching has been tremendous. Clemens is 3–0 already. The most important thing at this point in the season is preventing anybody from getting too far out front. Well, at least the other teams don't have to worry about us doing that.

APRIL 24 ★

Sometimes baseball can be a dangerous game, too. In the fourth inning of our game against the Twins tonight, Ken Davis, who was DHing, hit a line drive off the pitching shoulder of Denny Wilson. The ball hit Wilson square on the bone; it hit him so hard it flew into foul territory, bounced once, and went into the stands for a ground rule double. I could hear the clunk of ball hitting bone from my seat in the pressbox. They rushed Wilson to the hospital, and preliminary X rays indicated it was a broken collarbone. It was just awful. I hate to see anybody get hurt, particularly a solid starting pitcher like Wilson who isn't even in our division.

But maybe the worst thing was that Davis hit the ball so hard that his bat broke in half. When home plate umpire Joe Brinkman picked up the barrel, he saw that the bat had been doctored. Apparently someone had inserted a long, hollow metal tube in it, then put mercury in that tube. When Davis swung, centrifugal force sent the mercury to the top of the bat, giving him extra weight on the bat end, adding to his power. When the bat broke, the mercury spilled out onto the field. Brinkman confiscated the bat and ejected Davis from the game. I have to admit, even under the circumstances, it was pretty funny watching Brinkman down on his knees, trying to pick up the mercury for evidence. It was like watching a little child chasing a dog that doesn't want to be caught—every time he touched a drop of the stuff, it would scoot away. He was getting angrier and angrier until a member of the grounds crew shoveled it up for him.

We won the game, beating Rick Aguilera in relief of Wilson, to break our two-game losing streak. But a serious injury like that can take some of the joy out of winning.

Some, not all.

APRIL 27 ★

This job of owning a baseball team can be difficult sometimes. Yesterday and today, for example. Wilson's collarbone is officially broken, and he's out for the season. They operated yesterday morning and inserted a steel pin. Yesterday afternoon an attorney served Davis and me, as owner of the Yankees Corporation, with legal papers. Wilson's attorney contends that the fact that Davis used an illegal bat caused the ball to travel at a higher rate of speed than normal, making it extremely difficult for Wilson to get out of the way, and therefore contributing to the severity of the injury. He's suing the Yankees because, he claims, we should have prevented Davis from using that bat.

Davis was really shaken up by the lawsuit. I spoke to our insurance people and they're not sure our liability policy will cover him, or the team, if it can be proven that he knowingly broke the rules.

I think the whole thing is ridiculous. I remember when sports took place on the field, not in the courtroom, and the best team won, not the team with the best attorney. Sometimes, it seems to me, with the constant stories about contracts being broken, teams being sued, agents being sued, they should print the major league standings in the law journal. I saw Davis after the game—Twins 6, Yankees 3; Piniella ejected for arguing a call at first base—and told him not to worry about it. "Let me worry for both of us," I suggested.

Then, at 7:30 last night, the phone rang in my suite. Clifford Campion of the New Jersey Sports Development Corporation called just to say hello, and ask if I'd thought about moving the Yankees to the Meadowlands? I told him hello, I hadn't thought about it because I wasn't the slightest bit interested, good-bye. So in this morning's *Daily News* Bill Madden wrote, "A usually reliable source told the *News* that discussions concerning the Yankees moving to the Meadowlands Complex as early as next season are under way," and that "Yankee owner Albert 'Sparky' Lyle had spoken with Meadowlands officials about the move as recently as last night." Only in New York does hello, no, good-bye qualify as a discussion. I had a longer discussion with Graig Nettles yesterday, and he's not even talking to me.

Naturally every reporter traveling with the team called me today to try to confirm Madden's story. I told them all the same thing: I spoke to somebody for a few seconds and told him that I wasn't interested in moving the team. And that's all that happened.

"So," the *Times*'s Mike Martinez asked, "you're not denying that you spoke to them?"

What can I do?

Apparently every New York TV station has called my office at the Stadium today to try to set up an interview. Annie told them all that I was traveling with the team and was not available. So tonight, on the six o'clock news, *Eyewitness News* sports anchor Chuck George reported, "Lyle confirmed today that he had spoken to Meadowlands officials, but denied telling them that he intended to move the team to New Jersey next season, as has been reported. *Eyewitness News* attempted to contact Sparky, but his office repeatedly told us he was . . . unavailable for comment."

When they switched back to news anchor Samantha Chong, she asked Chuck if he thought there was any truth to the story. He frowned and sighed, "Well, Samantha, Sparky has been in New Jersey several times. I think we're just gonna have to watch this one as it develops."

APRIL 28 ★

The phone rang in my office at nine o'clock this morning, Annie told me. It was someone named Fred Rappoport, who said he was the chairman of the Mayor's Council for Economic Development. The message he left was, "Please don't do anything with New Jersey until you've spoken with us."

APRIL 29 ★

We had our first promotional day of the season tonight, "Entenmann's Big League Crackers Night." Every fan "under 90 years of age" attending the game was given a giant-sized box of Big League Crackers. It's a new product, sort of like animal crackers, except that instead of being in the shape of animals, the little vanilla cookies are shaped like baseball players hitting, fielding, pitching, or sliding, and instead of the box looking like a circus animal cage, it looks like a dugout. The gimmick is that inside every box there's at least one "Famous Player Cracker Collectible," that shows an identifiable Hall of Famer in some characteristic pose. For example, in the first box I opened I got a leaping Willie Mays, his left arm completely extended over his head and the ball in the pocket of his glove. I took off his arm with my first bite. Willie's arm was delicious. The object is for kids to collect the whole forty-eight-cracker set of these Hall of Famers. I like the cookies, but I don't understand how they're going to do that. They certainly can't paste them into an album. I can just see some kid who finally got his last cracker pasted down, happily slamming his album closed.

Chicken doesn't think the "collectible cookie" idea will work. "First of all," he asked me, "how are the kids going to get the stars to autograph their cookies?"

"As far as I know," I told him, "they haven't licked that problem yet." Chicken immediately invoked the 24-hour Bad Joke Rule, so now he's not talking to me either.

At least people can't complain this promotion was in bad taste.

Promotional events have become a very important part of the financial success of a major- or minor-league team. In the old days we'd have special days with reduced admissions, like Ladies Day or Senior Citizens Day; or we'd have some special event like an Old-Timers' Game, or Dairy Day, on which we had cow chip–throwing and milking contests. Today it's much easier to attract fans—you just have to give them something. Each team probably has more than thirty special promotional days a season now. The real beauty of this for the team is that the sponsor provides the item or pays a substantial part of its cost, as well as paying a fee, in return for being allowed to associate their corporate name with the team and certain other benefits—like getting great seats for their guests, and recognition on the message board. The team gets the fee in addition to the extra revenue from the additional fans drawn by the promotion.

I think Bat Day was the first great giveaway, but now they give away everything at the ballpark. Over a season a young fan can get a bat, a ball, a glove, a uniform jersey, a lightweight jacket, a hat, a wristband, sunglasses, a beach towel, a transistor radio that only gets WABC (the station that broadcasts our games), a beeper that only receives scores of Yankee games, a device that can be added to any standard telephone that provides direct dialing to the "Yankee Hotline" (a 900 number with all the up-to-date Yankee news), and an umbrella.

As a player I hated Bat Day. All I remember about Bat Day is 50,000 kids banging on the metal seats with their bats. But the single worst promotional event I remember was Horn Day. Want to hear a stupid idea? Give 35,000 kids those long plastic horns as they come *in* to the ballpark. Horn Day was a monumentally stupid idea. Sometimes, late at night, when the wind is blowing from the right direction, I think I can still hear it. And it's not a pretty sound.

One of the things I've enjoyed about this job was deciding which promotions we were going to have this season. Believe me, some advertising agencies have proposed some pretty ridiculous ideas for their clients. KeepFresh Refrigerator Bags, for instance, wanted to sponsor "Leftovers Night," on which we'd hand out hot dogs that had been left over from the night before and stored, "piping hot," in an insulated KeepFresh refrigerator bag. One of those law firms specializing in personal-injury cases wanted to sponsor "Negligence Night," on which any fan attending the game could consult with attorneys sitting behind desks in the rotunda behind home plate. We had one very rich

New York real estate owner who was so thrilled when his divorce became final that he wanted to underwrite "Divorce Day," and let anybody who came to the ballpark with his divorce papers in free.

We turned down all those proposals, but among the new promotions we've added this season is Yankee Marriage Day. Any couple with a valid marriage license will be invited to participate in a pregame marriage ceremony that will take place right on the field. A nondenominational justice of the peace will conduct a mass ceremony. Every couple that participates will receive a "Yankee Marriage Giftpack," filled with promotional-sized soaps, a sewing kit, and a shower cap, all with the Yankee insignia, as well as four box seats to a future Yankee home game. We've ordered 500 pounds of rice, so we're hoping as many as thirty or forty couples will take advantage of our offer.

We've also added Sleeko's Baseball Sneaker Night, on which we'll be giving away children's low-cut expandable sneakers designed to look just like baseball spikes, and Pope Picture Day, on which every fan will receive a commemorative picture taken during the Pope's visit to Yankee Stadium.

But the simple fact is that the best promotion in the world is exciting baseball. Nothing draws fans like a winning ballclub. And in New York, if you don't win, that's what you draw, nothing. And we're not winning. If the baseball season is an engine, right now we're like the old outboard motor I used to have on a rowboat. I'd pull that drawstring and I'd pull it again, and that engine would sputter and spark and finally start turning over. Then I'd go to sit down in the boat and as soon as I got settled, it would stop. I just couldn't get that engine to keep going. Right now, that's us, a rowboat in the middle of a lake with a stalled engine.

MAY 1 ★

I'm not panicking. I'm not panicking. Okay, I'm panicking a little. Today we traded Andy Hawkins and Jesse Barfield to the Mariners for right-handed pitcher Gene Kline. I don't think we had a choice. If our pitching doesn't improve soon we'll drop right out of the pennant race. Chicken came to see me two days ago to talk about this deal, although at that point it was still Espinoza to the Braves for outfielder Hubba White, which evolved gradually into this deal. With Winfield proving that he is over all his injuries, we have an excess of outfielders, and Barfield just never hit for us the way he had in Toronto. Hawkins pitched well at times, but he was never able to establish himself as the ace of the staff. I think Chicken finally decided to move him two nights ago when, in the middle of a tough situation, he walked to the back of the pitcher's mound and just stood there. When Lee went out to see what was wrong, Hawkins told him he'd forgotten his mantra and didn't feel confident pitching without it. Piniella was furious. He expects every player to be prepared every day, and that preparation includes knowing your mantra. Biondo got so shook up by Piniella's outburst that yesterday he went out and had his mantra tattooed onto his left thumb. So that if he forgets it, all he has to do is read his thumb.

I really didn't want to make the trade, and the TV and print reporters are all over my butt like vanilla icing on a birthday cake. The problem is that reporters don't really understand the pressure I have to deal with. The fans of New York have supported the Yankees in good times and in fairly good times for almost a century; they deserve a winner and I have only one year to produce it. The future may still be ahead of us, but I've got a ballpark to fill right now. Chicken and I both think that Kline can finally realize his potential and become the star everybody has predicted he would be. We've already got Lee and former Yankee pitching coach Mark Connor working with him to eliminate the flaws we've discovered in his windup.

I spoke to the team before the game tonight to explain the move to them. I told them I wanted them to feel secure as long as they were doing their job, but I also wanted them to realize that anybody who didn't produce was vulnerable. Unfortunately, in the middle of my speech, just when I really got rolling, Joe V yelled, "Could you hold it

up for a second, Sparky, I got to put a new tape in my recorder."
While I stood there waiting for Joe to change tapes, Mattingly decided,
"If he's going to include this meeting in his book, I have to put it in
mine, too," and we had to wait a little longer while he went to his
locker and got his recorder. Sometimes I wonder if I'm running a
baseball team or a publishing house.

"Look around you," I finally told the team. "These are the people
who are going to be your teammates for the rest of the season. Believe
me, except for this trade, stability is the key to our season. I'm
convinced we've got enough talent in this room to win if we play to
our potential, and play as a team."

"I can do it!" Reggie shouted from the back of the room—I didn't
even know he was there—and one by one, the whole team took up his
cheer. "I can do it! I can do it!" It was a roar of self-confidence.
Reggie's done a good job for us.

In fact, the cheering was so loud that it actually woke up Raoul
Rojas, who had fallen asleep in the flotation tank. And that tank is
supposed to be soundproof.

After my little speech we went out and pounded the California
Angels 9–2, as Tommy John picked up his third win against one loss.
Tommy has practically kept us in the race single-armedly.

MAY 2 ★

Sometimes I wonder what my life as an owner would be like if there
wasn't a little trouble every single day. The Angels announced after the
game last night that they intended to file an appeal with the Commissioner's office this morning, claiming that by allowing Tommy John
to pitch we gained an unfair advantage. Their press release
stated, "Baseball is a beautiful game that has evolved slowly over
decades to allow players with natural skills to excel above their peers.
Tommy John's technologically improved performance represents a real
threat to the game as we all know it, as it allows players to perform at a
level far greater than their natural, human abilities would permit.
Tommy John has been a great player, a great competitor and a gentle-
man, but his continued presence on the field makes a mockery of the

game and threatens the very foundations on which it is built. If he is allowed to continue competing against unimproved players, the Yankees will gain an unfair advantage. More importantly, a precedent will be established allowing technologically improved players to participate in major-league baseball games. These TIPs will be able to easily shatter all existing records, which have been compiled by completely unimproved players. Therefore, the California Angels request that the Yankees forfeit all games in which Tommy John participated, that Tommy John be barred from baseball for life, and that guidelines be established as to what technological, scientific, or medical improvements to players will be permitted in the future. Sincerely . . .''

Tommy John, "a threat to the game as we know it?" That's ridiculous. This great player has a little spring put in his arm and they try to make a lawsuit out of it. I can see the point of their argument, that at some point in the future there will be an implant or drug that can turn an average player into a superstar, but I would hardly call Tommy John a TIP. Who knows, maybe his fastball would have come back without the operation.

The Angels' protest went to Commissioner Vincent's office this morning, so obviously it's too early for any response. I've asked our attorneys to begin searching for a precedent we can use if it becomes necessary, but I really don't think it will. Every time there's been an improvement in baseball somebody complains about it. When they put in the lively ball the pitchers complained; when they manufactured bigger gloves the hitters complained. This is different, but it's really the same.

I told Tommy not to worry about it, that he should make sure he keeps his arm well oiled, and we'll take care of the legal problem.

We tried something brand-new in the game tonight. A few days ago Duke came into my office and told me she'd been doing extensive reading about motivational techniques, particularly about positive and negative reinforcement.

I told her I'd just finished reading Robert Ludlum's new spy novel.

She ignored me. Then she said her research had convinced her that we could put the message board on our scoreboard to better use than sending birthday greetings to fans or welcoming office groups. She said, "Suppose we use the message center to emphasize the positive accomplishments of our players and the negative things our opponents have done. Look at this, for example. Pete Simpson's only hitting .150

against Chuck Cary. If we put that on the board when Simpson comes to bat against Cary, it has to make Cary more confident, and maybe make Simpson press just a little. In a game as precise as baseball, that subtle difference could have a real effect on the game."

"Is that legal?" I asked. Our lawyers were already busy with the Davis case and the Tommy John situation. I didn't want to give them any more work.

"I checked," she told me. "There's no rule against it. That's as good as being legal."

So tonight we loaded the scoreboard message center with notes like, "Felipe Suarez is batting .333 lifetime against Chuck Finley,"—we didn't mention that he'd only been to bat three times; "Don Mattingly has 15 lifetime home runs off Angels pitching"; "Gene Kline has never lost to the Angels"—he's never pitched against them, either; and "Dick Schofield is a lifetime .215 hitter against the Yankees." Anyone reading the message center would think we hadn't lost to the Angels in years. The truth is that they've won the season series from us the past two seasons.

We put up about twenty-five messages like that during the game. Who knows if it really affected the outcome, but we won 4–1 as Kline, Tsumi, and Taft combined for a four-hitter. Taft still isn't pitching well, though; he gave up two hits and the only run the Angels scored in the inning he pitched.

We also used the cellular glove for the first time in an official league game tonight. The Rules Committee finally decided it was legal equipment this afternoon, and Dave Winfield wore it in the game. Everybody thought it worked very well. The coaches used Duke Schneider's defensive tendency charts, even though they were based on very little information, to telephone Winfield and tell him exactly where he should be playing. They also told Winfield exactly where Kelly and Verola should be playing and he shouted instructions to them. As soon as we can we'll equip all our outfielders with these gloves. I heard that late in the game Winfield was playing so deep when Wally Joyner came up that he was in a different area code. I heard that; I didn't make it up.

MAY 4 ★

Tonight in Baltimore, we had our first game with Trish Todd, the female umpire, behind the plate. I've heard that she's really having a tough time breaking in. There are a lot of players who believe women don't belong in the big leagues, and they're making it as difficult as possible for her. In her very first game in the majors, for example, the count went to 2–2 on the batter, and Oakland A's catcher Terry Little turned and asked her, "The batter's got two balls on him, right?" Then he keeled over laughing. They had to stop the game while he went into the dugout to catch his breath. And that was one of the nicer things players have said to her. Every time somebody thinks up a new insult it spreads around the league in a day: "Bert Blyleven has better curves than you do, lady." "I've seen your face; no wonder you went into a business where you could wear a mask." Every time she cleans home plate somebody yells, "Don't forget to sweep in the corners." In Boston, Danny Giancarlo got a big laugh by screaming, "I've seen her off the field. I don't know why she bothers using a chest protector, she's got nothing to protect!" She's managed to hold her temper so far; the only person she's ejected was Orioles manager Frank Robinson, who came out to argue with her and insisted on calling her "ma'am."

Lou held a team meeting before the game to discuss how to deal with Todd. "Umpires aren't men and they aren't women," he explained. "They're umpires. That's all. And a female umpire is no better than a male umpire. Remember what the directive from the league office said, there's no sex on the baseball diamond. So don't hesitate to say the same things to her that you'd say to any of them."

Frank Biondo leaned over to Winfield and asked, "Does that mean that you can call a girl umpire a homo?"

Bob Geren asked if it was proper to refer to her as, "the umpiress, you know, like a female vampire is a vampiress?"

Rosey Rogers seemed to be the player most upset about her. "The only women I like in a ballpark are the ones I give tickets to. They don't belong on the field. I'm not against them, but just like women who are in favor of women are feminists, I'm in favor of macho, so I guess that makes me a masochist."

The game itself was pretty uneventful. A few players didn't like some of her calls; they say she squeezes the plate on both corners, but her strike zone was consistent the whole game, and that's really all any player wants from an umpire. It wasn't much of a game anyway. We couldn't hold a four-run lead and got blasted by the Orioles, 11–5. In the clubhouse after the game Lou finally lost his temper. He threw over the table with the whole postgame meal on it. "I want you guys to be hungry," he screamed at them. "I want to see you fight for something. I don't want people around here who aren't as hungry as I am."

On the scale of Piniella tantrums, I'd give it a 6.5. But it's early in the season. If we keep losing, I think Lou can go for a perfect 10.0.

MAY 5 ★

How do you know when a slump is just a slump? By that I mean, how do you know when a player is just temporarily not producing, instead of having lost some of his skills? And when does a slump become a bad season? And when does a bad season become the best that player can do? And how many bad seasons mean the end of a career? Chicken and I were trying to figure that out at lunch today. Sometimes it seems like just when you're ready to give up on a player he suddenly comes back. Keith Hernandez had two very mediocre seasons in a row, and just when everybody decided he was through as a productive player, he got hot again and is hitting about .340 right now.

We've got the same problem with Mattingly. "The Hit Man" always starts out slowly, but eventually gets hot for the rest of the season. I just don't remember him ever starting out this slowly. The season is a month old and he's still hitting just below the Mendoza Line—about .200, with almost no power. How do we know this isn't the season that his bad back prevents him from hitting, and we wait for him, and wait, and by the time we realize this isn't a slump, it's a bad year, it's too late, and he carries us down like an anchor in a featherbed?

Chicken didn't know any better than I did. "That was one good thing about never being much of a hitter," he said, talking about his own career. "No one could ever tell when I was in a slump."

I knew when I was losing my stuff. I had a few bad outings with the Phillies and I realized I wasn't in a slump—that that was the best I could do. I could still make my slider drop, but I couldn't throw it as hard, so it didn't drop as abruptly as it once did. So I got hammered. The hitters up here are too good for that.

It's not just Mattingly we're worried about, either. It's Winfield and Taft, and we're not getting anything out of our third basemen. If we don't start scoring runs soon, this slump will become a bad season.

Nobody's happy. Losing can really make a clubhouse an unpleasant place to be. I mean, every team has players who don't get along with some teammates or the manager, and over a whole season there are always going to be arguments. In 1969, I heard, one player on the Cubs got so mad at manager Leo Durocher he went after him with a knife. The other players tackled him at the door to Durocher's office. We haven't had any problems *that* bad—and we only use plastic knives in the clubhouse—but we did have our first real argument before the game this afternoon. What happened was that the Commissioner's Office announced that, in response to the Angels' protest, Commissioner Vincent had asked the Competition Committee to set guidelines for future TIPs. But he also rejected their protest, based on the fact that at this time there's nothing in the rulebook prohibiting Tommy John from playing, and declared that Tommy John would continue to be an eligible player until the Competition Committee meets in July.

When the decision was announced, Don Mattingly started interviewing TJ for his book. Verola saw them talking, so he got his tape recorder and went over to John's locker. When TJ told him that he wanted to give an exclusive interview to Mattingly, Joe V got very upset. He started yelling at TJ, claiming that his publisher was bigger than Mattingly's. Then Donnie started defending his publisher. The screaming got louder and louder, and finally Winfield took off his Walkman headphones and stepped between them. The truth is that my publisher is bigger than both of theirs, but I didn't see any need to tell them that.

Finally Donnie got so fed up with the whole thing that he grabbed a bat and went to the cage to take some extra batting practice. When he came back about twenty minutes later, he discovered that someone had jammed his tape recorder with used chewing gum. He was furious. He figured it had to be Joe V, and he went after him. Joe V swore he had nothing to do with it. "Hey, man," he said, taking his gum out of his mouth and showing it to Mattingly, "I'm a Doublemint man. Anybody with half a nose can tell by smelling that recorder that that's Juicy Fruit, and swear to God, I never touch that stuff." Mattingly seemed to calm down a little, until Joe V added, "Besides, I don't have to do things like that to write a better book than you. My ghostwriter's much better than yours." That was when Mattingly went after him again.

Piniella grabbed him from behind and was able to hold him back, but Donnie kept screaming at him, "Oh, yeah? Well, let's see whose advance is bigger, smart guy."

I'll say this for Joe V, the kid didn't back down. He's got guts. "Screw the advance," he screamed right back at Mattingly. "Let's see who ends up with more royalties." It was really getting pretty rough— and then Hanko Tsumi stepped between them holding his own tape recorder. Guess who's writing a book about a Japanese baseball player in the major leagues?

"My publisher own both your publisher," he said happily. "So please should yell into my microphone."

This whole thing is ridiculous. I'd like to forbid them all to do books, but if I did, when this book is published they'd think I did it because I was worried about competition. Besides, when I spoke to Joe V's agent, David Braun, about the situation, he reminded me that the Constitution guarantees freedom of speech, freedom of expression, and a free press.

"Yeah?" I asked, "then how come I have to pay for the newspaper?" He didn't get it. Or if he did, he didn't think it was funny.

I have to wonder if Mattingly's slump has anything to do with his book. I know that if he thought it did he would drop the book project right away. That would mean, of course, that my only competition—in the American book market—would be Joe V. But where would Donnie get that idea?

After the fight we went out and beat the Orioles, 5–3. Tonight we played like a championship team. We hit, we ran, sacrificed, hit the cutoff man, did all the small things it takes to play winning baseball. We just can't seem to play that way two days in a row. I know we're better than a .500 ballclub, but we haven't even been able to get back to the break-even point after our terrible start. And believe me, if we don't start winning soon, it won't matter whose book is best. There's an old baseball adage it's worth remembering right now: Losing teams don't sell books!

MAY 6 ★

Sometimes I feel like the guy who handed over every single penny he had to the IRS and figured things couldn't possibly get worse—and then went to the men's room and discovered they only had pay toilets. Until tonight we'd managed to avoid the "injury flu" that had struck almost every other team. For some reason, there have been more unusual injuries this season than in a long, long time. The Cardinals have already lost three of their five starting pitchers: Joe Magrane suffered a broken wrist when he got confused and gave catcher Todd Zeille last year's high-five while Zeille gave him the new version. Magrane smashed his wrist against Zeille's elbow, breaking it. Danny Cox fractured his ankle when he slipped off a wet pitcher's rubber. And Jose DeLeon was lost for at least a month when a speck of rosin from the rosin bag got into his eye and scratched his cornea. The Dodgers lost Kirk Gibson for six weeks when he accidently stabbed himself in his leg with a ballpoint pen during an autographing session and got blood poisoning. Jack Clark is out indefinitely because he strained ligaments in his arm reaching across his body to swat a mosquito. Eric Davis is lost for approximately a month because the Reds tried to poison the pigeons that live under the roof at Riverfront Stadium. The groundskeepers put poison seed on the roof, assuming the pigeons would eat it and die. Unfortunately, one of them died in midair and landed on Davis's right shoulder, causing a deep bone bruise and making it impossible for him to throw. Toronto lost pitcher Al Leiter for anywhere between a month and the rest of the season when he dropped the jar of pickle brine in which he was soaking his fingers—to harden the skin and prevent blisters—on his foot, breaking two toes.

Our turn came tonight. We lost Eric Plunk for an indefinite period of time, and he wasn't even in the game. Like a lot of major leaguers, Plunk is just a little superstitious. The Orioles were beating us 6–1 in the seventh inning when Randy Velarde led off the inning with one of those nine-hoppers through the infield. Plunk happened to be sitting in a very awkward position, his legs crossed, his arm stretched over his head scratching his back, when Velarde's hit went through the infield. So Plunk decided that sitting in that position was good luck. He figured the luck would change if he uncrossed his leg or moved his arm. So he sat that way, without moving a muscle, through our biggest inning in two years. We scored ten runs on eight hits, two walks and an Oriole error. Frank Robinson made three pitching changes in the inning, which lasted about thirty-five minutes. When Roberto Kelly finally made the third out, Plunk couldn't move his left leg or right arm. He'd managed to stop his blood circulation and his muscles were frozen. His arm had actually turned blue-black. They had to carry him into the training room in that position, where Gene Monahan managed to restore his circulation by alternating hot and cold packs. But evidently Plunk had damaged some tissue and we had to put him on the 14-day disabled list, retroactive to last Tuesday.

I have to admit something. I've never understood how the disabled list works. How could Plunk have been on the disabled list last Tuesday when he pitched Wednesday? But the rules say he was, so he didn't. Chicken called up right-handed pitcher Tommy McKeever from Columbus to take Plunk's place in the rotation. McKeever's a six-year minor-league veteran, a breaking-ball pitcher who depends mostly on control and changing speeds to win. He's not going to overpower anybody, but Chicken and Woodley don't want to rush any of the kids up here and maybe destroy their confidence. McKeever really isn't a prospect, but our superscout, Clyde King, thinks he's clever enough on the mound to get past some teams the first few times they see him. If he can just keep us in the game for six innings, and do it three or four times, we'll be very satisfied.

We held on to win tonight's game, 11–7. But even when we win, we lose.

MAY 9 ★

Baseball certainly is changing. We got a request today from the Competition Committee asking us to supply copies of the X rays and blueprints of Tommy John's arm. After making some phone calls, we discovered that the surgeon who developed the Teflon spring mechanism has patented the operation, and TJ's arm has been registered with the United States Patent Office in Washington, D.C., as a prototype. That means that if another doctor performs this operation without compensating the surgeon, Tommy's arm will be used in a trial as evidence. The surgeon is faxing us copies of all his designs and patents, as well as the X ray, which we'll submit to the committee.

We also introduced the newly selected members of the Yankees Advisory Committee to the media this morning. The group consists of two men, two women, and one 12-year-old boy. The oldest member is 78-year-old Joseph Maresca, a retired gardener who remembers getting Babe Ruth's autograph, and the youngest woman is 22-year-old Joanie Silver, who wrote that she thinks "Joe V is the dreamiest outfielder in baseball." We tried to include representatives of as many groups as possible, while keeping the committee a manageable size.

After everybody had been introduced to the press, Chicken, Woodley, and I joined them for a private lunch in the Stadium Club. I'll be honest, we expected to make small talk for about an hour, then shake their hands, remind them we'll see them next month, and send them home. That's what we expected to do. But in the middle of a conversation, Geri Simon, a mature investment counselor, interrupted me and said, "None of us here really cares what the Mayor said to the Cardinal. What we want to know is what you intend to do about this team."

Chicken started to explain that we didn't intend to make any immediate changes, that we wanted to stress long-term stability, but that we were making plans . . .

"Plans, shmans," Ms. Simon said. "Look, Chicken, we're all busy people and we're here for a reason. If you want to jerk us around, fine, but tell me now because I don't intend to waste my time. I think we're all taking this committee very seriously, and we have some ideas. . . ."

"I got a good idea," 12-year-old Alex Langsam said. "I think we should trade Clay Parker to the Twins for Kirby Puckett."

"Me too, Alex," I told him. "I'm just not sure the Twins want to do that."

"I want to talk about the food in the ballpark," Louis Dominick DiGiamo, a movie character actor, said. "You've absolutely got to do something about those hot dogs."

"Like cook 'em, maybe," Joe Maresca agreed. "But food isn't that important. . . ."

"Maybe not to you," DiGiamo said.

Maresca ignored him. "What I want to know is what you're going to do about those ushers who extort money from you to wipe off your seat which isn't even dirty or wet, then sell the empty seats to kids who bought cheaper seats and don't want to do anything but smoke marijuana anyway. . . ."

"If you'll just give me . . ."

"I want to know how I can meet Joe V," Joanie Silver interrupted. "All my friends think he's adorable. I think you should have big posters. . . ."

I could see Ms. Simon was getting upset. "Are we here to talk about her social life or the American League pennant?" she asked. "I'm sorry, but I have to be at the beauty parlor by 4:30, so if we're not gonna get serious . . ."

"Who are you to call extortion not serious?" Maresca asked. "Is it a crime not to want to have to pay for a seat I already bought?"

"And when was the last time you tried to eat one of the soggy knishes?" DiGiamo asked. "The only thing soggier than the knishes is the ice cream." Then he turned to me and wondered, "Is the plural of 'knish', 'knish' or 'knishes'?" I shrugged.

It probably wouldn't be accurate to describe the meeting as a big success. I just remember sitting there for almost an hour while everybody shouted at me. Finally Annie got me out of there by interrupting the meeting to tell me I had an emergency call from the commissioner's office. After the meeting we released this press notice: "A wide range of subjects of great interest to Yankee fans was discussed at the first meeting of the Yankees Advisory Committee, ranging from team personnel to the conduct of Stadium attendants. Team owner Albert 'Sparky' Lyle commented after the meeting that he thought the gathering had been "thought provoking and tremendously beneficial, and I believe our fans will see many of the suggestions made here today implemented in the future." Lyle added that he is anxiously awaiting the next meeting of the Advisory Committee, which is scheduled to take place the first week in June."

The plural of "knish" is "knishes."

MAY 12 ★

I met with Fred Rappoport, chairman of the Mayor's Council for Economic Development, first thing this morning. Rappoport looks a lot like a college professor, but he's all business. "I don't want to expend your time or my time unnecessarily," he said, "so let me be frank with you. The Mayor intends to keep the Yankees in the Bronx and we're prepared to meet, or better, any offer you receive from the Meadowlands."

"I'm glad to know that," I said.

"Working together, we can ensure a bright future for the Yankees in New York. Working apart"—he spread his hands far apart and frowned—". . . nothing. So let's get down to it. What have they offered; what do you want?"

"Look, I'll be honest with you, I'm not moving the Yankees to New Jersey. The Yankees belong in Yankee Stadium. Moving the Yankees out of the Stadium would be like moving the King and Queen out of . . . out of wherever they live. I have no intention of moving the team anywhere except to the top of the standings."

He smiled. "Naturally, I'm pleased to hear you say that. Just as pleased as I was to hear Mr. Steinbrenner say almost exactly the same thing. But when it came down to converting that statement into a binding commitment, zippo, nada, adiós, amigo. Get my drift? So let's cut right to the chase. What do you want?"

Actually, there were a few things that I thought needed to be done around the Stadium. And as long as the city was offering, "Well, do you think it's possible for us to get a few more parking spaces around the Stadium."

He took a brown leatherbound notebook out of his briefcase, opened it carefully and started writing in it. "We can do that."

"And um, I think, you know, we definitely need improved lighting around the neighborhood, and maybe some more police before and after the game."

"Done."

"Oh, and I know that some conversations took place about adding access roads on and off the Major Deegan and the Bronx River Parkway."

"That's done, too." He looked up at me, his hand poised to keep writing. So I couldn't stop there. "Okay, okay, let's see now." I was speaking with a little more confidence, "I'll tell you, you should have seen our Con Ed bill for just a few games last month. Do you have any idea how much it costs to turn on all those lights for a night game? And nobody ever remembers to turn them off. I couldn't believe it."

"I think we can arrange with Con Ed to supply low-cost power. Next?"

"Have you been down the subway station lately? I don't think it's as clean as it should be." I leaned back in my chair, way back, and put my feet up on my desk.

He nodded. "Okay, next."

I was doing very well, but I was running out of things to ask for. Nothing else struck me immediately, so then I sort of blurted out, and honestly, I don't know where this came from, "How 'bout twenty-five million dollars?"

That's when he stopped writing. "I thought you wanted to stay in Yankee Stadium?"

"Twenty million?" I said.

He curled his lips over his teeth and kind of whistled through the opening. "I'm going to have to get back to you on this, Mr. Lyle." He almost spit out the "Mr." "But I guess those people from . . . New Joisey . . . have made you a similar offer?"

I didn't say a word. I had the feeling that, in this case, silence really was going to be golden. We agreed to meet again; then he stood up to leave. "I see you know how to play hardball," he said evenly. "But if you really are sincere about keeping the Yankees where they belong, I'm sure we can work something out. You know as well as I do that there's something really wrong with the name New Joisey Yankees."

He put his notebook back into his briefcase. "And besides," he concluded, "you just don't look like a guy who wants to spend the rest of his life being known as . . . The Man Who Raped New York City."

Some great thought. I waited until he left my office. I even peeked out the door to make sure he'd left the outer office. Then I closed my door and screamed, as loud as I could without being heard by anybody else, "TWENTY MILLION BUCKS! I don't believe it! I don't believe it! I do not believe it!" Baseball is some great game.

MAY 14 ★

Baseball history was made at Yankee Stadium last night. A miracle took place. Last night is a night that is going to live in baseball history forever. Very smart baseball people always say things like, "Expect the unexpected. The only thing you can be sure of in the game of baseball is that there's nothing you can be sure of." Well, the unexpected certainly happened last night. Last night Tommy McKeever, a career minor-league pitcher with only an average fastball and curveball, pitched a perfect game in his major-league debut. A gem. An absolutely perfect game. Twenty-seven Red Sox batters went up to the plate, twenty-seven Red Sox batters went back to the dugout. No runs, no hits, no errors, no walks, no baserunners. Two strikeouts. This is the only time in the entire history of big-league baseball, from the day they started writing it down, that a pitcher hurled a perfect game in his first appearance in the major leagues.

It was one of the most incredible games I've ever seen. McKeever wasn't fooling anybody. Believe me, they hit some rockets off him. But he had the atom ball going for him last night—everything they hit was right "at 'em." Line drives, ripped ground balls, but everything was hit right at somebody. When Roberto Kelly caught pinch-hitter Danny Heep's drive with his back against the wall at the 406 mark in centerfield, the whole ballpark erupted. Fans poured out of the stands to celebrate and McKeever ran off the field screaming, "Now I'm going to Disneyland! Now I'm going to Disneyland!"

During the first few innings of the game I just couldn't help thinking about my first game in the big leagues. When I got called in from the bullpen my hands were sweating so much I started looking for the rosin bag to dry them off. I couldn't find it; I walked all around the mound and didn't see it. Pitching coach Sal Maglie asked me what I was doing. "If this is the big leagues," I said, "how come they don't even have a rosin bag out here?"

Maglie reached down and picked up the rosin bag, which had been right in front of me. "What's this?" he asked.

What was I gonna tell him, Inca treasure? I took it and wiped off my hands and got the batter out. I pitched a perfect batter. McKeever pitched a perfect game.

The minute the game ended we went right to work. Since nobody had ever done anything like this before, we had to figure out what to do as we went along. In the old days, if somebody had pitched a perfect game, the reporters would interview him for an hour, he'd probably have been asked to appear on the *Today* show the next morning, and all the papers would carry his picture on the back page. In the old days.

The first thing we did was keep the sportswriters out of the locker room and set up a press conference in the clubroom. Our public relations director, Chris Mackerodt, spoke to the newspaper people and promised them all the time they needed, but asked them to let the TV guys ask the first questions so they could make the late local newscasts. Pixie, WPIX, our free TV station, got a remote crew out there and carried the entire press conference live, preempting a *Honeymooners* repeat.

But before McKeever went in to speak to the press, I went downstairs to introduce myself to him. He seemed like a nice kid, maybe a little overwhelmed by the whole thing. "Who's your agent?" I asked him. "Is he here tonight?"

"I don't have an agent," he told me. "I never needed one before."

I smiled. "Well, you will now. Do me one favor, okay? People are going to be sticking contracts in front of you to sign. Don't sign anything with anybody until you've spoken to me or Chicken. Believe me, when the agents find out you're not represented, they'll be camping out on your doorstep."

Evidently I said something funny, because he laughed. "Oh, they can't do that, Mr. Lyle," he said.

"Why not?"

"I don't have a doorstep. See, my wife just had our baby, the neatest little girl, and we don't have a whole lot of money. I didn't know how long I was gonna be up here, so I've been living in the back of my van, you know. Like, I've been saving some money. And vans don't have doorsteps, they got bumpers."

I smiled again. I don't think McKeever has the slightest idea of what is about to happen to him. He was great in the press conference, telling the writers, "I was too scared to be nervous. You know, I've been waiting a long time for this night. I was just hoping to pitch good enough to earn another start." He smiled at that thought. "I guess you could say I did that, right?" The whole room started laughing. He'd instantly won them over. I thought to myself, just wait'll they hear his wife just had a baby and he's living in the back of his van to save money.

After the press conference got underway I went up to my office to meet with our director of promotions, Arthur Richmond. Arthur had been on the phone with several videotape duplicating facilities and distributors. The best offer had come from a distributor who estimated he could move 25,000 tapes of the game for $19.95 in the next month—if he could get them in the stores in the next four days. The duplicator said he could turn out 5,500 units a day and could start work immediately. Arthur also woke up the artist, Michael Witte, in the middle of the night, and got him to work designing the package. Witte promised to fax us some roughs in the morning.

I stayed in my office all night. The phone never stopped ringing. According to McKeever's contract, a standard agreement, we basically own all performance rights. Anything that has to do with reproductions of the game, any video recordings, films, still photographs, sound recordings, we own. Anything in which he is performing in a Yankee uniform, we own. Other than that, we can't force him to make any appearances at places other than the pitcher's mound, or do any promotional work. Obviously, we'll have to sit down with his agent, when he gets an agent, and work out an overall deal.

Baseball is a lot more complicated than I'd originally thought.

Everybody wanted McKeever. The *Today* show, *Good Morning, America,* and *CBS This Morning* were desperate to have him in the morning. One of the very first calls came from Barbara Walters's producer on *20/20,* who wanted him for their final show of the season next Saturday. Robert Morton, producer of the Letterman show called, the Johnny Carson show called, and Arsenio Hall called. Merv Griffin called, and he doesn't even have a show anymore. A segment producer from Geraldo called to find out if McKeever had ever been divorced and remarried the same woman, had been an abused child, or had a "hidden biological time bomb," for example a severe allergy. Oprah's producer wanted to know if he had ever been cheated out of money by a sibling or parent, or had considered having cosmetic surgery. At least half a dozen movie producers called to offer money for the rights to his life story. *Time, Newsweek, Business Week, 7 Days, The Village Voice, National Lampoon,* and *New York Magazine* all wanted to set up interviews. Editors from Bantam Books, William Morrow, Putnam, and Prentice Hall Press all called to find out if book rights to McKeever's autobiography were still available. It went on and on and on. Chicken worked one phone, I was on the other line, and we couldn't keep up. By my count eighteen commercial agents called to offer an overall representation deal—one agency even offered a guaranteed $500,000 up front. All nine baseball-card manufacturers registered with Major League Baseball Promotions and the Major League Baseball Players Association called to get photographs for special cards for the next series, including the manufacturer of those new talking and video baseball cards. Several magazine publishers wanted to put out Commemorative Editions. I'd estimate we recorded more than 150 offers within five hours of the last out of the game.

And that doesn't even begin to include the personalities who called. I answered one call and a very official sounding voice ordered, "Please hold for the Vice President." I was trying to figure out the Vice President of what when Dan Quayle got on the phone. "Congratulations, Tarky, on winning that championship." I heard a voice in the background correcting him. Then he laughed and told me, "The President asked me to tell you that he watched the game and he thought it just might be one of the best pitched games he's ever seen." He paused. "Something like that." I gave him the phone number of the locker room so he could speak to McKeever himself. The second I hung up a call came in from an assistant to Donald Trump. This person told me that Trump was so thrilled about the game that he wanted to send McKeever a personally autographed picture, and they needed to know the correct spelling of his name.

"T-r-u-m-p," I said. Whoever I was talking to was not amused.

Malcolm Forbes called. Richard Nixon called. Sammy Davis, Jr. called. Former mayor Ed Koch. Socialite Jerry Zipkin. Zsa Zsa Gabor.

Shelley Winters. Leona Helmsley called collect. Jay McInerny. Tama Janowitz. Even Tiny Tim. And then the telegrams started arriving. Not only didn't the offers stop coming, as word started spreading the phones got even busier.

Besides the video we made only one very tentative deal. Leroy Neiman is going to do an original lithograph, which will be marketed in four editions: an unsigned and unframed numbered edition of 2,000 at $250 each; an edition signed by Neiman only, unframed, 1,000 prints at $500; an edition signed by both Neiman and McKeever, unframed, 500 prints at $750; and a handsomely framed litho, signed by both Neiman and McKeever, in an edition of 250 at $1,000. The deal is obviously subject to McKeever's agreement, but the printer is going to advance him $15,000 up front, which will at least allow him to move out of the van into decent housing.

And wouldn't you know it, right after we closed the deal with Neiman, Peter Max called up to offer his own deal.

I was exhausted by the time the sun came up, and I knew another round of calls would begin as soon as people who had something to sell, but had missed the late news, got up and saw the headlines. So Chicken and I decided to go out and grab something to eat before we started again. And, maybe even more amazing than the perfect game, as we walked by a newsstand I saw the new issue of *People*. There, right on the cover, was Tommy McKeever. The cover line read: " 'Mr. Perfect' Strikes Out for Immortality. The story of the secret life of baseball's newest superstar inside." I thought, "Mr. Perfect," huh? I sure hope Reggie doesn't see this.

MAY 16 ★

The phone didn't stop ringing for two days. McKeever interviewed about twenty agents and finally signed with Creative Morris, the hot new superagency formed by the merger of Creative Artists and William Morris. Adam Rosenberg is in charge, but there are about five people assigned to McKeever business. I spoke to Rosenberg this morning and he told me that they didn't want to jump into anything; they wanted to take enough time to really analyze all the offers and determine how to maximize everything before committing McKeever to anything specific. So he didn't expect to finalize anything before tonight. He did agree to proceed on the Neiman deal and gave McKeever to Letterman. "Every agency in the ad business is calling. They all want Mr. Perfect for their commercials," he told me. "I'm telling you, if we do this right, this could be the biggest thing since they got that little girl out of the well in Texas."

An unauthorized paperback biography, an "instant book" they call it, came out this morning. It's called *A Perfect Start.* Good title. McKeever is scheduled to start again day after tomorrow, but because we're on the road, in Chicago, we're probably gonna hold him back until we come home next weekend. If he starts a home game, we'll sell out. Bill Lee told Piniella that the rotation is going to get screwed up if we skip McKeever, but I pointed out to Lou the value of 25,000 additional fans. We're probably going to give out some sort of memento, maybe a Xerox of the box score with a facsimile of McKeever's signature on it, to everyone who buys a ticket.

The one thing we have to be really careful about is allowing this event to overshadow the rest of the season. It took a perfect game to beat Boston, but then they came right back and beat us last night, 7–1, to take two out of three games. So, perfect game or not, we're still stuck in fifth place, six-and-a-half back of the Indians and not playing well at all. The Red Sox, Brewers, and Blue Jays are bunched up right behind Cleveland. The Orioles are a half game behind us, and the Tigers are in the basement.

I do have a little reason to believe things are about to get better, though. As I was walking down the hallway to my office yesterday afternoon I saw Duke Schneider with her head down on her desk. She looked like she was crying. So I went in to try to cheer her up. "Hear the one about Tommy Lasorda and the baked clam?"

She nodded. "And it wasn't funny." When I asked her what was wrong, she told me that she'd been working day and night on her computer project, and was convinced that she had developed some important information, but that none of the players would take her seriously. "If they would just look at some of my work," she said seriously, "they'd see that the whole key to success is right here. It's all in the numbers; all they have to do is listen to me."

"You've tried?"

She frowned. "Rosey Rogers said he'd look at my stuff if I looked at his. Oh, Sparky, they think just because I'm a girl that I don't know anything about the game. They're wrong; they're the ones who don't understand. They're stuck in yesterday." She tapped her index finger on a tall pile of papers. "I just want to show them tomorrow."

"Look," I said, "let me see what I can do. You got some stuff prepared for the game tonight?"

She searched through the pile and handed me several sheets of paper. "This is the way Dopson's gonna pitch us tonight."

I glanced at it, then I . . . then I looked at it again. This wasn't just some general scouting report. This was a pitch-by-pitch, batter-by-batter analysis of what could be expected. For example: Mattingly. With no one on base, Dopson will start with a fastball inside, trying to jam him. If the first pitch is a strike, his second pitch will be a breaking pitch, probably a slider in the same location. If it's a ball, his second pitch will be a fastball out over the plate. If there is a runner or runners on base . . . Mattingly went on for six pages, covering dozens of potential situations. "Where'd you get all this?"

"I didn't do it. I just fed the right information into the computer, then asked the right questions. Anybody with an advanced degree in computer science could have done the same thing. See, it's just an idea I have. Instead of tracking the pitcher like most scouts do, I started tracking the catchers. Catchers are the players who really establish the pitching pattern, and they do it game after game. They'll always start off certain hitters with the pitcher's best pitch; it doesn't matter whether that's a fastball or breaking ball, whatever the pitcher's best pitch is, that's what they'll see. And almost always in the same location. And then, depending on the outcome of the first pitch, different options are opened up. But this Geoff Lyons who's catching for the Red Sox, he's really easy to track. Believe me, I've got him here." She tapped the pile of papers a little more firmly.

"How many other people have you told about all this?"

"Nobody else would listen to me." Suddenly her face brightened; she had another idea. "Wait, here . . ." she started digging through the pile again. "I'm pretty sure I can also pinpoint which pitch in the count will be the best pitch for the batter to hit, the pitch on which there's the highest percentage that he'll be able to hit safely. See, I've also broken down the various hitting zones for each player . . . Here it is." She showed me a sheet of paper covered with numbers. "See, Mattingly's hitting over .400 when he swings at fastballs in zones 12, 15, and 16. And"—she grabbed Dopson's sheet—"that's where Dopson's going to come whenever he's two balls behind in the count. And see, if the count goes to 3 and 1, the odds rise to almost 80 percent. . . ."

"So," I interrupted, "what Mattingly has to do is get two pitches ahead in the count, then look for a pitch in . . . in these zones. And if he does the odds are heavily in his favor that's he's going to get a hit?"

"Or at least hit it hard. The proof is right here." She'd figured this out for every position player on the team. Naturally, she explained, there were some differentials that had to be factored in—the situation in the game, day or night, natural grass or artificial surface, left-handed or right-handed pitcher, the weather—but the basic elements of the system remained consistent. "It's just that people are very predictable," she said, "and computers are particularly well suited to interpret those patterns."

I took all her Mattingly data and told her I'd do whatever I could with it. I made no promises. "Your job is to get us to Milwaukee tomorrow as quickly and cheaply as possible. This . . . this is all extra."

Don Mattingly is one of the nicest people in the game. I found him working in the video room, comparing tapes of his at bats made last season during his 31-game hitting streak with tapes made in the last two weeks. He was matching them frame by frame, trying to isolate the subtle differences that turn line drives into pop-ups. "Find anything?" I asked.

He frowned. "It's like looking for a penny in a bank. You know it's right there, but there are so many other things that attract your attention."

I handed him Duke's work. "Here. If you have a few minutes, why don't you take a look at this. Maybe there'll be something here that'll help."

"What is it?" he asked as he took it.

"Oh, just some data that Duke Schneider worked out on her computer."

He tried to give it back to me. "C'mon, Spark, be serious. I've got work to do."

I pushed it right back at him. "Just look at it. What's the big deal?"

He sighed. "You know as well as I do that all the computers in the world can't tell you if you're dropping your shoulder on an inside pitch. That's what I need. Look, I get letters from fans every single day, and every one of them tells me what I'm doing wrong. I'm lunging, I'm sitting back, I'm too far from the plate, I'm too close to the plate. I got one the other day that said the brim of my hat is too long and it's affecting my vision.

"Duke seems like a nice girl. I guess she's a pretty good traveling secretary. But what does she know about hitting? You know as well as I do that if women could hit, they'd make baseball uniforms with skirts. But they can't." He held out the papers to me. "Here."

I wouldn't take them. "Do me one favor, okay? Just take five minutes and look at this stuff. Do it just this one time and I give you my word, I'll never ask you again."

He paused. I knew he was just too good a guy to say no. "All right," he agreed, "but just this once." He glanced at the page on top. "What do all these numbers mean?" So I sat down and started explaining Duke's system to him. And something pretty surprising happened. He seemed to get really interested in it.

Then he went out and got two of our five hits off Dopson, and hit another ball as hard as he's hit a pitch all year. Unfortunately, it was right at Ellis Burks. I saw Don leaving the ballpark after the game, and he called me over. "I want to tell you something," he said. "That stuff you showed me? It isn't as crazy as I thought. First time up I took three pitches, just to see if there was anything to what she said, you know. She was close, pretty close. Second time up I took a couple of pitches, then decided to commit myself to her charts. She said that in that situation he'd throw me an off-speed pitch away. So I cranked up for it and sure enough, that's what he threw me, and I just rode it the opposite way. Same thing happened the third time I got up. I'll tell you something, Sparky, if she really can figure out which pitch is the best one to go after, these charts could really be valuable. Tell her I said thanks, okay, and tell her that I'll look at whatever she puts together."

"Tell her yourself. She'll appreciate it a lot more if it came from you."

"I . . . you know . . . the guys . . . if they hear I was paying attention to her charts . . ."

"If you keep hitting like you did tonight, they're gonna want to know where you got them. Imagine what a big strong kid like Suarez would hit if he knew when to sit on a fastball?"

Mattingly considered it. "That's not a bad idea." He nodded. "Maybe I'll casually mention it to a few of the guys, just to see their reaction."

"That'd be great," I said. "We might as well try it; if we don't do something soon to get going, we're gonna get buried."

I watched as Mattingly walked alone down the long cement stadium corridor, holding a bat loosely by its knob, letting it drag behind him. Well, I thought, it's a start.

MAY 20 ★

When I walked into the office this morning Donny Osmond's new hit, "The Ballad of Mr. Perfect," was blaring on a receptionist's radio. Mr. Perfect, huh? If any one of those line drives the Red Sox hit had been six inches to the right or left, Donny Osmond would be singing a different tune. But that's what makes history.

Things have finally started to settle down to a manageable chaos. But it seems like whatever we do about McKeever, somebody objects. We wanted to give Yankee fans a chance to see his next start in person, so we announced that due to the excessive demands on "Mr. Perfect" 's time since his perfect game, he had not been able to maintain his normal conditioning schedule. Therefore, rather than risking his valuable arm, we were going to skip his next turn in the rotation. Instead, his second major league start would come when the team returned from its brief road trip.

What's the big deal? From the reaction of the press, it seemed like I personally had destroyed the foundations of baseball. The *Times* actually ran an editorial claiming that I was symbolic of everything that was wrong with America because I was letting my greed for a few more paid admissions become more important than the game itself. "By bypassing Tommy McKeever's next scheduled start on the road to ensure a sellout crowd at Yankee Stadium, Mr. Lyle is continuing the very disturbing trend in sports of putting the dollar before the game. Apparently the difference between winning and losing is no longer as important as the bottom line. Even during the wildest of Mr. Steinbrenner's shenanigans it was quite clear he wanted to win at all costs. Sad to say, this latest episode shows that that is no longer true in the Bronx." Mike Lupica wrote in the *National* that I was "selling out for the almighty dollar," and wondered, "What's happened to that old Sparky who would have celebrated McKeever's epic feat by sitting naked on a cake?" Well, I hope Lupica's right—I hope we do sell out. And based on advance ticket sales, it looks like we might. Okay, I admit it, I am exploiting the situation. Since when is that a crime? This is the United States of America, and the right to exploit a situation is a basic constitutional right. I'm pretty sure.

Besides, based on the results we've gotten from the 900 number we set up to allow Yankee fans to vote on whether McKeever's next start should be at home or on the road—$1.95 for the first minute, only 45¢ a minute afterwards—our fans overwhelmingly support our decision.

I just don't think the writers really appreciate how tough it is to run this business. Let them sit in my chair for a few days and I suspect they'd become a lot more understanding.

Fortunately, the team has been on the road for the past few days, and except for this McKeever controversy, the office has been pretty quiet. The reality is that the day-to-day operations of a baseball team aren't that exciting. A baseball team has to be run like any other business—and that means making sure payroll taxes are deducted, medical insurance is current and comprehensive, getting the leaks in the stadium roof fixed, changing the water in the flotation tank, all the same mundane tasks the president of General Motors has to worry about.

It was really a very typical day. Joe V's agent, David Braun, called to tell me that Joe was very unhappy about platooning in left field with Felipe Suarez. Braun said the situation was intolerable and Joe couldn't stand it, so he wanted either a guarantee that he would get an opportunity to face some right-handed pitchers, or a contract extension. I told him that the manager decided who to play and the general manager decided who to pay. "So what do you do, then?" he asked.

"I hire the manager and the general manager."

Just before lunch we got back the results of all the medical tests we had Tums Taft take. Whatever's wrong with him isn't physical. He just isn't getting batters out in critical situations. Let me put it this way: If he was the person we were depending on to keep his finger in the dike, glub, glub. This year, the bull, she wins a lot.

Early in the afternoon I was pleasantly surprised when Pete Rose called from the University of Cincinnati campus, and proudly told me that he'd gotten an "A" in social studies. That didn't surprise me, Pete was one of the most sociable people I'd ever known. "Nice going, guy," I said, "everybody in baseball's proud of you."

"Yeah, I just love being here. I'm thinking about running for freshman class office; I should win—I'm the freshest guy I know."

We both laughed. "So you're enjoying it there, huh?"

"I wouldn't give it up for nothing. Until now, baseball was all I knew. I'm learning so much. Hey, you hear about World War II?"

"What about it?" I asked.

"It happened." Then he changed subjects, "So how's it going?"

"You see the standings. Not so good."

"Yeah, well, I did notice something about that. Not that I have a lot of time to read the sports section, what with all my homework. I'm even learning to work a computer. So far I've got 'on' down pretty good." He cleared his throat. "So how's Lou doing?"

"Fine," I told him.

"Good, glad to hear that. I always liked Lou, even if he did take my job. So I guess you're pretty satisfied with him, huh?"

"We're not winning," I pointed out. "Not that it's all his fault."

There was a long, long silence. Then he said, "Well, I'm real happy here, real happy. But you know me, I've got baseball bats in my belfry. So if you wanted me, I could find somebody to turn the whatchamacallit off . . ."

"I know that, Pete, and I appreciate it. But right now . . ."

"Oh sure, sure, but you know, things change and. . . . Wait a second. Listen, I got to go. The guys in my fraternity pledge class and I are playing a prank—we're blowing up the frat house . . ."

A few minutes after I'd hung up on Pete, I got a call from a vice president at the investment banking firm of Roberts & Tarlov. Brian Something, I didn't write down his last name. He told me that he was representing "a party who wishes to remain anonymous, but a man of substantial means," who wanted to know if I would consider selling the corporation. When I told him that the Yankees were not for sale, he suggested, "You should at least give it some thought. You know, these businesses with a substantial amount of sentimental value attached tend to be overvalued by their owners."

I said I didn't understand. Not that I was nervous or anything, just because the rest of my life was tied to the value of the team, but it certainly wouldn't hurt to listen to Brian Something's proposal. Dan Hunter's United American held an option to buy; they hadn't made a commitment.

Brian Something explained that companies are valued by the total their assets would bring in the marketplace. "Think of the Yankees as a conglomerate," he said, "and each of your players as separate companies owned by that conglomerate. If you were to spin off each of these players individually to other like concerns, then throw in the Stadium lease, minor league operation, etc., you'll see that the total income doesn't approach the overall value you've set for the corporation. The intangible, of course, is what's known in the business world as 'goodwill.' The value of your name and reputation." He lowered his voice. "Mr. Lyle, I've seen your corporation play this year, and it's my considered opinion that with your pitching you're squandering your goodwill."

This was all very confusing. "Okay," I said. "Suppose you're right. What about our broadcasting contracts? We've got more than half a billion dollars in long-term television and radio contracts."

"Discounted for inflation, I'm afraid. You see, due to the size of the national debt, a deficiency in tax revenues, and the emergence of the Far Eastern cartel, we're entering uncharted economic waters. A lot of people see storm clouds and rough seas ahead. The tide is no longer coming in. . . ."

Bells started clanging in my head. Water? Rough seas? Tides? A party who wishes to remain anonymous? It all began to make sense. What goes on the water? Boats. And who did I know in the boat business? "Uh, Mr. Something," I said, "that client of yours, his name wouldn't begin with a George, would it?"

"Mr. Lyle, please! You know I can't break his trust."

I was right. The Boss was trying to buy back the team. Well, I'd been sort of expecting him to do something like this, and I was ready for it. "I'm very sorry," I said firmly, "this corporation is not for sale. Good day." I had always wanted to say "Good day" in a huff, like they do in the movies.

"Then you wouldn't reconsider that position?"

"Listen, the only thing I want to hear about positions is who's playing third base. Thank you."

I started to hang up, but he stopped me, "Mr. Lyle! I want you to understand that this is business, not baseball. I expect you've heard the term 'hostile takeover'?"

"And I expect you've heard the term 'Up yours'?" I think I heard him gagging as I hung up the phone. But for some reason, for a long time afterward, I couldn't shake the chill that ran down my spine.

After hanging up I spent some time with Chicken going over the roster. "Maybe it's time to shake things up a little," I told him. "Nothing major, just something to get their attention."

Chicken wasn't sure. "We don't want to risk upsetting the delicate balance we've got."

"Delicate balance? It's about as delicate as a twenty-pound lead weight. I don't know why, but for some reason the chemistry just doesn't seem to be there."

We agreed to put out a few feelers, just to see who was available. If we want to make a move, there are a lot of directions we can go. Who knows, maybe this whole stability thing is overrated.

And then, last night in Milwaukee, we dropped another game behind. Doyle Alexander won his first game of the season, shutting us out, 3–0. Doyle Alexander? One of the things that has always fascinated me about baseball is how a team can have a personality that transcends its players. And they do. The Yankees, for example, have always had trouble beating pitchers who throw a lot of off-speed stuff, junk. That's been true as long as I remember. Not just Alexander, but Kenny Holtzman, Ed Dickson, Marty Bell. Hoyt Wilhelm pitched a no-hitter against the Yankees as a starting pitcher, and he's in the Hall of Fame as one of the greatest relievers of all time.

It's amazing to me that a team can change its entire roster—every player, every coach, even the manager and general manager—yet still retain its personality. Not just the Yankees. The Red Sox' entire history revolves around breaking the hearts of their fans. The Cardinals have played basically the same type of running game from the Gas House Gang of the 1930s to Whitey's carpet sweepers today. For some reason the Dodgers have always managed to produce great pitchers and no offense. The Indians consistently come up with good young players who burn out quickly. The Reds have always been a power team. And strange things always seem to happen when the Mets are playing.

Of course, maybe it isn't fair to use the entire history of the New York Yankees as an excuse for losing to Doyle Alexander. Maybe the real story is that we're evening things out a little more this year—this year we don't hit power pitchers just as well as we don't hit pitchers who throw junk.

The only good news is that Mattingly had three of our five hits and seems to be out of his slump. It looks like that material Duke gave him really helped.

MAY 22 ★

As of today, I think I can say without any doubt that I have now seen everything. It started out to be just a typical day in the growing saga of "Mr. Perfect," as Tommy McKeever is now known. This morning Nestle's introduced its Mr. Perfect Bar. For the record it consists of a milk chocolate outside, a layer of caramel, then a layer of semisweet chocolate, a layer of marshmallow, and a thick bittersweet chocolate center. Of course, if you don't like chocolate you probably won't enjoy it that much.

As usual, each of the papers had a couple of stories about him. Today they were mostly focused on the fact that he was scheduled to make his second big-league start tonight at the Stadium. Phil Pepe had a nice column in the *News* about McKeever's relationship with his teammates, several of whom admitted they hadn't met him yet. The *Post* had a long interview with his Little League coach, who remembered him as "a nice kid, easy to coach, he wasn't one of them who was always spitting at the other kids." And even the *Wall Street Journal* had a long piece about him, speculating on how much money the perfect game will be worth to him and quoting several investment counselors on the best way to conserve that income.

I was in my office with Chicken about 5:30. The gates had just been opened, and the real baseball fans were just beginning to pile in to watch batting practice, when McKeever and his new agent, Adam Rosenberg, knocked on my door. The truth is that it took me a few seconds to recognize McKeever. I've only seen him about four times in my life. His life, too. "We need to talk to you," Rosenberg said.

I'd sort of been expecting this visit. I didn't know if Rosenberg was going to ask me to renegotiate McKeever's contract or simply demand a bonus, but I knew that any agent worth his Mercedes was going to get something special for his client. I invited them into my office; they sat on the royal blue couch, and Chicken and I pulled up chairs. After we'd all settled down, McKeever stared at the carpet and said in a very low voice, "I'm not gonna pitch tonight."

"Excuse me?" I said.

He looked up at me, and I really think there were tears in his eyes. "I'm not gonna pitch tonight, or tomorrow, or whenever. I'm done. Finished."

I asked the obvious question. "Did Bill Lee put you up to this?"

"He's serious," Rosenberg said. He didn't look very happy about it either.

"I don't understand," I said.

"Look, Mr. Lyle," McKeever began, still speaking softly. "I want you to know how much I appreciate the chance you gave me to pitch up here in the big show. Believe me, I'll never forget it. But the truth is, I know exactly what I am. I'm a journeyman pitcher with very average stuff who got incredibly lucky. You saw the shots they hit off of me. If Plunk hadn't gotten hurt, I'd still be in the minors. And except for . . . for . . . you know, the game, when he came off the disabled list you'd send me right back. And you'd be right.

"But right now, I'm Mr. Perfect. That's now. If I go out there again though, chances are I'm gonna give up a hit or a walk or something, and that's it, no more Mr. Perfect. So I'll get a few more starts, maybe I'll even win a few more games. Who knows, maybe I'll fool everybody and even stick up here for a few seasons. But I'm never gonna be a star; I'm never gonna be the ace of somebody's staff. I'll just hang on for as long as I can and then they'll hand me my release and there'll be a few nice stories in the paper about what might have been and I'll go back to Tampa for keeps. If I go out there and pitch again, that's what's gonna happen.

"Now look at it the other way. If I quit right now, I'm the only player in baseball history who really had a perfect career. Not just one at bat or one inning, a perfect career. That's a record nobody'll ever beat. I'll be a solid gold legend." He wrote in the air with his index finger, as if he were scripting a movie title, "They'll call it *The Legend of Mr. Perfect.*" He looked right at me, "And that's forever."

"Think you can walk away from it that easily?"

He nodded firmly, "Oh yeah, I do think so." He pointed over his shoulder with his thumb. "I've got maybe half a million bucks in offers sitting back there in my locker. You think if I walk away now they'll disappear? No way. I'll spend the rest of my life working autograph shows, appearing at banquets . . ."

Chicken finally spoke. "But what about . . ."

McKeever didn't let him finish, "Listen, I've earned this luck. For six years I've been riding buses, working winters, watching my wife work so we could keep the van running. You know what I made last year? $17,000. So, believe me, luck or no, I've earned this. And I'm not embarrassed to pick up my chips and walk away from the table. Let me ask you, how many people get the chance to walk away at the absolute peak of their career? Remember 'The Bird?' Fidrych? I'll bet you'd remember him a whole lot better if he'd walked away after his first season. See, kicking around the way I have, I know something about the world. There's always going to be a market for 'Mr. Perfect.' Nobody cares about 'Mr. Almost Perfect.'"

I looked at Rosenberg for help. "You agree with this?"

He held out his hands in a gesture of helplessness. "It's his decision. It's not my idea."

I looked at McKeever again. Losing Abramowitz to his passion for fixing teeth was one thing, but losing a decent starting pitcher because he'd done too well in his first start was even tougher. "It doesn't bother you that you'll never know how good you could have been?"

He smiled. "I know I'm not gonna get any better."

I was running out of arguments. I think I might have been about to ask him if his mother knew about this decision when Chicken looked him right in the eyes and said, "One million dollars."

"What?" McKeever said.

"What?" I said.

Chicken nodded. "Two years, one million three, all guaranteed. We'll call the three a signing bonus."

"And he stays in the big leagues?" Rosenberg asked.

"This season, guaranteed. Next year he's gotta make it."

"A million three?" I finally managed to blurt out.

Chicken turned to me. "He's worth it. We're gonna have 55,000 people here tonight, that's maybe 25,000 more than we'd normally draw. At fifteen bucks a head, including concessions, that's almost $400,000. Three or four starts, we'll break even. Who knows, maybe he's better than he thinks he is. You can go a long way on a lot of luck."

"A million three?" I said again. That was even more, much more than I'd been paid not to broadcast for ten years.

"All I know is that there're gonna be 55,000 people in this ballpark two hours from now," Chicken continued, "and if Chuck Cary walks out to the mound in the first inning they're gonna be mighty disappointed." He paused, and had a thought that made him chuckle. "Hey, Sparky, if you ever wondered exactly what 55,000 real disappointed New Yorkers might do, this could be the night you find out." He gave me a sort of friendly punch on the shoulder. "C'mon, you'll be the big hero. We'll announce that you gave him a million-dollar bonus for pitching the game, that's got to be the biggest bonus in history, and the rest is a contract extension." He turned and faced McKeever. "So? What do you say?"

McKeever didn't say a word; he just stared at the carpet. I could see he was having a very tough time making a decision. I really felt very sorry for him. He was probably right. He was maybe one pitch away from immortality—if he never threw it, he'd be remembered forever in baseball history as "Mr. Perfect." But one million three meant lifetime security for himself and his family. Finally Chicken broke the silence, pointing out, "That's a lot of candy bars and autograph sessions, son."

I thought I saw McKeever's head bounce up and down just a twitch. Then a second time, a little more firmly. And finally, he nodded. "All right, I'll do it." He looked at Rosenberg. "You get the papers ready, I'll sign 'em." I couldn't believe it. I was paying him one-point-three-million dollars, basically for pitching one game, and he had me feeling like I was doing something rotten.

After they'd left the office, I looked at Chicken. The expression on his face told me he wasn't too happy about the situation either. "Well," I said, "that's baseball."

And then McKeever went out to face the Mariners. The ballpark was sold out, we had press people from more than a hundred papers and TV and radio stations, ESPN was broadcasting the game instead of the scheduled Red Sox–Angels game. In the first inning he struck out Harold Reynolds leading off, got Henry Cotto on a pop-up to Sax, and then Scott Bradley flied out to Suarez in left. Thirty consecutive batters. In the top of the second, Ken Griffey, Jr. hit a hard shot into the hole. Espinoza backhanded it and made a great throw, getting Griffey by half a step. It was a great play, one of those plays that make you think, Maybe? Two in a row? And then Jay Buhner walked on four straight pitches. Just like that, onetwothreefour. The string of perfection was over. No more "Mr. Perfect." The ballpark shook from the ovation he received. It went on for about three minutes. McKeever went behind the mound and wiped off his brow. Mattingly went over to him and said a few words.

Then Shane Connors lined his next pitch to left-center field for a clean single. End of no-hitter. And once more, every person in the stadium stood up and cheered. Me too.

I'll tell you the surprising part. McKeever fooled a lot of people again. He threw a six-hit shutout, walking only two, and beat the Mariners 5–0. Maybe he's no longer "Mr. Perfect," but as far as I'm concerned he's still "Mr. Pretty Damn Good."

MAY 26 ★

Just another typical day: In the afternoon we put Clay Parker on the 15-day disabled list and recalled Ed Holliday from Columbus. That meant moving Plunk from the 15-day DL to the 21-day DL, but we made it retroactive to a few days before he went on the 15-day DL, so he's actually eligible to come off the 21-day list a day before he'd been eligible to come off the 15-day disabled list. I think the rule is that you're not allowed to have two people injured for the same period of time.

Parker really hasn't been complaining about that tightness in his arm, but he's been pitching so poorly that Lou and Chicken figured it had to be tight, and told him so. Holliday has been sensational at Columbus. Some people think we might be rushing him, but he's already had two consecutive quality starts, and it seems to me he doesn't have that much left to prove down there. Besides, we've got to do something to get some stability in our rotation.

Then, two hours before the game, Lou gave Felipe Suarez permission to go home to the Dominican for three days to be with his wife, who gave birth to their first child this morning. Lou and I both know that one of the most difficult parts of professional baseball is having to spend so much of your life away from your family. So we agreed before the season to try to give the guys a break whenever possible. Hey, umpires get vacations during the season; why shouldn't players?

Then, during the game in Toronto, Yogi tried to call Joe V in left field on his cellular glove to tell him to come in a few steps, but he kept getting a busy signal. At first he thought he must be dialing the wrong number, so he called the cellular information operator; but she didn't have the number. Apparently Joe V was using an unlisted glove. Finally, Yogi got so upset about this busy signal that he asked the operator to check to see if the number was in service. She checked, and reported that the line was in use—people were talking on it. So Yogi requested an emergency interruption and finally got Joe V on the phone. The kid admitted to Yogi that he had figured out a way, by rubbing two fingers together, to get an outside line. While he was in the outfield, he said, he was talking to his stockbroker on his glove.

Lou was livid when he found out. He fined Joe V $500 plus the cost of the call, and warned him that if that ever happened again, his cellular glove privileges were going to be suspended.

We managed to hold on and win the ball game, 8–6, moving us back into fourth place, seven games out in the loss column. Once again, we were lucky to hold on to win. Tommy John started and, for the second straight time, he just didn't have it. He struggled through four innings, giving up four runs and leaving with the bases loaded. When Biondo came in to relieve, Lou reminded him that the bases were loaded. Frankie looked around and used the great old line, "Gee, Lou, I didn't think they were extra infielders." But he got out of the jam and gave us four strong innings. Then Lou brought in Taft to close it out. Unfortunately, the bull, she win again. Tums gave up two runs and left with the tying runs in scoring position and one out. Big John came in and saved it.

Toronto, according to Nicholson, has "contractor ants" in their bullpen. "They're like carpenter ants," he says, "but they're so big they run the job."

MAY 27 ★

"Mr. Perfect" gave up the first runs of his big-league career this afternoon, one day after he signed a deal for a TV movie. Supposedly he's going to be played by Richard Chamberlain, and they're trying to get Lindsay Wagner to play his wife. The rumor is that Danny Aiello is going to play Piniella and Robert Prosky, from *Hill Street,* has agreed to play Yogi. McKeever won the game, though, pitching his third straight complete game, beating Toronto 4–2, to give us our first series sweep of the season.

After the game the Kangaroo Court, presided over by Judge Reginald Martinez Jackson, fined McKeever $5 a run for his effort. I don't know if it's a coincidence, but since the court went into session we've started to play a little better. Kangaroo Courts have been a part of baseball a lot longer than I have. For those people who don't know what it is, it's a meeting of players after every winning game at which fines are arbitrarily levied for such crimes as missing a signal, misplaying a ball, getting picked off base, getting caught looking up a female fan's skirt, and appearing on television without saying hello to your mother.

When I was with the Yankees we had a Kangaroo Court. I was the presiding judge. I was a tough judge too. I automatically doubled the fine of anybody who appealed one of my decisions, for "wasting the court's time." I fined players for wearing ugly shirts, for showing up at the ballpark with bad haircuts, for allowing a batter to get a hit on a no ball–two strike pitch. I fined anybody seen with an unattractive woman before midnight $10; there was no fine after midnight. Participation in the court was totally voluntary. Nobody had to be part of it and you couldn't be fined if you didn't. At the end of the season we threw a big party with the fine money.

I always thought the court was great for a team. Not only did it bring everybody together, but it forced you to think on the field. I'm serious about that. When I was pitching and I had an 0–2 count on the batter, I'd think, if I let this sucker get a hit on this pitch it's going to cost me $10. That's a cheap reminder.

I think it was Sax who suggested convening this court. They asked Reggie to serve as judge because, as Bob Geren tells everybody, "We all know that the Bible says let him who is without sin cast the first stone. Well, a lot of us watched Reggie play when we were growing up, and we know that if he tried to throw a stone at us, he'd miss the cutoff man." So Judge Jackson called the court to order and began handing out fines. Besides McKeever, Espinoza was fined $5 for failing to sacrifice successfully in the seventh inning. Piniella was fined $10 for allowing Reich to hit in the eighth inning against a right-handed pitcher instead of pinch-hitting Rojas. Kelly was fined $5 for wearing his pants too long. Verola was fined $25 for being on his glove during the game, retroactive to yesterday. And Rogers was fined $5 for "Failure to Blonde," a fine automatically imposed when somebody spots a great-looking woman wearing a very short dress that rides up on her legs when she sits down, and subsequently fails to alert his teammates. Finally, Nettles was fined $10 for G.P. G.P. stands for "General Principles," meaning that they didn't catch him doing anything wrong, but they know that he did because they know him.

Incidentally, Nettles and I made up with each other just before the team left on this road trip. Neither one of us was willing to apologize, so I got him and Hanko Tsumi to come up to my office. Tsumi sat between us. After a few seconds Hanko turned to me and said, "He thinks you should not criticize him in public newspapers for his deeds."

Then he turned to Graig and told him, "He thinks you are taking this too seriously, and anyway he is sorry for the distress it has caused you."

Then he turned back to me and said, "He thinks he will forgive you this time, but that you should know better than to criticize a teammate to a reporter."

Then he turned to Graig again and said, "And he hopes that you will become a better third base coach in your future."

Maybe the best thing about Tsumi is that if I ever have to release him, or we trade him, I won't even have to tell him.

MAY 30 ★

The White Sox made a strange announcement this afternoon: They're going to try something radically different. Since the platoon system— using batters or pitchers against players who throw with the opposite arm or hit from the opposite side of the plate—has proven to be so successful on the playing field, they're going to try it in the dugout.

Owner Eddie Einhorn said that they were going to be platooning managers. Instead of the traditional lefty-righty platoon, this one is going to be offense and defense. Something like football, I guess. When the team is at bat, Carlton Fisk will be in charge and make all the decisions. When they're in the field, Ray Miller, the great pitching coach and former Twins manager, will run the team. Einhorn's thinking is that the game has gotten so complicated it takes more time than any single man has to fully understand everything that is going on. Allowing the manager to specialize in either offense or defense will give him the time to devote himself fully to that aspect of the game.

Fisk and Miller will make up the starting lineup together. If the White Sox have the lead after the fifth inning, Miller will be in charge of making all substitutions—although Fisk will still be responsible for choosing the pinch-hitters when Miller wants one—in an effort to hold onto the lead. If the team is tied or losing after the fifth inning, Fisk will run the game in an attempt to get even or go ahead.

I guess it's an interesting idea. I sort of remember that the Cubs once used seven or eight managers in a season, with each one running the team for about a month. But this is very different. Of course, George has had as many as three managers in one season and has rehired Billy five different times, so I suppose that two managers at the same time isn't really that bizarre.

Duke called me from Toronto last night all excited because Keith Reich and Winfield had asked her before the game if they could take a look at her charts. Winfield had a double and hit two other balls hard. Reich didn't play. As the season progresses and Duke is able to feed more information into her computer, the information it spits out will be even more accurate. I don't know if it's really beneficial or not, but Mattingly's batting over .400 since he started paying attention to her charts. Maybe the most important thing these charts do is reinforce a player's confidence. I've always believed confidence is as important as any skills a player has. If a pitcher *knows* he is going to get a batter out, he might be able to do it. If that same pitcher *hopes* he can get the batter out, his infielders better make sure their health insurance is fully paid, because they're likely to get hurt. The reality is that no machine ever got a base hit or threw a pitch, and that includes the "New, improved Tommy John," as we now refer to him, but if players believe they can play better because they have this information, then they can.

I also found out today that the rookie pitcher we brought up from

Columbus, Eddie Holliday, is a very religious man. I mean, a very, very religious man. Apparently the first thing he did when we brought him up was ask Nick Priore, our clubhouse man, if he could wear uniform number 3. That happens to have been Babe Ruth's number, and it's retired. Holliday said he wanted it because he said it placed him closer to God. "Babe was pretty good," Priore said, "but not that good." Holliday explained it reminded him of the Biblical verse, John 3:16. That's the sign fans hold up on television, it has to do with a belief in the Resurrection. Then Holliday asked for 16—he couldn't have that because it was Whitey Ford's number, and it's retired too. He settled for 27, his wife's age.

What a lot of fans don't realize is that the makeup of a baseball team is no different than the makeup of a factory crew or a school class. It's just a group of people brought together by circumstance. In baseball, the only thing members of a team have in common is superior athletic skills. Other than that, you get every different type of personality on a team. I've played with good guys and bad guys, very religious people and thieves; I've played with extroverts and very shy people, really smart people and really dumb people—and none of it has anything to do with their ability on the field. So what you do is try to keep the opposites apart and hope, somehow, that it all works. And if it should come together, if that group manages to become a team, it's wonderful and special, and it's the best feeling in the world.

I've actually played with several very religious people. When I was with the Yankees in '74 and '75, we had a very useful utility infielder named Bob Schaeffer. And "Snuffy," as we called him, was always leaving little tracts—a prayer message, called "Pitching for the Master"—in my locker. Now, I've always respected everybody's religion, but I just never thought it belonged on the field. So whenever I found one of these pamphlets in my locker I'd return it to him. "Look, Snuff," I'd tell him, "I don't read this stuff at all. So why don't you just save the paper and not leave it in my locker, okay?"

"Eventually everybody comes home to the Master," he told me.

"Maybe so," I agreed. "But they don't do it in my locker." So eventually he took me off his distribution list. Look, there's always been a very important place for religion in baseball. Every team I've ever played on had a Sunday chapel service, both at home and on the road. The Fellowship of Christian Athletes has always been active in pro baseball. There have even been some good players who demanded to be traded when they found out their team was illegally stealing the other teams' signs.

Does faith have any effect on the game? There's never been any proof that it does; on the other hand, sometimes there is absolutely no logical explanation for things that happen on the field. For example, the ground crew rakes pebbles off the infield two or three times every day, yet somehow a ground ball hits a pebble and takes a crazy bounce and the outcome of a ballgame is reversed. I've seen balls hit exactly the same spot on the fence and rebound in completely different directions. Some great pitchers go an entire career without throwing a no-hitter, yet Tommy McKeever throws a perfect game in his first start. Maybe it's just luck. Or fate. Or maybe it is something else. I believe that if a player believes that putting his faith in a Higher Power is going to make him a better player, it might. I'll guarantee you one thing, there is absolutely no way I'm going to become the first owner in baseball history to bar God from the clubhouse. If He wants to come in, He's welcome. He just can't wear uniform number 11 right now.

I'll tell you the strangest religious experience I ever had in baseball. After Fritz Peterson retired, he became a very religious man. I don't think he was actually a minister, but he conducted chapel services for the White Sox when I was with the team. One day he came over to me and said, "I know you never go to the chapel meetings, but would you come for me today?" I asked him why. "I've got a special guest scheduled and I think you might enjoy hearing him," he told me. "He's a trombone player who talks about God through his trombone."

How do you say no to a trombone player who talks about God through his instrument? So I went to the meeting. After a few minutes of silent prayer, someone would shout out the number of a Bible verse or commandment and this man would play his interpretation of it on the trombone. For example, the Fourth Commandment sounded like this: Waaaaaaaaaaaaaa! It was the silliest thing I ever heard. But I finally understand why, when God handed down the Ten Commandments, He wrote them on a tablet instead of playing them on a trombone.

You know what the Eighth Commandment sounded like? Waaaaaa-aaaaaaa!

Holliday is very tall, very thin, and very soft-spoken. And very polite. We found out how religious he is when he started his first game for us tonight against the Brewers. Before every pitch he'd make the sign of the cross, like a lot of batters do. Whenever a hitter got on base he'd go behind the mound, get down on one knee, and pray. And everytime he did, the whole crowd quieted down. It was tough on the umpires; they wanted to keep the game moving, but they also didn't want to interrupt a man's prayers. Whatever he was doing, it didn't do him much good, because he gave up five runs in four and one-third innings before Lou pulled him.

At the end of the inning Nettles went back into the clubhouse to make sure Holliday was okay. Holliday was sitting in front of his locker, his head bowed between his legs. "I must have sinned very badly for the Lord to do that to me," he said.

Nettles didn't know what to say to that. "Ah, they didn't hit you very hard. Those sins probably weren't that big." He pointed out happily, "Hey, they didn't hit a home run off you. It was just a lot of dinks."

"Just His way of telling me that I'm still a sinner."

Graig tried a joke. "Who knows, maybe next time He'll send a telegram." Holliday didn't laugh, so Graig continued, "Well, maybe some of the Brewers just prayed a little harder."

Holliday looked up. "And maybe they were praying that they'd get to hit off me."

After Graig left the clubhouse Holliday found the latest addition to Nicholson's collection, a jar of large Milwaukee County Stadium barflies, and released them. Later he explained to Nicholson that we are all God's creatures and we all have a right to live.

"Even umpires?" Nicholson asked.

JUNE 1 ★

I've always thought that a baseball season was a lot like an airplane flight: The takeoff in April might be a little rocky, but by the middle of May or June you've reached cruising altitude, and except for some occasional turbulence, the rest of the flight is smooth—until you have to pack up and get ready for a landing in September. Well, so far this flight we've had to keep our seatbelts fastened. It's been pretty rocky. Win one, lose one, we can't get a winning streak started. At 25 wins and 26 losses we're as close to .500 as we've been all year, but we just can't seem to get there. The good news is that nobody else in the Eastern Division has been able to grab the season, so we're only seven-and-a-half games behind the Blue Jays. The pitching staff is still disorganized, Bill Lee's attempt at vitamin therapy doesn't look like it's working, and Mattingly is the only player hitting consistently. Winfield's been hitting the ball a little better the past few days, but we're still not getting any real production from the rest of the batting order. Kelly is at .240. Sax is stuck in the .230s. Espinoza's been terrible and is right around .125—and he's still hitting better than Reich. It's reached the point where opposing pitchers are semi-intentionally walking Mattingly when he leads off an inning, to get to everybody else.

We completed another deal today, getting David "Mad Man" Madden from the Rangers for Deion Sanders and, believe it or not, 1,000,000 frequent flyer miles. I really hated to give up Sanders, who's going to be a good player the day he decides he wants to, but the future is beginning to get away from us. Madden is a good veteran left-handed power hitter who can play a little first base, a little outfield, and DH. With Madden, Rogers, and Davis, we now have three really dependable veteran left-handed power-hitting first basemen–DHs. The usual critics will complain that we didn't need another slow veteran, but I really don't think we had a choice. When you can get someone like the Mad Man, who hit 31 home runs only three years ago and looks like he's getting his stroke back, without giving up a front-line player, you have to take the chance. You just can't have too many left-handed power hitters at Yankee Stadium. If Lou can figure out how to get them all enough at bats, and we don't have to face too many left-handed pitchers, we're going to be very tough to beat at home.

In order to make room for Madden on the roster we had to release Jim Sundberg. He did a good job for us in his two at bats, but he was obviously having problems getting down in a catcher's crouch. Every time he crouched down some loose bone rubbed against some stretched ligaments and he sounded like a frog with a sore throat croaking.

That makes Jorge Burns our backup catcher. We think he can be a pretty good player, even though he has the strangest way of hitting I think I've ever seen: Unlike some great players like Mel Ott and Darryl Strawberry, who raised their front foot in the air and stepped directly into the pitch, Burns lifts his back foot when the pitcher goes into his windup, then sort of falls backward, planting his foot as he lands, and shifting all his weight onto it. He claims that by planting his foot either closer to or farther away from home plate, he keeps the option of hitting to any field. It's a very complicated swing, but he's had good success with it in the minors, and our hitting coach, Jon Boswell, doesn't want to try to change him until he's had a chance to watch him hit against different types of pitchers.

We had the second meeting of the Yankees Advisory Committee today. It was only slightly less hectic than the first one. Two people wanted me to fire Piniella, two people wanted me to extend his contract, and the 12-year-old, Alex Langsam, wanted me to find out why the Chicago White Sox' new exploding scoreboard was still standing after it exploded. Lou DiGiamo presented me with a petition signed by about 300 people complaining that the pizza is usually colder than the ice cream. Geri Simon wanted us to find a sponsor for a one-page handout listing all the players in the game by their numbers; either that or she wanted us to put players' names on the back of their uniforms. I started to explain that we didn't put names on the back because the Yankee pinstripe is the most recognized uniform in sports, and we didn't want to tamper with tradition, and we also didn't want to tamper with the revenue we got from selling about 1.5 million scorecards at $1.50 each, which is an even better tradition. But before I could finish, Ms. Simon said she had to leave to get to the hairdresser. Joanie Silver suggested we have a "Date Night" promotion, in which female fans could win a date with their favorite single Yankee. And finally, Alex Langsam wanted to know why, since we have a Senior Citizens Discount, don't we have a Junior Citizens Discount?

About the only thing we agreed upon was that at our July meeting we'd have a wider selection of luncheon meats.

JUNE 3 ★

We got back the full report on Tommy John's physical examination from the mechanical engineer this morning. It seems like the reason he's been losing velocity on his fastball is that there is a slight flaw in his Shuster Valve. In fact, according to this report, it seems to be rusting. So for the first time in baseball history, it would be accurate to say that a pitcher throws like a rusty gate. If it's not repaired it's going to get progressively worse, and eventually he'll lose as much as forty or fifty miles per hour off his fastball. Apparently there are several things they can do to correct this. A medical carpenter can operate and replace the valve, which would put Tommy on the DL for three to four weeks. Or they can do basic silicon therapy. Silicon therapy is an industrial operation which involves injecting a silicon-based liquid into the valve—sort of futuristic arthroscopic surgery—in which case Tommy would be out six to eight hours. When I told Tommy the options he asked for a little time to think about it, telling me, "Before I make any decisions I really want to talk to my family." He told me he'd let me know tomorrow.

The team came home late last night, and first thing this morning Bill Lee conducted an exorcism around the pitcher's mound. It's an attempt, he told reporters, "to exorcise the evil spirits that have inhabited the bodies of the Yankee pitching staff. I admit that we haven't actually found proof of their existence, but you can't see air either—except in New York and Los Angeles—and I can't find any other logical explanation for our poor pitching this season."

When I spoke to Lee after reading the stories in the afternoon papers, he reminded me that a lot of teams—the Indians, the Braves, the Cubs—had hired local witches to help them break losing streaks. He said he couldn't find a certified witch, so he'd hired Doctor Devino, a well-known East Bronx faith healer, to do the exorcism. "Don't worry about it, though," he told me. "I warned him, no chickens." The real reason he did it, he explained, was to try to take some of the pressure off the pitching staff. "I've just got to get them to relax a little. Everybody's so tense. And nothing else I've tried so far has worked. I just know we've got a better staff than we've been showing. I just know it." Then he smiled and added, "And you never know, maybe there are some evil spirits out there."

I tried something myself. I asked Tums Taft to come up to my office to talk about relief pitching. Relief pitching is probably the only subject in the world on which I really am an expert. The moment he walked into the office I knew he was suffering from the dreaded "Relief Pitcher Depression." That's the disease you get when you start giving up runs in the eighth and ninth innings. The symptoms include an inability to sleep at night, loss of appetite, complete loss of your sense of humor, a tendency to snap angrily at people for innocent remarks, maybe even a rash, loss of your sex drive, and a total loss of your self-confidence. When you've got it, all you can think about is the last ballgame. And whenever you're brought into a game, this disease makes you pitch defensively—you don't concentrate about winning so much as worry about losing. "Been using the frustration room at all?" I asked him.

"I moved a cot in there last week," he said. "Next week I'm gonna put up some curtains, maybe hang a few pictures. . . ."

I really sympathized with him. "You have any idea what's wrong?"

"The usual," he said, nodding sadly. "I think my release point is a little off, I've had bad location, I'm not getting ahead in the count so I have to come in with the pitch they're waiting on, I've either been gripping the ball too tightly or not tightly enough, the mound's a little too high, I've lost my concentration, I've been tipping off my pitches, either I've been used so much that my arm's tired or I haven't been used enough and I'm so strong that I'm overthrowing, the mound's too low, my fastball is flat, my curveball isn't breaking, and my slider isn't sliding, I think there's a slight flaw in my delivery, I'm opening up my shoulder or dropping down too much, I'm definitely not following through, and the umpires have been squeezing the plate on me. Other than that, I think everything is okay."

I smiled knowingly. "Bill Lee put you up to that, right?"

"I don't know what's wrong. But whatever I'm doing wrong, I'm doing it a lot, 'cause those suckers are hitting the shit out of that ball. The infielders think they're funny complaining about line drives. Well, hell, I'm a whole lot closer to the plate than they are, and the way I'm throwing, that's a dangerous place to be." He shrugged his shoulders. "I don't know anymore. I've tried everything I can think of. You got any ideas?"

"Maybe," I said. "I've been thinking about it. I think maybe it's your character."

He took it wrong. "Hey, buddy, thanks a lot. What's wrong with my character?"

"Well, for starters you don't have one."

"I don't have character? *I* don't have character?"

"No, you're not listening. Sure you've got character. What you don't have is *a* character. Look, it's simple. Being a short reliever is one of the strangest jobs in the world. You only get to pitch when the game's on the line, you rarely pitch more than an inning, and you're one of the most important players on the team. These days nobody can win without a stopper coming out of the bullpen. I mean, tell me another job that takes so little time and is so important? Now, I don't know if you've noticed, but most of the really good short relievers have had a character. Al Hrabosky was 'The Mad Hungarian.' Remember, with the beard, he'd go behind the pitcher's mound and stomp around psyching himself up? I was 'The Count,'—whenever I came into a game the organist would play 'Pomp and Circumstance.' Tug McGraw . . . he was his own character. Mitch Williams took his character from that movie, you know, about a crazy baseball team, and he became . . . 'The Wild Thing!' Remember Ryne Duren, who pitched for the Yankees in the 1950s? He wore very thick glasses and he'd pretend he couldn't see the catcher and throw his first warmup pitch over the catcher's head against the screen. And it isn't just Chuck Perschetz, it's Chuck Perschetz, 'The Curve Master!' See, short relievers are the professional wrestlers of baseball. They've got to have a gimmick. Not just for fun. I really believe those little acts help build up their confidence. You know as well as I do, when Tom Henke comes into a game, it's not just Tom Henke. It's . . . 'The Terminator!' Honestly, when I came in from the bullpen and I heard them playing my music, I would really get psyched up, I'd get cocky.

"But you. . . . You just come into the game. How can you be a stopper, you don't even have your own theme music. So I think if we could find something that boosted your confidence, something that really got the fans into it . . . See what I mean?"

"Yeah, okay. I think . . ."

"Besides, what're Mattingly and Verola and Hanko going to do with their books if we don't have a zany character coming out of the bullpen? Without a really colorful relief pitcher the movie rights to those books won't be worth anything." I didn't even mention my book.

I could see he was interested in the idea. "What about bullfighting?" he asked. "Like, you know, I could be . . . Mr. Matador! Dum dum!"

I shook my head. "Sounds like a comic-strip character. Let's think about this for a minute." And then it came to me, boom, just like that. "What about this? Listen, this is really good. First, Lou comes out to the mound. . . ." I got up and I walked purposefully across the room; I was Lou walking out to the mound. "Then he signals to the bullpen." I raised my right hand as if I was signaling to the bullpen. "And then, over the loudspeaker, the crowd hears the beginning of a low roar. MMmmm. MMmmm. It gets a little louder. MMMMmm.

MMMMmm. Finally, it becomes a roar. MMMMMMMM! Then the bullpen gate opens and out comes . . ." I couldn't think of the right nickname, but I knew it would come, "Whatever. But there you are, wearing a black leather jacket over your uniform, and sunglasses, and a black helmet, and pasted on the side of that black helmet is a skull and crossbones sticker for every save you've gotten this season. Then you rev up the bike"—I twisted my hands at the wrists as if I were revving up a bike—"and then you rev it again. MMMMMMM! MMMMMM! And then the loudspeaker system bursts into . . . into . . ." I searched the air for an answer. And found it. ". . . into 'Leader of the Pack!' And suddenly your back wheels start spinning, raising a cloud of dust in the bullpen and you come roaring out of that cloud on your Harley . . ."

Taft saw it too. He stood up and took over, twisting his own hands as if he were on that bike. "And then I roar around the warning track, kicking up a trail of dust, until I get right in front of the dugout. Then I do a complete 360° spin and stop. The batboy comes running out and takes the bike and the jacket and the helmet and the sunglasses and I . . ."

"Keep the sunglasses!" I yelled at him.

"Yeah, right, I like it. I *keep* the sunglasses on and stomp to the mound . . ." He stomped across my office until he reached the pitcher's mound. Then he leaned over and sneered in at the catcher. Finally, he stood up and looked at me. All signs of Relief Pitcher Depression were gone, replaced by an aura of complete confidence. Then he just sort of curled his upper lip and said with just the right touch of threat in his voice, "Mr. Cool is back."

"Mr. Cool," I repeated. "The Ice Man. Nothing shakes him up."

"No matter how tough the situation is, he's the coolest dude in town." He held out the palm of his hand. I slapped it hard and he slapped me coming back. "I think I've found the flaw in my delivery," he said.

"The team gets a percentage of poster rights," I said.

JUNE 8 ★

We won our third straight game tonight, coming back from four runs down to beat the Angels, 7–5. This was the first game of a nine-game western swing, and it's a very good way to begin. Holliday started the game for us and for the third straight time he just didn't have very much, giving up four runs in two-plus innings. After Piniella yanked him, he sat on the bench talking to himself: "How can they expect me to pitch against Angels? Don't they know that angels are God's attendants in heaven? How can I pitch against God's pals, tell me that? That's why I need to pitch against the Devils. . . ." I guess it could have been worse for him. He could be in the National League and have to pitch against the Cardinals and Padres.

Tsumi and Biondo held them to a run while we came back, and Taft finished up with a solid inning. Taft's brand-new Harley is going to be delivered while the team is on the road, but he already looks like a different pitcher. Self-confidence is just so important in sports. If you think you're better than you really are, you really are.

We had eleven hits, including Mattingly's home run and Winfield's two doubles, so it looks like we're finally starting to break out of that hitting slump we've been in since the beginning of the season. Maybe it's just a coincidence, maybe it's simply a matter of self-confidence, but every batter who's used Duke's computer readouts has improved. Every one of them. By now her program is in its second generation and has become much more accurate. The computer is able to correctly predict the location of the pitch 78 percent of the time and the type of pitch 71 percent, allowing it to correctly predict the location and type of pitch 55.8 percent of the time. More important, the computer is able to pinpoint the "batter's ideal pitch to hit," and predict the exact location, plus or minus two zones, and the type of pitch almost 60 percent of the time. And when the count is 2–1 or deeper, that percentage increases to 77.6. So the more selective our hitters are, the higher the odds that they will get a pitch they can hit. Computers are absolutely incredible.

So far only five players are using the charts every day, but several more people are looking at them seriously. In fact, the only person who doesn't like what's going on is Piniella. And he doesn't like it at all. He called me from Anaheim this morning to complain that Duke was undermining his efforts to teach discipline and bat control at the plate, and that she was confusing his players with all kinds of silly statistics that had nothing to do with hitting. "That stuff is just a crock," he said. "There isn't a mother-blanking computer in the whole world that can make somebody a better hitter. I mean, who knows more about hitting, me or IBM? How many hits has IBM ever gotten in the World Series, Spark, tell me that?" He didn't wait for my answer. "None is how many. Listen to me, hitting is a combination of coordination, instinct, intelligence, hard work, and even some luck. It takes hundreds of hours of preparation and repetition, doing the same thing over and over and over again, to make a good hitter. I'm just worried that some of the guys are going to start relying on those numbers she shows them instead of doing their work. Sure, it might help them in the short run, but believe me, in the long run it's going to hurt them."

"What do you want me to do about it?"

"It's gotta stop. I want her to do what she's supposed to do and leave the players alone. I've spent my whole life in baseball, I know about these things. This isn't gonna help anything."

I took a few seconds to collect my thoughts. If the players believed Duke's charts were helping them, they were. Now that we'd finally started hitting, I didn't want to change anything. "Well, you know, Lou, Ted Williams always said that hitting was a science. And you know how important computers are in science. So maybe they can help hitters a little, you know, by adding some predictability."

I could almost hear him shaking his head. "I don't think so, Spark. Hitting really isn't a science. If it was, Einstein would have been a .380 hitter. I think hitting's actually more of an art, and when was the last time you heard of a computer that could create art?"

"Well, if it's an art, how come Picasso never played in the big leagues?" I knew I had him there. "Look, Lou, who's she hurting?"

"Right now? Probably nobody. But you've seen what happens when hitters start believing in false coaches. They do fine for a little while, then . . ." He whistled, sounding like a plane going down for a crash landing.

"Listen to me, Lou. I understand what you're saying. And maybe you're right. But the world of baseball is changing, and I don't want us to get left behind. You're much more of a traditionalist than I am. You'd like it if there were still sixteen teams, with no designated hitter, playing doubleheaders on grass. But sometimes change is a good thing. You remember how many people had to get hit in the head before players started wearing protective helmets. . . ."

"Yeah," he agreed halfheartedly, "so maybe they should start wearing computers now."

I ignored that remark. "So for now, I think, let's just leave things alone. I'll tell her to step back a little. And as soon as we see that she really is getting in the way, I promise, I'll pull the plug."

"You know, if you're not happy with the way I'm running things around here . . ."

"That's not what I said, Lou. I think you're doing a great job holding things together. But let's just leave everything alone while we're winning." Reluctantly, he agreed with me.

Tommy John didn't travel with the team. Instead he checked into Lenox Hill Hospital to have medical carpentry done on his arm. The carpenter said that the operation was a complete success, that they'd removed almost two grams of rust, and that TJ shouldn't have any more trouble with his valve this season. He also pointed out that Tommy's arm was still under warranty, and that he should get a replacement installed during the winter. TJ should be able to crank it up for us again in two days.

JUNE 13 ★

Yesterday, while we were sending Eddie Holliday back to Columbus and recalling Bruce McDonald, the Mets got Greg Swindell from the Red Sox in exchange for Tim Teufel, Phil Lombardi, and a minor-league pitcher. That makes the Mets' starting rotation Dwight Gooden, David Cone, Frank Viola, Orel Hershiser, and now Swindell with Bret Saberhagen in the bullpen. That just has to be one of the top three or four pitching staffs in the National League. I just don't understand how the Mets get so lucky. It certainly makes it very tough to compete with them in New York.

We think McDonald could be a good one. He's a big kid, 6'4", 220, and throws very hard. If he can just improve his control and come up with another pitch, maybe a slider, he can win some games in the big leagues.

Another tough night last night. Not only did we drop the second straight game to the Mariners 9–6, but Bob Geren suffered a seriously sprained forehead when he squinted up into the halogen lights in the Kingdome. Trainer Gene Monahan immediately sprayed Geren's forehead with the anti-inflammatory ethyl chloride, freezing his wrinkles in position, but after the game the whole area swelled up badly. We had to put Geren on the 15-day disabled list, which meant we had to move Clay Parker to the 21-day DL and Eric Plunk to the 30-day DL. Parker insists his arm is fine, but after throwing in the bullpen for almost an hour before the game last night, he admitted his arm felt "a little tired." We put Plunk on the 30-day list retroactive to last month, so he was actually eligible to come off that list before he went on. He was ready to pitch a few days ago, but because of the long layoff he's had we've decided to give him a few more days to work himself back into condition. That's why we put him on the longer list. The worst thing you can do with a pitcher is rush him back into action before he's ready, and as long as we're staying in contention we can wait until Plunk is 100 percent.

To replace Geren on the roster, we brought Jim Sundberg out of retirement.

Then, after the game, we had our first problem with dissension in the ballclub. Kenny Davis told reporters that he wanted to be traded. "I want outta here," he said. "The trade for Madden was a slap in my face. They just don't give you a chance around here. You go a couple of months without hitting and they bury you on the bench. I'm the kind of hitter who needs to play to get out of a slump, and I can see that isn't going to happen here. So I think it would be better for everybody if they made a deal and got me out of here. I don't think any team really needs four left-handed hitting first basemen. I hate to say it, but I think the people running the club are just stupid. They're dumb. They don't know anything about baseball."

I think I know what Davis is trying to say; he isn't satisfied with some of the things that have taken place around here. Believe me, if The Boss was still here, Davis would be gone before the ink was dry on those stories. But these are new times. I understand his frustration, so I'm not going to take it all that seriously. I'll give him some time to cool down, then we'll get together and talk about it. Working together, we'll try to find a solution that will satisfy everybody. The Boss never understood how sensitive some major-league players really are, and that they sometimes say things they don't mean, or don't say exactly what they do mean. But Chicken and I played the game, so we know exactly what Davis doesn't mean.

I read in the papers this morning that Adam Rosenberg, Tommy McKeever's agent, announced that McKeever will be appearing as a guest star on The Pete Rose Show on the Home Shopping Network next month to sell his autograph. Not autographs, autograph. One. It seems that during the brief time McKeever was with Columbus, and in his first few hours with the big club, nobody knew who he was, so they didn't bother asking him for his signature. After he pitched his perfect game he was overwhelmed by the media, then isolated by his agent, so he still didn't sign any autographs. In other words, he hasn't signed a single autograph all season. Rosenberg decided McKeever was going to take advantage of that by committing himself to sign only one autograph "this perfect season," as Rosenberg put it. So he's going on the show with Rose to auction it off. Experts have estimated the value of that one signature will be between $3,000 and $50,000, depending on the rest of his career and how many other autographs he signs in the future. But the experts believe his autograph will instantly become one of the most valuable signatures of a living person.

I'm sure the whole thing has the promoters of collectibles shows terrified. If players realize that the fewer autographs they sign the more valuable their autograph becomes, and that they can make more money by signing fewer autographs, the collectible business will be in trouble.

Rosenberg did announce, by the way, that "a substantial percentage" of whatever is received will be donated to the newly established Mr. Perfect Foundation, for the help of less than perfect children.

That reminded me of some of the problems we've had satisfying charities this year. Until I sat in this chair I just never realized how many requests for contributions a major-league team gets from fundraising organizations and charities. They want anything we're willing to give them—money, tickets and equipment that can be sold or auctioned off, and personal appearances by our players. Whenever possible we've tried to help out, but sometimes I have to remind myself that I'm trying to run a business here. One of the first things I did was institute a team policy of sending bats that were broken in games to charities for their "celebrity auctions." I'll tell you a little secret, when we found out that bats broken by Mattingly and Winfield sold for the most money, we sent a card with each bat claiming that it had been broken by one of them. When we began running short of broken bats we started sending out used equipment—torn jerseys and pants, sweatshirts, discarded spikes, even used sweat socks and sanitary hose. Then these organizations informed us that these items lose some value to collectors if they've been washed after being used in a game, so now we're sending dirty sweat socks to people who sell them for substantial amounts of money. That pleases me, because I've always felt I was very lucky to be able to play in the big leagues, and I always wanted to give something back to the community, even if it is dirty sweat socks.

Nettles told me that that's what people mean when they talk about "the sweet smell of success."

We've also encouraged our players to work with the charities of their choice whenever possible. We can't demand that they make personal appearances or donations, but a lot of them do it on their own. The Dave Winfield Foundation, for example, does a great job helping underprivileged kids. Don Mattingly donates $1,000 for each home run he hits to an organization that provides medical treatment to kids in the inner city. Tums Taft sends $1,000 for each save he gets to Save the Bulls, a sort of retirement home for bulls who survive the bullfighting ring. Felipe Suarez is very active in the Boys Club. Unfortunately, some of our other players haven't grasped the concept: Joe V, for example, wanted to set up an organization called Bail Bonds for Brooklyn. His idea was that every time he hit a home run or knocked in the winning run, he'd put up a $250 bail bond for a deserving Brooklyn native. Chicken managed to talk him out of it, explaining that it might cause a "public relations flap."

The biggest continuing program is the Con Ed Kids, in which Con Ed and the Yankees provide free tickets for needy kids. It really works out very well for everybody; the kids get to see a ballgame, Con Ed gets good publicity out of it, and we get a great tax deduction.

JUNE 16 ★

A losing streak is like a bad haircut. You know that eventually it will disappear, but while it's there it's absolutely the only thing you can think about. Every club, every season, goes through at least one long losing streak. It's as natural and normal as the leaves changing color in the fall or, as we used to say, The Boss changing managers. There's no obvious reason why a team suddenly goes into a losing streak; no one has ever figured out why an entire team goes into the dumper at the same time. But all of a sudden the hitters stop hitting and the pitchers start getting racked.

The most important thing a team can do during a losing streak is not let things happen that might destroy the rest of the season. A losing streak is like a headache that doesn't go away. It gets under your skin and in your teeth. It makes your food taste bad and music sound off-key. Somehow, during a losing streak you get caught in bad traffic jams, your airplane flights are cancelled, and your home appliances break down. Old tax bills arrive in the mail during losing streaks. Everything is magnified way out of proportion: In the clubhouse radios play songs you don't like too loud, obnoxious teammates say the wrong thing at the wrong time, and every move the manager makes turns out wrong. And everybody's temper gets shorter and shorter. Just one spark could ignite a fight or wreck a team for the whole season. It's that time of year when one player asks another player to pass something, and the second player demands, "What'd you mean by that?"

After getting swept by the A's in Oakland, we've lost seven straight. Worse, after the final game in Oakland, Duke had the team fly a two-hopper across the country, stopping in Denver and Iowa City. Piniella woke me up at 5:45 this morning to ask me why I wasn't at the airport to greet the team. "If I'm up at this hour, you son of a bitch," he told me, "you're gonna be up."

Supposedly Rosey Rogers got so mad at Duke that he told her, "Believe me, the only thing standing between me and homicide are your great legs."

During this losing streak we've lost ballgames in ways I've never seen before. Last night, for example, Gene Kline pitched a solid ballgame, but we were losing 4–3 with two out in the ninth. Suarez was on first base when Kelly lined a base hit to right field. When Canseco misplayed it, Kelly kept going. The ball bounced into the corner and Canseco kicked it around. Kelly put his head down and rounded third and took off for home plate. He made a great diving slide around A's catcher Scott Finnegan to score what should have been the go-ahead run. The only problem was that Suarez was still standing on third base. Kelly was ruled out for passing a runner; so instead of being a run ahead, the game was over and we'd lost.

The Mariners beat us when Taft and Mattingly collided going after a slow ground ball toward first that would have been the last out of the game. Either one of them could have made the play easily; instead, the runner was safe and the tying run scored. The runner on first went to second on a passed ball and scored the winning run when M. L. Blanks broke an 0-for-22 streak with a broken-bat flare just over Mattingly's head. I hope Blanks made some charity happy.

There really is only one thing you can do to break a losing streak—win a game. The longer a streak goes on the more difficult it is to break it, because the pressure grows and everybody becomes tense and tries to do more than they're capable of doing. That's when batters try to hit six-run homers and pitchers figure they have to pitch a no-hitter to win. Instead, they end up making small mistakes, and somehow those small mistakes end up costing the team the ballgame. There's an old saying around the clubhouse, "When you're winning even your underwear smells good." That means that when a team's on a winning streak players are not supposed to change anything—including their underwear. They're supposed to do everything precisely the same way they did it the day before, and the day before that. I remember when I was with the Yankees in 1978 and we got red hot in August, somebody complained that he wanted our winning streak to end because he'd had to sleep with his wife every night for two weeks.

But when a team goes into a losing streak players are supposed to try to do everything differently to break the unlucky streak. So they sleep on the opposite side of the bed, drive to the ballpark by a different route, put their spikes on before their pants, skip batting practice, sit in a different spot in the dugout, use somebody else's bat or glove. None of it makes any real difference, of course, except that a lot of people tear their pants with their spikes. It usually takes an outstanding pitching performance, and maybe just a little luck, to end a losing streak.

Piniella has tried everything. He's juggled his starting lineup, he's rested some of the regulars to try to loosen things up, he's played his "Tommy Lasorda Sings Italian Love Songs" cassette in the clubhouse, he's yelled, he's begged, he's even tried to shake things up by letting Rosey Rogers try to steal a base. But nothing has worked. Eight straight.

When he called me from the airport this morning he told me he wanted me to keep Duke away from the players. "You see what I told you?" he said. "Whatever she's doing, it isn't working. You told me you didn't want to change anything while we were playing well. Maybe you've noticed, but we're not playing well anymore. Do something."

I told him he was completely wrong. "Now would be the worst time to tell her to stay away from the players," I explained. "You know as well as I do that the most important thing we can do right now is stay calm. If the team thinks we're panicking, we might as well pack our bags and go home. We've got to show them that we've got a plan and we're going to stick to it."

"And what's our plan?"

"Letting them think we have a plan. And not panicking. Let's just keep cool for a while. If I were to make a big deal about Duke right now, the players would think we were blaming the losing streak on her. We can't do that. Let's just wait until we've won a few games, then I'll tell her."

Before Lou could argue with me, the telephone demanded another nickel. He didn't have it, so we were cut off. Remind me to send Ma Bell a Mother's Day card.

Duke got to the office from the airport about ten o'clock. She looked terrible, which is not an easy thing for someone as attractive as she is to do. I went into her office and told her about my conversation with Piniella. "Maybe you could sort of keep a low profile for a while," I suggested. "Besides, you know, maybe he has a point."

"What do you mean?"

"Well, all this . . ." I indicated her computer setup. "It doesn't seem to be doing us much good. We've lost eight straight, you know."

"Oh, but I knew that was going to happen," she protested. "It's nothing to worry about. Here." She handed me another one of those sheets that made as much sense as my high school trigonometry textbook. "Look at that. It's all right there."

"What's all right where?"

"The losing streak. It was all in the computer. I just had to find a program to bring it out. Remember what I told you? Everything that happens in baseball can be translated into statistics. That's why all those statistical analysis books have sold so well. But compared to what we've got right here, they're just elementary school primers." She put her hand gently on top of her terminal. "This is the future of big-league baseball. The laws of probability cannot be repealed. They're irrefutable. And that sheet tells you everything you need to know about the losing streak."

"What does it say?"

"It says it's over. See, while we were on the coast I ran a study of every losing streak five games or longer in the last fifteen years. Besides proving that a losing streak of less than ten games has very little impact on the pennant race, it estimated that there is a better than 97 percent chance that we're going to win our next two games."

"So you're saying we're going to win tonight?"

She smiled shyly. "I'm just the channel." Then she nodded toward her computer. "That's what she says."

"Let me ask you something, Duke. If you're so sure about all of this, why don't you just pull a Pete?"

"Gamble?" She shook her head. "Not me. I've been waiting my whole life for a chance at the big leagues, and I'm not going to jeopardize it to make a few bucks." She paused, and for an instant I thought she was trying to decide whether to say anything more. Finally she spoke again, and when she did there was a determination in her voice unlike anything I'd ever heard before. "Believe me," she said, "this is only the beginning."

Today's *Post* was on my desk when I returned to my office. A big headline on the back cover read: "Lou Through?" I couldn't believe it. When Lyle Spencer called me yesterday to ask me if Piniella's job was safe, I told him, "Lou Piniella is my manager. Period. I've got complete confidence in him." Spencer's story quoted me accurately, pointing out that I had given Lou a vote of confidence. "Which," he continued, "in the crazy world of baseball means they're measuring his neck to make sure the rope fits around it snugly."

Coincidentally, Pete Rose called me this afternoon to tell me the bad news he'd just heard in summer school: "President Roosevelt's dead," he said, "I wanted to tell you about it right away."

I told him I'd heard something about that, then asked him how he was doing in his other subjects.

"Pretty good," he told me. "I'm taking new math. But even with that I can't figure out how a .230 hitter's worth $850,000 a year."

JUNE 21 ★

Duke was wrong. We didn't win two in a row. We swept all three games from the Brewers, then won the series opener against Baltimore last night. It's amazing how different the world looks during a winning streak: All food tastes great and all music is a symphony. Somehow you never get caught in traffic jams, planes arrive early, broken appliances suddenly start working and unexpected tax refunds arrive in the mail.

It seems like everybody has started hitting at the same time. The pitching is still barely adequate, but all we have to do is keep scoring one more run than we give up. The highlight of last night's game took place in the ninth inning. We were up 6–4, but Cadaret opened the ninth by walking Cal Ripken. Lou strolled slowly out to the mound and signaled to the bullpen. A few seconds later a roar rose from the bullpen, the gate opened, and Tums Taft came speeding out of a cloud of dust in full gear. It was tremendous. The crowd went absolutely wild. The public address system started blasting "Leader of the Pack" throughout the whole ballpark. It was baseball at its very best. Finally Tums did a very small wheelie in front of our dugout, and spun to a stop. Then he took off his jacket and helmet and marched out to the mound.

Meanwhile, the message board noted, "The Orioles have not scored a run off Taft today," and "Tettleton is batting .000 in this game."

Tums's first pitch to Tettleton was a strike. Suddenly Frank Robinson came running out of the dugout screaming at home plate umpire Richie Garcia. At first I thought Robinson was arguing about the call, but after the game Garcia announced that Robinson had protested the game on "G.P." Robinson seemed to think that there was a rule prohibiting pitchers from wearing sunglasses on the mound. He's wrong, there's no such rule. Every other player is permitted to wear sunglasses on the field—even indoors—so there's no way they can discriminate against the pitcher. When Garcia explained that to Robinson, Frank decided to protest on "general principles."

The whole thing got Taft really pumped up. He retired three consecutive batters without allowing a ball out of the infield. Not only did he look like a different pitcher, his act seemed to pick up the whole team, as well as the crowd. Everybody was getting into it. It was great fun, nobody got hurt, and it seemed to work. The only problem is that if Tums continues to pitch so well, we're going to have to change his name to No-Tums.

Maybe the only person on the team who isn't happy right now is Kenny Davis. I asked him to come up to my office this afternoon so we could talk about the things that were bothering him. He showed up with his agent, Mike Garcia. "We've got four left-handed hitting first basemen," Davis said, "and Mattingly is the best player in the game. This is my option year and I'm nailed to the bench. I want to play."

"I understand that," I said sympathetically. "But you're not playing because you're not hitting."

"I can't hit if I don't play."

"You can't play if you don't hit."

"That's not the way we see it," Garcia said. "If you played him, he'd hit. And obviously you've been stockpiling left-handed hitting first basemen, so you don't need him. That's why we'd like you to trade him."

"Even if we wanted to trade him," I said, "which we don't, we wouldn't trade him when he wasn't hitting because we can't get his full value. So we have to wait until he's doing well before we can think about trading him."

"So you're saying that if he starts hitting, you'll try to trade him?"

"That's right. We'd only trade him if he was going good."

"But he can't start hitting if he isn't playing."

"And he's not playing because he isn't hitting, so we can't trade him. You know what I'm talking about. Believe me, if he were really hitting we'd be glad to get rid of him. But as long as he isn't hitting, he's going to be a Yankee."

I could see Garcia getting frustrated. "You know, if you don't make a deal now, at the end of the year he'll become a free agent and walk away, and you won't get anything for him."

"Yeah, that's right, but if we trade him now we won't get anything for him, and if he goes somewhere else and starts hitting, we'll look like we really got Mookied. Look at it our way; as long as he isn't hitting we can't get his real value for him, so we're better off taking our chances that he'll start hitting."

"Just hold it a second," Garcia said. "I want to make sure I understand exactly what you're saying. You're telling us that Kenny isn't playing because he isn't hitting, and you can't trade him while he isn't playing because he's too valuable; but if he starts hitting, then he'll get to play and he won't be as valuable so you can trade him? And then you're telling us that you'd rather lose him to free agency, and get nothing in return, than trade him now and get something in return, because if Kenny goes to another club and starts hitting people will blame you for not getting more in return?"

"Isn't that what I said?"

Garcia let out a low, respectful whistle. "This is some tough game."

I nodded. "And you don't know the half of it." I looked at Davis, who seemed a bit confused. "Think of the bright side of this," I suggested, "we're paying you $750,000 this season to sit on the bench. There are a lot of people who'd be thrilled to earn that kind of money for not playing in the big leagues."

"Maybe," Garcia answered, "but he won't be able to get near that much money next year unless he shows he can still play."

"But what if he plays and doesn't hit?" I pointed out. "In that case he'd be much better off not playing this year. He could make a lot more money." I reminded them that it's a long season, that before the end of the year we were going to need contributions from everybody on the squad, that it was his job to be ready to play when Piniella needs him, that tomorrow's hero is today's goat, that you can't win 'em all, that the game is never over till the last fat lady is out, that . . . well, I'd just about run through all the good clichés when Garcia yawned and stood up. As I walked them out the door, I told Kenny, "Just remember that it's impossible to keep all twenty-four men on the roster satisfied. This is baseball, and only ten men can play at the same time."

JUNE 25 ★

I feel so sorry for Dave Steib. He's been such a tremendous pitcher for the Blue Jays for so long, and just about the only thing he hasn't done on the field is pitch a no-hitter. He's thrown seven one-hitters, and three times he was within one out of a no-hitter when he gave up the first hit. In fact, in two of those games he was within one strike of a perfect game. But last night was probably the toughest one of all. Pitching against Texas in the Skydome, he was one strike away from a perfect game for the third time. Steve Buechele was the batter. With the count on Buechele 1 and 2, Steib threw a perfect slider. Home plate umpire Jim McKean called strike three, and the Skydome erupted. Fans piled onto the field. Steib's teammates picked him up on their shoulders and carried him into the locker room and doused him with Gatorade. Toronto GM Danny Dengate handed him a bonus check for $10,000. Film crews were pushing and shoving to get close enough to him to get usable postgame footage. There was bedlam in the clubhouse.

Suddenly Jim McKean managed to fight his way through the chaos and told Steib that third base umpire Trish Todd had called time just before his last pitch to Buechele because a tennis ball had bounced on the field. The game wasn't over, McKean explained. Steib put on a dry uniform and returned to the field. Because of the unusual circumstances he was given about ten minutes to warm up. Then Buechele stepped into the batter's box and play resumed.

Buechele lined Steib's first pitch into center field for a clean single, ending the perfect game and no-hitter. That's the closest Steib has come yet.

During our game against the Royals last night—we lost 5–2—Yogi tried to call Joe V on his cellular glove to bring him in a few steps. The glove rang three times, then Yogi heard a recorded announcement telling him, "This is Joe V. I'm not here right now, but if you'll leave a message at the beep telling me the time and date of your call, and your phone number, I'll be glad to call you back. Don't forget, wait for the beep. And have a grand slam day."

Yogi didn't know what to do. While the message was playing he was looking at Joe V standing out there in right field. He did the obvious thing. He left a message: "This is Yogi Berra. It's a little after nine o'clock and I'm in the dugout at Yankee Stadium. Give me a call when you get this message." Then he left the number.

Because Yogi is in the first-base coaching box while we're at bat, he didn't get a chance to ask Verola about that message. But two innings later Yogi's dugout phone rang. "Hey, Yog," Joe V said, "this is Joe V. You know, in right field. I just got your message. What's up?"

"Hey Joe, how you doing?" Yogi said. "Thanks for calling back. I was just calling to tell you to move in a few steps."

"Oh, sure," Joe told him, "I'll be glad to." And then he did. "Listen, thanks for thinking of me. I'll speak to you later."

I don't think Yogi ever realized that Joe was just impersonating an answering machine. After the game he went over to Joe V's locker and started examining the cellular glove. Reggie happened to walk by and asked Yogi what he was doing. "Oh, nothing," Yogi said in kind of a perplexed voice. "I'm just looking to see if there's an answering finger in this glove."

Sometimes I think the fine art of the practical joke is being lost as baseball becomes more of a business. When I was playing you really couldn't trust anybody, and I'm sorry baseball isn't like that today. In those days the majority of practical jokes involved snakes and hotfoots. People were always buying rubber snakes and putting them in somebody's carry bag or uniform or glove. Once when the Yankees were out in Anaheim I bought a rubber iguana at Disneyland and put it out by second base. When Sandy Alomar saw it he refused to go out and play his position. Moe Drabowsky wasn't satisfied with rubber snakes—he used live snakes. Once he buttoned a small garter snake in the back pocket of Luis Aparicio's uniform pants. As Drabowsky describes it, Aparicio was half dressed when he discovered the snake. "And that was the first time I ever actually saw a man run out of his pants. I knew Luis was quick. I just never knew he was that quick." A few years ago Drabowsky even brought a snake to a dinner honoring the old Orioles. He was sitting on a dais, a few seats away from Brooks Robinson, when Brooks asked him to pass the breadbasket. Drabowsky quietly slipped his three-foot king snake under the napkin covering the breadbasket, and passed it to Brooks. "It was quite a sight," Moe remembers. "That's when we found out that Brooks still moved pretty good for an old ballplayer."

Drabowsky was one of the legendary practical jokers in baseball history. He was the kind of man who would sneak into an opponent's hotel room and put sneezing powder in the air-conditioning system, or call the hotel operator pretending to be a player on another team and tell her, "I have to get up every two hours during the night to take some medicine. Please call me every two hours, and do it even if I try to tell you to stop."

Personally I was a cake and mask man. I had a good collection of horror masks. Once, I remember, when the Yankees were in California we stayed at the Charterhouse Hotel, and in order to get into the hotel you had to walk up a little ramp. There were bushes next to ramp, and sometimes, late at night, I'd put on my werewolf mask and hide in the bushes. And wait. When one of my teammates walked past, sometimes escorting a young lady, I'd leap out of the bushes screaming as loudly as I could. I guess I ruined a few nights that way.

John Lowenstein did much better than that. One night when he was with Texas, the team checked into a hotel and Jim Bach went down the hall to get some ice. "Bones" made the mistake of leaving his door open, so Lowenstein snuck in, climbed onto the closet shelf, and waited. "Bones" came back, got into bed, read for a while, maybe watched a little TV, and finally turned out the lights and went to sleep. After a few minutes he heard some hangers clinking softly in the closet. Then, silence. A few minutes later, the hangers clinked again. Then, again, silence. Finally, when the hangers started clinking again, he couldn't take it anymore. He got out of bed, turned on the light, and opened the closet door—and Lowenstein screamed and came flying out of the closet at him!

Of course, Lowenstein probably wouldn't have done that if he had known that Bach was an epileptic. That's what made the whole thing dangerous. "Bones" had actually had his first seizure while he was playing golf. They rushed him off the course and he was fine. Afterwards, though, he was talking to his partners and he asked them how they did. "We don't know," one of them said, "you bit the scoring pencil in half."

In those days we were always doing something for laughs. Sometimes, before a game, we'd stand in the outfield throwing balls at players who weren't paying attention, and after the games we'd have rough hockey games in the clubhouse. Now, as an executive, I can understand how silly we were, risking our careers just to have fun.

We did all kinds of things to rookies. I remember when the Yankees brought up a kid pitcher named Dave Pagan. Before a game one day, we told him that there was a big dinner at the Stadium Club and he had to speak at it. So, dressed in his uniform, including his spikes, he went upstairs to the Stadium Club, which was filled with people enjoying their dinner. Pagan went over to the podium and started making a little speech telling everybody how happy he was to be with the Yankees. The maitre'd kicked him out of the place.

Then we would teach every rookie the Lift. That was an elaborate routine which ended up with the rookie lying on the ground with his privates covered with red-hot balm. Of course, we were always very nice about it. We'd always hand him a bottle of rubbing alcohol and tell him to use it to get the balm off.

They don't do anything like that today. Today everything is so professional. When Saxy told this kid that we just brought up, Bruce McDonald, that he had to go upstairs and speak at the Stadium Club dinner, McDonald told him, "That sounds like fun, but I can't make any personal appearances until my agent has made all the arrangements." And nobody is crazy enough to try the Lift on him. He's easily one of the strongest players in our system. He told Winfield that he was on a special "non-vegetarian diet." That means he's not allowed to eat anything green, only red meats. It's the same diet used by the Russian Olympic weightlifting team. He's also an expert in El-Haiku, the oriental art of elbow fighting. He did a little demonstration in the frustration room. The key to successful El-Haiku, he explained, is keeping your elbow jabs short and maintaining the proper angle. "When your arm is bent at exactly 135° your elbow is the strongest point in your entire body. But angle is everything; even a few degrees less will cost you power in direct relationship to thrust and distance."

We've certainly come a long way since the days of sending rookies out to search for the keys to the batter's box.

The other thing that happened today was that we finally got an official ruling from the commissioner's office on Tommy John's arm. Commissioner Vincent took the White Sox protest very seriously, and acknowledged that in the future baseball is going to have to deal with the existence of technologically improved players. According to the decision, the Baseball Rules Committee is going to set up a series of guidelines that can be applied to any TIP. Anything that allows a player to artificially improve his natural abilities will be prohibited.

In his three-page decision Commissioner Vincent explained that it is currently impossible to predict what forms these technological and medical advances will take, but that by examining statistics and anecdotal evidence assembled over the last decade, a Scale of Human Capabilities will be created. This scale will be used as a basic form of measurement, and will include: how far a player with major-league ability can throw a ball and hit a ball, how fast a player can run, and how fast a pitcher can throw. Any player exceeding the top ranges of that scale by more than 5 percent will be subject to medical examination, and if that examination should detect any form of technological or medical enhancement, the player will be considered to be a TIP and banned from the major leagues. "Otherwise," the statement read, "all existing records that have been achieved by normal human skills will be shattered." The Scale of Human Capabilities will be periodically updated to reflect normal improvements in human performance.

Additionally, an independent testing laboratory will be established at the site of the National Baseball Hall of Fame and Museum in Cooperstown, New York, to test any mechanical devices to be inserted in players. These devices will be tested for stress, force, pressure, tension, compression, resiliency, and any other factors that might potentially enhance their performance. Any device that is proven to improve performance beyond the predictable range on the Scale of Human Compatibilities will be banned.

Commissioner Vincent also grandfathered Tommy John's arm, meaning that these regulations do not apply to him, and that he'll be permitted to play major-league baseball "so long as his abilities enable him to." Besides, TJ's fastball, which has been clocked at a high of 96 mph, is well within the acceptable range.

I guess the really surprising thing is that TJ was terribly upset by the ruling, even threatening to challenge it in court. I found out later that if the ruling had been more positive, Tommy was going to act as spokesperson for General Electric in a series of TV commercials based on the theme "When better players are made, General Electric will make them." With this ruling, though, those commercials will never be filmed. After Tommy read the full text of the commissioner's decision he started storming angrily around the clubhouse, which is really out of character for him. Supposedly he told "Plug" Reich that he really wanted to go into the frustration room and punch a few bags, but he was afraid of stretching the tension out of his springs.

JUNE 30 ★

Old-Timers' Day at Yankee Stadium is always one of the highlights of the baseball season, and today was no exception. I don't think The Boss has ever received full credit for his contribution to the success of this day. Thanks primarily to him, the Yankees have the largest number of old-timers in baseball. The fact is that because of George Steinbrenner, there are more ex-Yankees than there are former members of any other team, which gives us many more people to choose from.

The theme of the game this year was "Yankees of Yesterday vs. Yankee Broadcasters." Actually, we stretched the truth a little. It wasn't so much the stars of yesterday. It was really the last couple of years. In addition to inviting back all-time Yankee favorites like Mickey Mantle, Joe DiMaggio, Yogi, Whitey Ford, Catfish Hunter, Mel Stottlemyre, and Moose Skowron, we had recent Yankee favorites such as Ron Guidry, John Candelaria, Rich Dotson, Charlie Hudson, Jamie Quirk, Mike Pagliarulo, Wayne Tolleson, Tom Brookens, Steve Shields, Tim Stoddard, Dale Mohorcic, Bob Brower, Steve Balboni, Gary Ward, Steve Kiefer, and Ken Phelps. I sat around with them in the clubhouse before the game listening to them swapping lies about the good old days. I'll tell you something, most of these guys looked great. They were still in good shape and looked like they could go out there right now and play in an official major-league game. Except Balboni, of course.

The Yankee Broadcasters team included Reggie, Bobby Murcer, Phil Rizzuto, Gene Michael, Mickey Rivers, Tony Kubek, Dooley Womack, and Jim Kaat. Piniella, Chicken, Yogi, Catfish, and I played with the broadcasters and we won the three-inning game when Scooter laid down a perfect sacrifice bunt, 10–9. I pitched an inning and couldn't get my slider to break at all, so I gave up six runs, all earned. Under different circumstances, I think they might have taken me out, but it was my ball and my ballpark. The Stadium was completely sold out, and I think the fans all had a good time watching the old-timers stumble around the field. The most surprising thing to me was how good Catfish looked during his ⅓-inning stint on the mound. His pitches had good velocity, and his control was excellent. As I watched him throw I turned to Chicken and said, "You know, if . . ."

"Don't even think about it," Chicken warned.

In the real game that followed the present-day Yankees beat the Indians, 10–9. I think, finally, our hitting slump is over, and a lot of the credit for that has to go to Duke Schneider. Almost everybody is using her charts now, and in the seven games we've hit .293 and scored 47 runs. I think the other players began taking Duke's charts seriously when Winfield started using them and got hot.

The difference between a good hitter and a great hitter is the difference between Winfield and Mattingly. Winfield has holes in his swing. If you pitch to his weakness you can get him out—but if you make a mistake he can hit a ball a long way. When Mattingly is swinging well he has no weaknesses, so pitchers try to make him swing at a bad pitch, or walk him, or change speeds to try to keep him off balance, or pray. The other players know they're not going to be able to hit like Mattingly, so they really weren't convinced that Duke's charts were responsible for him breaking out of his annual early-season slump. But when Winfield picked up the charts and started hitting, they got very interested. Everybody could see a big difference in the way Winfield approached each at bat. Dave is a notorious free-swinger, but as soon as he started using the charts he became much more selective. "Those charts force you to think about what you want to do when you go up there," he explained to Kelly and Suarez. "They provide you with a plan. Soon as I realized how accurate they were, I began trying to work the count in my favor, trying to force the pitcher to throw me that pitch of maximum opportunity. You guys should try it."

Even Lou has grudgingly accepted Duke's contribution, although I'm pretty sure he still doesn't like it. He hasn't said a word to me in a week about keeping her away from the players, and she's been spending a lot of time in the clubhouse before the game. Nettles told me that Lou doesn't believe the charts are really responsible for the way we've been hitting, that their only real benefit is that they force batters to concentrate more when they're at bat, making them more selective.

I know that the rest of the league is beginning to get curious about Duke's charts too. I've gotten several calls from front-office people telling me there's a rumor going around that the Yankees have discovered a new system that might revolutionize the game. "Believe me, it's nothing," I told Dodger general manager Myles Horn. "Our new traveling secretary, you know, that pretty girl, Duke Schneider, she's been fooling around with a computer. She's just made up some charts, some predictions; that's all it is."

He laughed. "Now, you wouldn't be trying to put one past me, would you? I want you to know you're talking to a man who saw *Damn Yankees* three times. 'member?" He started singing, "Whatever Lola wants, Lola gets, da da dum. So I don't have to worry none, right? You didn't make a deal with the Devil?"

"Not unless he's willing to offer pitching," I said, and Myles laughed again. He hung up whistling a few ominous bars from "Lola."

Pitching, pitching, pitching. No matter what we do, we just can't seem to get our pitching rotation settled. We scored 47 runs in seven games but only won four of them. If we don't do something to improve our pitching soon, this season is going to get away from us. As it is, we're stuck 9½ games behind the Fred McGriff–led Blue Jays. We just can't seem to climb more than a game or two above .500. Tommy John and Tommy McKeever are the only two starters we can depend on to keep us close, and Tums has pitched well in his two appearances as "Mr. Cool." Everybody else has been inconsistent. In fact, after watching our pitching staff I think I've finally figured out where the expression "hit or miss" comes from—our pitchers either get hit or miss the strike zone.

Bill Lee has tried everything he can think of to straighten out the staff: He's had them running, not running, running backward and walking; he's given them new mantras and had them chanting individually and as a group; he's switched vitamin doses; he's had them throwing a football and a basketball before the game; and he's worked with them in the exercise room, the bullpen, the video room, the mood room, and the dining room. He's worked with them to improve their control, increase their arm speed, and smooth out their deliveries; he's had them experimenting with different grips and emphasized the importance of changing speeds. He's even tried to teach them how to throw the slider. "I'll tell you something, Sparky," he said the other night after we'd gotten blown out by the O's, "I'm running out of ideas. I just can't figure it out. In the bullpen this is a pretty good pitching staff; the problem is that the umpires are making them pitch in the game. It just seems like every time they make a bad pitch, somebody hits it into the upper deck."

"So I guess we can say the exorcism didn't work, huh?"

He tried to smile. "You know, that's a strange thing. Ever since we did that, Tsumi claims he hasn't been able to read minds. He said that instead of seeing thoughts, all he gets are test patterns." He shrugged. "Least, I think that's what he said. It was either that or that he wanted to take a submarine sandwich to the Great Lakes."

We put most of the team on waivers yesterday. It really doesn't mean anything, and every team does it almost every year. It's just a way of finding out which players other teams are interested in. If any team shows a real interest in a player, we'll withdraw the waivers and try to make a deal for pitching. So far, though, the only players anybody has shown an interest in are pitchers. I've also spent so much time on the telephone that my ear now has the pattern of those little dots on the receiver pressed into it. I found out that just about every general manager in baseball was feeling very well. I also found out that they are willing to help us out by taking a couple of our top minor-league prospects in exchange for pitchers with earned run averages only slightly lower than the national debt. Jim Freydberg in Kansas City actually tried to convince me that the only reason he was willing to trade Robin Ullman was because Ullman had grown up in Los Angeles and was allergic to the fresh air in the Midwest. "The doctor says he has a carbon monoxide deficiency," Freydberg told me, "which makes him very weak. That's why he usually gets hit hard after facing a few batters. So he'd do much better pitching for a team in the Northeast or Southern California."

Seattle even offered us Gaylord Perry. I pointed out to their assistant GM, Doc Curtis, that Perry's been retired for eight or nine years. "Sure he has," Curtis said. "That means his arm must be in great shape."

The local papers are criticizing me practically every day for not being able to get some pitching, but I'm running out of places to look. I've searched the big leagues, the minor leagues, the Mexican leagues, I even looked under "Pitching" in the yellow pages, between Pipe Cleaning Articles and Pizza Equipment Suppliers. The yellow pages doesn't have any pitching either. Maybe the only thing left is advertising in the *Sunday Times* employment section. Can you imagine, under "Pitcher: MLT desperate for RH or LH starter or reliever. Some professional experience desirable but not mandatory. Must have good control, live fastball, and ability to learn a slider. Salary negotiable. Contact Box 20 wins."

It's days like this that make me wonder if Herbie Abramowitz has had his fill of cavities.

JULY 7 ★

A very excited President George Bush called the clubhouse two days ago to tell Tommy McKeever that he's officially decided that McKeever's perfect game is probably almost definitely one of the greatest games he's ever seen pitched. Of course, he also added that that decision is still subject to the latest opinion polls.

McKeever sold his one autograph on the Home Shopping Network last night. Donald Trump bought it for $36,750. A very happy Trump told viewers that he was going to have McKeever sign a photograph of Trump standing in front of Trump Towers with the words, "From one 'Mr. Perfect' to another." Then Trump said he was going to have a limited edition of the autographed picture printed and give them to customers of the Trump Shuttle.

Amazingly, just when we thought our pitching problems couldn't get worse, we had to put Hanko Tsumi on the disabled list with what has been diagnosed as very bad karma. Hanko says he just hasn't felt right since Lee had the bullpen exorcised, and he thinks that might have upset the delicate balance between his yin and yang. His yin is all out of whack, and he can barely find his yang. Nettles said that that just goes to prove that "Yinning isn't everything." Obviously, bad karma can be a very serious problem if it spreads, so we're just hoping he didn't infect the whole team. As a precaution, Dr. Nelson is going to give everybody a vaccination shot.

In order to make room for Tsumi on the DL, we had to move Eric Plunk to the 60-day DL retroactive to spring training, Clay Parker to the 30-day list, and Geren to the 21-day DL. To replace Tsumi we recalled Ash DeLorenzo from Columbus. DeLorenzo's one of the "crown jewels" of our farm system. He had a great season with our Double-A Albany team last year, going 11–1 with a 1.12 ERA and 96 strikeouts in 110 innings. We really wanted him to get a full season of Triple-A experience, but the scouts are raving about his poise and maturity and tell me has all the tools necessary to win in the big leagues right now. And sometimes you just have to force-feed these kids. At Columbus he was 5–1 with a 2.98 ERA and 53 strikeouts and only 3 walks in 53 innings. We're going to be very careful with him, the one thing we don't want to do is destroy his confidence. But the consensus of our people is that he can give us some quality innings coming out of the bullpen without any risk to his future.

Keith Reich was also injured. When he found out we'd put him on waivers his feelings were badly bruised. He just assumed we were preparing to give him his unconditional release, and got so depressed he broke out in hives. I mean, major-league hives, big red spots all over his body. He looked like the world's largest connect-the-dots puzzle. "Plug" had already prepared his resumé and was getting set to start sending it out. Like just about every major leaguer who isn't a big enough star to get a broadcasting contract when he's released or retires, he's very nervous about his future after baseball. I can't blame him. One of the real problems almost every major-league player eventually faces is that, outside pro baseball, an expertise in playing third base is not a marketable skill. Being able to field a bunt barehanded and throw underhanded to first base doesn't have wide application in other fields. What's a potential employer going to say: "Oh, you can field bunts barehanded? Well, then sit right here behind this desk and work this computer"? Or maybe: "You know how to knock down line drives with your chest? That's great, we've got a real shortage of people with your experience, so we'd like you to become a staff physician"?

I explained to "Plug" that we'd put the entire roster on waivers as a formality, and that we had no intention of releasing him. But he's still pretty shaken up about it. The problem is that he's so worried about his future that he isn't doing the job for us. When that happens players often find out that tomorrow can get here today.

The Yankees Advisory Committee had its monthly meeting a few days ago and they actually came up with a couple of good ideas. For example, Joe Maresca suggested that we print a diagram of the ballpark on every ticket so fans would be able to find their seats. "And that way we wouldn't have to pay extortion to those ushers for leading us to the seats we've already paid for, and then dusting off the clean seat with a dirty rag."

Lou DiGiamo wants us to hang pictures over each refreshment stand showing what foods are available at that particular stand. That way people could decide what they want before they reach the counter, and not have to hold up the whole line while making their decision. "And another good thing," he pointed out, "when a stand runs out of an item, all they have to do is take down the picture, and nobody will waste twenty minutes standing in line like I did the other night, just to find out that the stand is out of ice cream."

Before Geri Simon left for her appointment at the manicurist, she reported that the people in the low-cholesterol section were very upset because the people in the low-sodium section had much better seats, and high cholesterol is potentially much more damaging than high sodium. I promised to look into that for her. Then she suggested that we run a tram, like the ones used at Disneyland and other theme parks, up and down the long ramps before and after the games to help handicapped or older people reach their seats.

Twelve-year-old Alex Langsam told me that he and his friends had decided that we should trade utility infielder Raoul Rojas and either Kenny Davis, Mad Man Madden, or Rosey Rogers to the Houston Astros for veteran pitcher Mike Sanderson. He said that all his friends thought this was a deal that would help both clubs without costing more than they could afford to give up. He's a cute kid, and as I started to explain to him that every club runs an expensive scouting network that rates players in both leagues, and that making a trade requires very complicated negotiations and involves balancing needs and surpluses and salaries and contractual commitments, I realized his suggestion made a great deal of sense. I made a note to have Chicken contact the Astros and discuss it with them.

Joanie Silver suggested we create a special "Singles Section," so that unattached fans could come to the game by themselves and maybe meet somebody. "See, what you could do," she explained, "is sell the odd-numbered seats in this section to men and even-numbered seats to girls, and that would guarantee that everybody will be sitting next to a person of a different sex that they don't know. See?"

There was a motion to serve corned beef at the next meeting, but it was voted down in favor of turkey. Then we adjourned.

Finally, last Saturday night we introduced our new mascot, "The Boss," to the fans. This is quite a costume. He looks like Humpty-Dumpty with a head, wearing a Yankee uniform. He's got a big mustache, which twirls around, ears that wiggle, and a Yankee cap that goes up and down. When it goes up, steam escapes from the top of his head. We've hired a phys ed major from St. John's University in Queens to be "The Boss" at all home games. Besides performing on the field before the game, he's going to walk through the stands during games handing out schedules. We're also going to give him a few dozen tickets for future home games to give away to kids and their parents. It'll cost us a couple hundred dollars, but the truth is that we're giving out tickets to our least desirable games. What we gain in public relations and what these fans'll spend on concessions while they're at these games makes it a great deal for us.

I actually wanted flames to come out of "The Boss's" mouth when he opened it—because nobody fired more people than The Boss. But the fire commissioner wouldn't allow it.

JULY 12 ★

One of the funniest scenes that ever took place on a baseball field happened in Minnesota's Homerdome the other night, and they've been showing tapes of it on the news for two straight days. Baseball teams tailor their ballparks for the type of players they have. If a team has no speed, for example, the groundskeeper will let the grass grow very long to slow down balls hit by the other team. The problem for teams playing on artificial surfaces is that no matter how much they water their plastic, it isn't going to grow. So the 3M Company, which pioneered the development of artificial surfaces for indoor stadiums, created a product called "Slow-Go." Slow-Go was originally intended to be a high-gloss wax that would restore a plastic surface to its original imitation grass-green color. In order to make the wax adhere to the plastic, 3M scientists used a small amount of the same glue used on the back of Post-it's, those little yellow notepads that stick to walls. But during testing they discovered that even small amounts of that glue substantially increased friction, causing objects moving on the plastic surface to slow down considerably. Naturally, larger amounts of the glue produced greater friction, slowing down objects even more. So they produced Slow-Go, a spray that does for artificial surfaces what sun and water do for real grass—it slows down baseballs bouncing on it.

Everybody in the game knows that the Twins have absolutely no team speed this year. You know, they time their runners to first base with a calendar. They couldn't outrun a glacier—downhill. Etc. So in order to gain an advantage in the Homerdome, they started spraying the field with Slow-Go. It's perfectly legal. But apparently a member of the grounds crew got a little overzealous. The Oakland A's were coming in for a big three-game series, and he decided that he was going to make sure Rickey Henderson didn't do any bunting or running. So he soaked the infield with that stuff.

There was one thing 3M's scientists hadn't considered. Because the dome was empty the air-conditioning system was off. The heat wave that has baked the Midwest for the past two weeks raised the temperature inside the dome to almost 100°, and that intense heat turned Slow-Go into No-Go, a kind of gooey superglue. Umpire Joe Brinkman's crew decided the field was playable, but the surface slowed everything down. I watched the game on ESPN and, believe me, it looked like it was being played in slow motion. The players moved like flies walking on flypaper. In the sixth inning Mark McGwire slammed a Dave West sinker onto the ground. It took one bounce and . . . and nothing. It hit the turf and stuck there. Solid. Nobody could pick it up. The tape of Kent Hrbek trying desperately to pull it off the ground while McGwire is sneaking cautiously from base to base is one of the funniest things I've ever seen. It took McGwire maybe four minutes to circle the bases for his inside-the-park home run. Inside-the-park? That was the first stuck-to-the-infield home run.

The ball must have hit a particularly gooey area, because Hrbek's spikes also got glued to the surface. He looked like he was nailed down. Finally he had to step out of his shoes, leaving them there. The

TV camera just focused on these empty shoes sitting near the pitcher's mound. Members of the grounds crew had to use shovels to get the ball and spikes loose. And when Brinkman decided to send McGwire back to second base, on G.P., both teams protested the game. Afterwards Brinkman told reporters, "It was a sticky situation, and I made what I thought was the correct ruling. There's no ground rule covering this kind of ground."

Naturally we had our own unusual event of the week in New York. What would life be like for the Yankees if we didn't? Just when I thought Bill Lee had run out of bright ideas for improving the pitching staff, he came up with the wildest one yet. Last Monday night, an off night, he invited the entire pitching staff and the catchers to a brownstone on West 44th Street between 9th and 10th Avenues. They went into a large studio apartment and took seats around a big wooden table. Several candles were lit, and the host, described by Chuck Cary as "either an old hippie or a young gypsy," told everybody to join hands and not let go. "Then she started chanting some mumbo-jumbo stuff."

"At first I couldn't figure out what was going on," Big John Nicholson told me. "And then . . . and then I heard her saying something about some spirit showing up. I thought maybe this was a pep rally. But then . . . then . . ." He shook his head in disbelief. "And then . . . I don't know how to describe it, but it was one of the most amazing things I've ever seen. This white mist drifted into the room, like a fog rolling in, then it started condensing, like in the movies when a genie goes back into the bottle, you know? Only this time it took the shape of a person, a man, and he was wearing a very old Red Sox uniform. I mean, a really old one, the kind that had the hats with the different-color brim? And he just sort of floated there for a while, and then finally he started talking.

"At first his voice was garbled and we couldn't understand anything he was saying, but then the gypsy woman told him he was talking to the wrong channel, and he made some adjustments and we could hear him clearly."

"Sparky," he said seriously, looking me right in the eye, "this guy was Cy Young."

All right, I admit it, I was a little dubious. Cy Young? The greatest pitcher in baseball history? Cy Young, who died in the 1950s? "What'd he look like?" I asked.

"He was much shorter than I thought he'd be," Nicholson said. Then, he continued, Young apologized for making them wait. "He said he'd been at a banquet with Ty Cobb and Cobb was making a speech and he wouldn't stop talking, so he just lost track of time. I have to tell you, I liked the guy. He was very friendly and he started by telling us a good joke. Somebody, I think it was Kline, asked him if there was any baseball where he was. 'Oh, sure,' he said. 'Every weekend the Devil comes up with his team and we play. We never beat them though, because the Devil's got all the umpires.'

"He asked if anybody had any questions. Biondo, I think, said, 'I got a question. How come I'm getting such bad mileage on my new 'Vette?' But before he could answer, Lee interrupted and told us that Cy Young was there to talk about pitching. So he did. He told us that the battle between the pitcher and the batter was like the battle between good and evil, God and the Devil, and it was everybody's duty to do everything possible to defeat the Devil/batter. 'He'll resort to tricks, he'll do anything to beat you, and if he does, he'll watch you starve without offering you a morsel.' Then he went on to talk about thinking on the mound, and not trying to strike out every batter. 'Like Walt Johnson did. Walter always thought he had to strike everybody out. I told him that wasn't necessary, I told him to use his fielders, but Walter was a very stubborn man. He had to prove he could strike out every batter. So he struck out a lot of people, but you'll notice that at the end of the season, when they give out the award to the best pitcher, they don't call it the Walter Johnson Award. Use your fielders; that's what they're getting paid all that money for.'

"He spoke for fifteen minutes; who knows, maybe it was an hour, it just went so fast. He talked about staying in condition, warming up properly in the bullpen, turning the batter's own strengths against him, gripping a curveball, never taking the upper bunk on sleepers. McDonald asked him how he gripped his curveball, and he snapped his fingers and a baseball appeared. He floated over the table to Bruce and showed him how to grip it, but when he handed the ball to Bruce it turned out to feel like a warm snowball. It just turned to water in Bruce's hand. Lee asked a lot of questions, everybody else asked a few, and Cy answered every one of them. Suddenly he asked what time it was, and when somebody told him it was almost midnight, he explained he had to get back to the cloud before curfew or Connie Mack was going to be furious. He told TJ it had been nice seeing him again, then he told McKeever that he had seen his perfect game. As he was starting to fade, Parker yelled out, asking him if he had any last words of advice.

" 'Oh, sure,' he said. 'Never hang a curve to Babe Ruth.' Then he was gone. Gone. The most amazing thing I've ever seen."

I asked Nicholson if he really believed what he had seen.

"Listen," he told me, "the day before yesterday I saw a baseball sticking to plastic while a guy circled the bases. Yesterday some cable station in California paid the Dodgers $575 million for the broadcast rights to their games for the next ten years. Compared to that, what's so strange about seeing a ghost?"

JULY 16 ★

Whatever advice Cy gave the pitching staff, it hasn't seemed to help very much. In our three-game series with Toronto at the Stadium we gave up 20 runs, including 6 home runs. We were really fortunate to win one of those games, so we only lost a single game in the standings. Ten and a half back, 81 to play. We are in trouble.

DeLorenzo made his major-league debut in the second game. Lou brought him in with two out in the fifth inning with runners on first and third and three runs already in. He walked George Bell. McGriff knocked in two runs with a single. Alvarez walked. Gruber knocked in two more runs with a base hit, and, finally, Roberto Kelly ran down Tony Fernandez's long fly ball in right center. Not exactly a great start. But the kid was obviously nervous out there. I'm sure he'll do much better his next time out.

One thing I'll say in defense of this team, they're not quitting. They've got some fight left. After Mattingly took Jimmy Key deep in the third game, Key came inside to Winfield. Knocked him on his tush. Dave got up, glared out at Key, then stepped back into the batter's box. Key dumped him again. That was enough. Winfield took off after Key. Home plate umpire Kenny Kaiser somehow managed to get in front of Winfield—Kaiser is a former professional wrestler and a very strong man—but Dave just brushed him out of the way, sort of like an agent brushing away a one-year deal with no guarantees. Key dropped his glove and waited on the top of the mound. I have to admire his courage. Both benches emptied. The bullpen gate opened, and Taft came riding out on his Harley, with McDonald on the back waving his cap like a rodeo rider.

Taft headed straight for the pitcher's mound. McDonald hopped off and dove into the mob, assuming the classic El-Haiku fighting position: both hands clenched into fists, knuckles intertwined in front of his chest, elbows raised just slightly, glistening in the afternoon sunshine. Nobody wanted any part of him—particularly those elbows.

It was a classic baseball brawl. A lot of people grabbing each other and holding on. There was a lot of very serious milling. Occasionally a hat would get thrown up in the air, and the crowd would react. When peace broke out Kaiser threw Key, Winfield, Taft, McDonald, and Tom Henke out of the game. When Blue Jay manager Cito Gaston asked him why he'd thrown out Henke, he said, "I figured one Henke is worth a Taft and a McDonald."

Meanwhile, while everybody was watching the fight, our mascot was mugged. He was walking along the ramp in the middle loge section when three guys jumped him and knocked him down, then stole all the tickets he was carrying. When the security people got to the mascot to help him, they took off his head to see if he was okay, and he immediately covered his face with his hands—as if he were a vampire afraid of the sun—and waddled off for the exit. He stopped just long enough to slip out of the costume; then he was gone. The thing is, that wasn't the real mugging.

About forty minutes later the kid from St. John's who was supposed to have been inside the costume staggered into my office. He told me in a shaky voice that when he'd arrived at his dressing closet before the game he'd found a box of chocolates, sent "by an admirer." After eating several pieces he got very drowsy. The next thing he remembers is waking up on the cold cement floor of the closet and realizing that the costume had been stolen.

Somebody had been masquerading as "The Boss"! I couldn't understand it. I asked him, "Did you see any suspicious-looking people on the subway or on the streets outside the Stadium?"

He nodded, "Several hundred. But nobody in particular."

I interviewed the security people who had helped the mascot when he was knocked down. One of them had gotten a good look at his face. "I'll tell you the truth," he said. "To me, he looked just like Richard Nixon."

Richard Nixon had mugged our mascot? Things were really getting confusing.

"Nah, nah," the guard continued. "I mean, like, he was wearing one of those Nixon Halloween masks."

Something was wrong, very wrong. Nothing made sense. Why would somebody mug a mascot for his outfit? Who would be wearing a Nixon mask under a costume? Why would somebody need to be incognito in Yankee Stadium? What was that person doing on the middle loge level—where our executive offices are located? And where could we get more pitching? I was absolutely stumped.

And then I felt that strange chill running down my spine. I took two aspirin, but it still didn't go away. Something was rotten in the Bronx.

JULY 18 ★

I arrived at my first All-Star Game as owner of the New York Yankees yesterday morning. All the other owners seemed very glad to see me. I noticed that the further an owner's team was out of first place, the happier the other owners were to see him. Or her. Atlanta's Ted Turner was the most popular person there, by 3½ games.

We had an owners' conference in the afternoon at which several pieces of business were discussed. Probably the most important report came from the Expansion Committee, which announced they had finally reached a decision to expand. They were going to add two new members to the Expansion Committee.

At the big dinner last night the thing most people wanted to talk to me and Chicken about was our "Fire Sale." In baseball, I found out, a "Fire Sale" is what people call those late-season deals between pennant contenders and teams out of the race, in which the contending teams get an established player who might help them win the pennant, in exchange for several young prospects. Apparently they're called "Fire Sales" because, by showing the public that they are already rebuilding for next year, a lot of executives don't get fired.

There's a lot of interest in all three of our power-hitting left-handed

DH/first basemen. But I told everybody that I didn't think we were out of the pennant race and had no intention of dealing anybody until we were mathematically eliminated. "Don't wait too long," Chris Carrier of the Cubs warned me. "Remember that he who trades last, gets least."

A lot of people reminded me of the baseball lore that says that the teams leading their divisions at the All-Star break will win the pennant. Just before I left my office for the airport, Duke handed me a readout proving that that was true only 34.8 percent of the time, which did not include the strike-shortened 1981 season. Of course, the only people who really believe that old lore are the people whose teams are in first place at the All-Star break.

The game itself was really enjoyable. Mattingly was the only Yankee voted to the starting team, but Sax and Espinoza were selected as reserves, and Frank Robinson picked Tommy McKeever for his pitching staff. The American League won the game, 6–3, Dennis Eckersley got the win by throwing two shutout innings, but the real highlight of the game came in the second inning, when Bo Jackson came up to bat against Dwight Gooden. Sometimes, during the season, when the team is losing, the writers are criticizing, the phones are ringing, the agents are demanding renegotiation, the Players Association is threatening a strike, and the plumbing system in the ballpark is stopped up and every rest room is overflowing—at those moments I sometimes forget how beautiful the game of baseball can be.

I think one of the reasons I loved it so much while I was playing it, and still do today, is that it's a pretty simple game; no matter how big the ballparks get, no matter how many people are watching the game on televison around the world, it always comes down to the pitcher, the batter, and the baseball. Even when you're on the field, it's not much more complicated than that. So here were two of the best young players in the game facing each other. It was a classic confrontation. Gooden vs. Jackson; the greatest young power pitcher in baseball facing the greatest young slugger in baseball. One on one, mano a mano, baseball style. I think everybody in the ballpark, and probably everybody watching the game on TV, realized what was going on: Gooden was going to try to throw his fastball past Jackson. Jackson was going to try to launch one. If this at bat had taken place during the World Series, Gooden would have used all his pitches; he'd mix in a few hooks, he'd change speeds, and Jackson would be selective, and look for a good pitch to hit. But this was the All-Star Game, an exhibition game. Gooden wasn't going to throw any curveballs; Jackson wasn't going to be selective. This was going to be heat, hotter and hottest. Gooden was going to crank it up; Jackson was going to try to crush it. The fastball vs. the home run. Maybe the last time there was such a great confrontation between a fastball pitcher and a slugger was in the 1978 World Series, when Bob Welch faced Reggie Jackson with the ball-game on the line and threw him nothing but fastballs and struck him out.

Gooden went into his windup. His first pitch was away. Ball one.

His second pitch was also outside; Jackson swung right through it. One and one.

Bo stepped out of the batter's box and wiped his hands on his uniform pants. He was just trying to break Gooden's rhythm. Gooden stood behind the rubber, staring at the plate, bent slightly forward at his waist, holding the ball in his glove. Jackson stepped back in. Gooden went into his windup and threw. High heat. High cheese, they call it now. A blur at the letters. Jackson unfolded; his bat whipped across the plate. And he swung through it again. Strike two.

Now it was Gooden's turn to make Jackson wait. He walked behind the mound. He took off his glove and shoved it under his right arm while he rubbed up the baseball. I've stood right there, doing the same thing, and I think what Gooden was really doing was savoring the moment. Finally, he stepped back onto the mound. He looked in at Benny Santiago to get the signal. That was just a formality; he was throwing lightning. He eased into his windup. He kicked his left leg high into the air. Around came his big right arm. He threw.

Jackson shifted all his weight onto his back leg and braced himself. He swung. He extended his arms out over the plate. And he got all of it. I mean, he crushed that baseball. The sound of ash striking baseball was as clear and crisp as the sound of a single bolt of lightning crashing directly overhead. The flight of the ball was majestic; it just disappeared into the night. In left field, Eric Davis just glanced up into the sky as the ball passed over his position. For a second, maybe even less, the whole ballpark was struck absolutely silent. Awestruck. The ball was hit too high and too far for anybody to really believe what they were seeing. Bo stood at home plate, holding onto his bat, watching the flight of the ball. Gooden sort of grimaced.

Calling it a home run would be like calling the Atlantic Ocean a puddle. It would be like calling the Grand Canyon a ditch. Like calling Queen Elizabeth a foreigner. Like calling The Boss shy. It wasn't just a home run, it was THE home run. The Clout, as the newspapers called it this morning, will forever be the tape-measure blast against which all long home runs are measured. It sailed far over the top of the left-field stands. It struck the side of a building, which stopped its flight, but statisticians estimate it would have gone 703 feet.

Jackson dropped the bat and started trotting around the bases. The crowd absolutely shook the ballpark. As Jackson rounded second Gooden looked at him, then took off his cap and wiped his brow. I like to think it was a salute.

In the radio booth, Reggie Jackson, who was doing anecdotal announcing for WABC radio, involuntarily screamed "Yeah!" when Bo hit the ball, then told his listeners, "That's just the way I used to hit them."

I was watching the game from the press box, and I was laughing to myself. I knew exactly what the writers were going to ask Gooden after the game: "Hey, Doc, how'd you hold that one to make it go so far?"

There are some baseball traditions that never change.

JULY 21 ★

I've always believed that the only omens worth believing are good omens. And to me, a good omen is something like being in first place by four games with three games left to play. But if I did believe in omens, I'd think we were in serious trouble.

We opened the second half of the season against the White Sox in Chicago last night. Rick Ricardo hit TJ's first pitch on the ground to third base—right through Reich's legs into left field. Suarez fielded the ball in the corner as Ricardo cruised into second base, and for some reason, Felipe threw behind the runner. As soon as he released the ball, Ricardo took off for third. Sax, at second base, was so surprised when Ricardo went to third that he took his eyes off the throw. It bounced off his glove into short right field and Ricardo scored. One run on no hits, two physical errors, and a mental error. We lost the game 9–2. The second half has begun.

Ash DeLorenzo made his second big-league appearance when Piniella brought him in to pitch the eighth inning. We were down 6–1 and I think Lou just wanted to let the kid throw without any pressure on him. DeLorenzo walked the first two batters he faced on eleven pitches, then grooved an 88-mph fastball to platoon-player/manager

Carlton Fisk, who hit a three-run homer. After the game a very shaken DeLorenzo told reporters, "I'm learning that you can't pitch from behind in the count in the big leagues. These guys can kill you when they know you have to throw a strike."

This is the second straight time the kid did not look good. If he's the crown jewel of our organization, I think we're on the verge of a revolution.

I also had a second meeting with Fred Rappoport from the City yesterday. He told me that Mayor Dinkins and Governor Cuomo had agreed to form a joint city-state bipartisan mediating committee to ensure that the Yankees will be tenants in Yankee Stadium for "the next fifty years."

"What happens after that?" I asked.

"We'll talk about it then."

Rappoport told me that Dinkins and Cuomo had agreed that Yankee Stadium was going to be the anchor of the new Yankee Stadium Complex, which would be the first step in the revitalization of the entire Bronx. The complex will include two office buildings, a residential tower with views into the ballpark from the upper floors, an additional 3,500 indoor parking spaces, a shopping mall with space for forty-two mid-sized stores, and a new subway stop that opens directly into the mall. "The mall'll provide about seven hundred permanent jobs and generate anywhere between eleven and fifteen million dollars in annual tax revenues directly to the city," Rappoport explained. "We'll also provide new lighting for the entire area, access roads on and off the Deegan, and, I know you'll like this, establish a new police miniprecinct in the area to which forty-five officers will be permanently assigned.

"See, Sparky, the way we figure it, the housing stock in the Grand Concourse area is still very good," he continued, "and rents are much lower than anyplace else in the city for a comparable apartment. It's a great place for young people who can't afford the rents in Manhattan. We think the new stores, the lighting, the additional police presence'll attract those people. You know, the urban pioneers. And when they come in, the restaurants and retailers'll follow." He looked at me as if he was waiting for a response. I raised my eyebrows. He obviously assumed that meant I wasn't satisfied. "Oh, and yes, we've discussed your situation with Con Ed and they've agreed to several million dollars in rebates, spread over the life of the contract, of course. Now, as soon as we can finalize this agreement with you to keep the Yankees where they belong, we can get to work on the complex."

It doesn't take much of a businessman to recognize a great situation when he steps in it, and I certainly wasn't much of a businessman. I couldn't believe how much the city was willing to give me for doing exactly what I intended to do anyway. "Uh, Mr. Rappoport," I started.

"Fred; call me Fred."

"Fred. Well, Fred, that's all great. But when you were here last time, there were a few things I sort of forgot to mention. You know, in the excitement of meeting you and everything. But the truth is, if we're going to be able to compete with those new stadiums, we've just got to have some luxury boxes for our corporate clients."

He wrote something down in his notebook.

"And, and you know what else would be great?"

"What?" he asked in a weak voice.

"Close your eyes for a second. Go ahead, do it. Now imagine this: a new upper deck on top of the outfield bleachers so all of those new people in the neighborhood will have a place to sit."

The color drained right out of his face. It was really an amazing thing to see. I hadn't seen anything like that since Chris Chambliss's home run off Mark Littell in the bottom of the ninth inning in the final game of the 1977 playoffs against Kansas City. But he wrote it down. The guy was a pro.

I thought, this is what Christmas is really supposed to be like. "And you know what else, Fred?" I said happily. "I don't know if you've ever thought about it, but honestly, don't you think it would be great if Yankee Stadium had a dome?"

I thought I heard sort of an involuntary groan, but I could have been imagining that.

"And you know what else? This one's important. The plumbing in the ballpark just isn't good enough to support all those rest rooms we're going to need for the people in the luxury boxes and the new upper deck. And let me tell you, it's impossible to get a plumber on Sunday morning a few hours before you're having 53,000 people in."

I know I heard him groan that time. He promised he would discuss my suggestions with the mayor, governor, and members of the new board, and get back to me. We agreed to meet sometime in August. He wasn't out of my office ten seconds when my private phone rang. It was Cliff Campion from the Meadowlands calling. He said one word, then hung up: "Double."

JULY 22 ★

We traded Ash DeLorenzo to the White Sox this afternoon for Rich Dotson. It was a very tough decision to make, but sometimes you just have to hold your nose and jump in the water. I remember, before I owned the Yankees, that I would read about trades that didn't seem to make a lot of sense, and The Boss would explain, "My baseball people were solidly behind this deal." The fact is that I didn't really believe him. I guess I thought that meant that his baseball people who wanted to keep their jobs were solidly behind the deal. Well, now I've learned the truth about that, too.

My baseball people, Chicken, Woodley, Piniella, the scouts who were in town, and the coaches when they were available, have been meeting on a regular basis to evaluate talent in the league and in our system. When I've been available I've sat in on their meetings, although I've rarely said anything. I hired them because they knew how to evaluate talent. I didn't want to impose my will on them.

They met yesterday afternoon specifically to discuss DeLorenzo. He hasn't looked like a major-league pitcher in either of his two appearances. And if he isn't going be able to pitch in the big leagues, the best thing to do is trade him while his value is still high. We gathered in Chicken's office. "You guys have seen him," I said. "Tell me truthfully, what do you think?"

"Same thing you do," Woodley said.

"Yeah, I think Woodley's right about that," Piniella agreed.

"What do you think, Sparky?" Bill Lee asked.

"Remember Dave Pagan?" I asked. "He had great stuff, but every time he was scheduled to start, he'd break out in hives."

"Sure, I remember," Woodley said. "Great story."

"Who could forget?" Chicken asked.

Lee was the only dissenter. "Hey, everybody," he interrupted, "this kid is only twenty-two years old, and he's only thrown two innings. Don't you think it's a little quick to be giving up on him?"

"Gooden was a 20-game winner when he was twenty-two," I reminded Lee.

Woodley nodded firmly. "That says it all, doesn't it."

"And just let me point out," I pointed out, "that if we pitch him again, and he gets hit again, he'll lose even more value."

"That's right," Nettles agreed. "So that means we can't risk pitching him anymore."

"And if we can't risk pitching him anymore," Chicken realized, "then there's really no sense in keeping him."

Piniella summed it up. "If we can't pitch him, and we can't keep him, I guess there's only one thing left."

Woodley actually said it. "I say trade him. Let's do it right now, while he still has some market value left."

And that is exactly how my baseball people made the decision to trade Ash DeLorenzo. Bill Lee was the only person against it. "Why don't we just send him back to the minor leagues, which is where he should have been all season. I told you he wasn't ready."

"Nobody's blaming you, Bill," I interrupted, "but there are some players who just can't pitch in the major leagues. I'm not saying DeLorenzo is one of them; that's up to you people to decide. But sometimes it's better to cut our losses now rather than wasting three or four years trying to find out."

"Just the way I would have said it," Woodley agreed.

"I think I know what Sparky means," Piniella explained. "He means that a headache hurts just as much in the first five minutes as it does in two hours. So you really don't have to keep the headache for two hours to know what it's gonna feel like."

The meeting continued for more than an hour as my baseball people discussed their strategy. They decided that the most intelligent thing to do was make a deal quickly, and settle for the best player we could get, rather than letting everybody in baseball know that DeLorenzo was available. If other teams found out we were trying to get rid of him, when only a few days ago we'd been so high on him, they'd assume we'd learned that there was something wrong with him. His value would diminish even more. So my baseball people decided to pick one team, in another division, a team that was not competitive with us, and try to make a deal with them. We all sat there trying to figure out what team made the best match for us. Suddenly, it came to me. I really don't know from where. "How about the Chicago White Sox?" I said.

Woodley snapped his fingers. "Of course. Why didn't I think of that?"

Everyone more or less agreed. Lee agreed less than everyone else. I think, under the circumstances, Chicken did a great job getting a veteran like Rich Dotson for an unproven kid like DeLorenzo. Dotson won 12 games as a Yankee only a few seasons ago, and I'd always admired his courage. Even when batters were knocking his pitches all over the ballpark, he'd stood on the mound proudly. I figured he was worth the gamble: He'd never really had much of a fastball, so we wouldn't have to worry about him losing it. Not like a lot of younger pitchers. And this move wasn't something that my baseball people did without considering the consequences or seriously discussing it. My baseball people have been in the game a long time, and they knew exactly what they were doing. Believe me, if they had vetoed this deal, we never would have made it.

JULY 25 ★

A preliminary hearing was held in court this morning in the matter of *Wilson v. Davis and the New York Yankees Inc.* Denny Wilson is suing Davis for $3.25 million, and Yankee Corp. for an additional $6.75 million, claiming that's approximately how much money he stands to lose because his injury is considered career-threatening. Ten million dollars for a pitcher who's never won more than 7 games in a full season? That's ridiculous. He's barely worth half that much.

A hearing was held this morning to determine the admissibility of the bat and ball into evidence. Our attorney, Glen Goldstein, told the judge that the bat should be inadmissible because Wilson had no way of proving that Davis even knew the bat was loaded. Wilson's attorney, Elyce Hagouel of Abby, Koorman, introduced photographs of the bat showing Davis's signature on it and his uniform number written on the bottom of the knob in Magic Marker, as well as Davis's baseball card, which pictured him swinging a bat with his signature on it. "It looks like his bat," she explained. "He's using it as his bat. I think it's fair to draw the assumption that it is his bat, over which he exercised dominion and control. I also intend to prove that the owner of a bat, just like the owner of an automobile, is responsible for operating that bat in a safe and prudent manner, and that he is responsible for the care and upkeep of that bat. I submit, Your Honor, that if this bat were a car, and the defendant failed to ensure that it had been properly maintained and was therefore safe to operate, he would remain responsible for the consequences. As Your Honor is aware, the courts have long held that the responsibility lies not with the automobile, but with the owner of the automobile. And in this case, I suggest that it is not the bat which is at fault, but rather the owner of that bat.

"Your Honor, we intend to prove that bats don't hit baseballs, batters do. I believe we've shown that Mr. Davis is the sole owner of that bat, and he is the sole user of that bat, and therefore the bat should be admissible. Thank you."

The judge asked both attorneys to submit briefs on the matter, including whether Wilson's civil rights had been violated, which would make this more properly a matter for the federal courts. He then asked both attorneys to waive their objections to having all pertinent evidence—the bat and the ball—fully examined by a neutral testing laboratory. They did. He gave them one month to submit their briefs, then set a hearing date for September.

Wilson limped out of court, until somebody reminded him that it was his collarbone that had been broken, not his anklebone.

We continued to have problems with injuries today. Hanko Tsumi came into the office and said he'd read in my mind that I wanted to see him. I told him that that wasn't true and I'd never thought it. He frowned, and sighed. "Then I must have read that someplace else," he said, and left.

We were all set to take Eric Plunk off the 60-day disabled list today, and Lou had tentatively penciled him in for a start later this week. But Plunk was so excited about finally coming off the DL that he couldn't sleep. According to Gene Monahan, in fact, he hadn't slept in four days, so as a precautionary matter we're going to move him from the 60-day list to the 10-day list for insomnia, retroactive till tomorrow morning. That means everybody else has to move up a list. Dotson is going to take his place in the rotation.

And finally, Duke came into my office this afternoon struggling under a load of readouts. She barely managed to dump them on my desk. "Here they are," she said.

"Here what are?"

"The answer to our pitching problems." She collapsed onto the couch and said, "I've been working on these six straight nights. I'm exhausted."

I just flicked the edges of the pages, causing a slight breeze. More numbers that meant absolutely nothing to me. "All right, what is it?"

She explained it to me like a teacher explaining basic addition to an elementary-school student. "Don't you remember? A couple of months ago when I gave you the Tigers' Tendency Charts, you told me to try to extend my research into pitching."

I didn't remember that at all. "Of course I remember," I lied.

"Well, I think these might just solve our pitching problems."

I certainly didn't want to discourage her, and, as any Yankee fan could tell you, it couldn't hurt. "Explain it to me."

"See, it's similar in conception to the original charts I did, just a lot more sophisticated. Thanks to ESPN, when I'm alone in my hotel room, I've been able to accumulate data on just about every regular player in the American League. I've established 15 at bats as a minimum, because statistically a batter faces 4.7 pitchers every 15 at bats, which I think provides us with a good sample. If you remember, I've divided the hitting zone into sixteen small areas, but with the larger sample I've been able to figure out the hitter's batting average for each of those zones, and for several different types of pitches within each zone. I've also computed the tendency of the batter to swing when a pitch comes into each of those zones, whether he made contact if he swung, and, on a scale of 1 to 10, how hard he was able to drive the ball.

"Now, here comes the wrinkle. I've also determined the likelihood of a batter swinging at a pitch in a zone following a pitch in each of the other zones. That's very important, because it allows us to establish a pattern. I've seen, for example, that some batters will absolutely never swing at a pitch in the outside zones directly following a pitch in the lower-middle zones.

"Of course, there are some variations based on the count, but with less than two strikes, they're too small to be statistically relevant."

It was all pretty confusing. To me, pitching was just "throw the slider." I flicked the edges of the pages again; that breeze was soothing. "How does all this . . . can you take into account the different pitchers? I mean, even if all this stuff said throw a fastball, I didn't have a fastball."

"I've programmed for that. I just broke pitching down into three broad categories: straight pitches, like a fastball and change-up; breaking pitches—curve, slider, split-fingered; and changing speeds. And then by cross-indexing the batter's statistically weakest zones based on the pitcher's best pitch, we pretty much can predict the highest percentage pitch for a particular individual to throw in any given situation. Of course, none of this guarantees the pitcher'll make a good pitch, but . . ."

"We? Who's we?"

She seemed surprised at the question. "Me and my IBM System 3 6000i with dual drives. Who'd you think I meant?" I shook my head, and she continued. "Look, I know this seems very complicated to you, but it's really just exactly the same kind of information scouts have been compiling forever. It's just that, thanks to ESPN and IBM, I'm able to do as much in a few nights as all the scouts in baseball history have accomplished in their lifetimes." She sighed. "And, honestly, I think we're probably just a little more accurate, too."

I have to admit that I was pretty impressed. If she could only get us to Boston without stopping over in Chicago, I'd probably consider giving her a raise. "You show this stuff to anybody yet?"

"Just a few of the guys. TJ was interested; Bruce McDonald . . ." Suddenly she sat up on the couch, her eyes opened wide, and she asked me, "Did you know that Bruce McDonald can eat baseballs?"

"Excuse me?"

"I said he can eat baseballs. It has something to do with all those martial arts he does. You know how some people show how strong they are by breaking bricks with their heads?"

I have seen that feat done many times, and every time I've seen it done I've wondered, why would somebody *want* to break a brick with their head? "Yeah?"

"Well, he can eat baseballs. He says he can also eat bats, but I've never seen him do that. He puts the baseball in his mouth and kind of jiggles it and then takes a bite out of it. It's not really a big bite, of course, and he doesn't swallow it. Those strings would be bad for you, right?"

"I think so. Sure." The thing that surprised me even more than the fact that McDonald eats baseballs was that Duke was talking about it. This was the first time she'd ever mentioned anything personal about one of the ballplayers. While I was thinking about that, she kept speculating about the digestive problems that could be caused by eating a baseball. Finally, I interrupted her and said, "So you've become friendly with one of the players?"

She blushed. This was the very first time I'd seen her respond in a naturally feminine way. "It was when we were in Chicago, we had dinner a couple of times. . . . He's . . . you know, he's . . . single, it was his first time in Chicago, and I just thought . . ."

"It's okay. It's fine. Only . . . I want you to . . . you should be careful. I've seen what women can do. . . . What I mean to say is, a baseball team . . . I guess what I really want to say is that men . . ."

"You don't want me getting involved with any of the players because it might cause some of the other players to get jealous, and create dissension on the team, right?"

I chuckled nervously. "Boy, those IBMs are even smarter than I thought."

"We're not involved," she told me, stressing the word "involved." "I think we were both a little lonely, that's all." Then she got defensive. "And just how long do you think a normal girl can sit in her hotel room watching ESPN with her computer?"

Obviously, I couldn't answer that question. Besides, it's sort of unfair for a person who used to spend his nights on the road hiding in bushes wearing a werewolf mask to complain about what other people do. But I thought I'd better exercise a little authority. Authority, it had taken me a long time to learn, is like a muscle—if you don't exercise it, it gets flabby. And I didn't want my authority getting flabby. "Just be careful," I told her, "you know what can happen." Then I changed tone. I pointed to the charts and asked, "What about all this? What do you want to do about it?"

She looked at me blankly. "Use it. That's why I did it."

I took a deep breath, blowing up my cheeks so that I looked a little like Old Man Winter blowing up a storm, then exhaled. "Okay, but let's introduce it quietly. Lou's a little sensitive about all this. . . ."

She closed her eyes and shook her head. "When are people going to get with the twenty-first century?"

We agreed that she would show her charts to a few pitchers and catchers. If they wanted to use them, they had my permission. But I wasn't going to make it an official team project. At least not until I was convinced that it would work.

JULY 28 ★

It's been an eventful few days. President Bush called McKeever again last night to tell him that now he was really absolutely sure that McKeever's perfect game was one of the best games he'd ever seen, and he wanted to be among the first to offer his congratulations. McKeever was very pleased to hear from the president again, and promised to send him an entire set of the limited edition set of official St. Lucia coins bearing his likeness.

Eric Plunk's insomnia seems to be getting worse. I happened to be in the clubhouse when he came in to see if he could get some sleep in the flotation tank. He looked terrible, and he told me he hadn't been able to sleep all night. "I was having this awful nightmare," he said. "Every time I drifted into sleep, I'd dream that I was Ed Whitson and I was in a car surrounded by Yankee fans. Then, thank goodness, I'd wake up."

We're thinking about moving him up to the 15-day DL. Clay Parker is throwing easily and looks like he's about ready to come off, so there'll be an opening on that list.

Joe V is up to his new tricks again. Yogi tried to phone him during our game with the Brewers last night, to move him into right-center. "The phone rang a couple of times," Yogi explained after the game, "but when it got answered, instead of hearing Joe, I heard this girl with a bad case of asthma. I figured she had to have asthma because she was breathing so heavy. And then she told me, 'My name is Magic, and I want to be your sex slave.' I thought that was pretty silly, what kind of name is Magic for a girl? So when she said, 'I want to take your . . .' I hung up because I figured I must have the wrong number."

In the Kangaroo Court session after the game, Judge Reggie Jackson fined Joe V $10 for putting his glove on call forwarding, then fined Yogi $25 for hanging up.

The Kangaroo Court is working out pretty well. Reggie is a very tough judge. He fined Roberto Kelly $15 for missing a steal sign. It cost Winfield $10 for missing the cutoff man, and another $10 for wasting the court's time by appealing. Dotson was fined $5 for being traded from a last-place team. President Bush got fined $10 for mispronouncing McKeever's name when he called. Frank Biondo was fined $5 for "Possession of a Sammy Davis, Jr. at the Palace" cassette.

The biggest fine levied so far was against Rosey Rogers, who got caught with a woman, in the mood room watching an adult film on the big wall screen. Reggie fined him $100 for "Invasion of Public-cy." "That's the opposite of invasion of privacy," Judge Jackson told Rogers. "It means that you shouldn't have done something like that without inviting your teammates."

The only problem with the court is that it still isn't meeting often enough—court only goes into session after a victory. Since the All-Star break we've played one game better than .500, but still dropped to eleven back. Toronto is still leading the division by ½ game over the Red Sox, the Brewers are four back, and the rest of us are bunched up within a game or so of each other. Over in the Western Division it's Oakland and Texas on top as usual, with the A's leading by three games. Knuckleballer Charlie Hough has practically carried the Rangers by himself this season; his 15 victories are the most in the big leagues. TJ and Charlie were teammates on the Dodgers almost twenty years ago, and TJ told me that Charlie had called him recently to find out all about the Teflon spring operation. "If that spring got you throwing 95," Charlie told him, "then I could easily get my fastball up to . . . 35, 40. If there's a good wind blowing in from centerfield, 48." There's a rumor going around that Charlie's knuckleball has been so effective this year that he's been offered a starting spot in a dental clinic in Great Neck. Hough, who's almost 45 years old, likes to remind people that very few major-league pitchers have ever won as many or more games than their age, "Even if I have a great second half I can't do that, but I might get it up there around my I.Q." If Hough does have a big second half, and he gets a little help from those kids Bobby Valentine has, like Jason Klurfeld and Tommy Robbins, this could be the season Texas finally wins the division title.

In the National League Least it's the Cubbies, Cardinals, and Mets, just as predicted. Nobody really believes the Cubs are going to hold on again this season, but baseball experts have been predicting that they're going to fold for almost four years now. If the Cardinals can get a couple of their pitchers off the DL, everybody believes Whitey will have them in the hunt at the end. The Mets have the best pitching staff in the game, but the team batting average is at .198. I don't care what the experts say, I don't believe you can win without hitting. David Cone hasn't given up an earned run in 45 innings, covering parts of six games, and has no decisions to show for it. In every one of those games he's been taken out for a pinch hitter with the Mets either tied or behind. Mets manager Davey Johnson really looks like he could use an hour in the frustration room. A few days ago he told reporters, "I'd say we were in a batting slump, but we'd have to raise the team batting average about 25 points before we were hitting well enough to say we were in a slump."

In the National League Best, as the western division is known, it looks like the Los Angeles Dodgers' "Hired Guns" are going to fulfill their money-back guarantee this year. "The Guns," as George Brett, Eric Davis, Bobby Bonilla, and Joe Carter call themselves, took advantage of the quirk in the last Basic Agreement that allowed players to collude, to negotiate as a group. They posed for a photograph wearing old western outfits, holding bats instead of rifles, and called themselves "The Hired Guns." "Go for broke," was their motto—they demanded $14,000,000 for the four of them for one season, but offered a $2,000,000 rebate if the team didn't win the pennant or draw 3,000,000 fans. They advertised in *The Sporting News*, claiming, "Have bats, Will travel." The Padres signed them last season, but qualified for the rebate by finishing second and drawing only 2,800,000. This year, though, "The Guns" look like they're going to win the division title for the Dodgers. LA's in front of both the Giants and the Astro's by seven games. And Bonilla, with 22 home runs and 78 RBIs, looks like he's on his way to the MVP.

Right now we're hitting the ball as well as we have in several seasons, and I have to think that Duke is at least partially responsible for that. Pretty much everybody is at least checking their readouts before going up to bat. The charts are getting better too; the more games Duke sees, the more raw data she feeds her IBM, the more accurate her readouts become, the better we hit. Of course, I think Lou is at least partially correct when he claims that the charts make players better hitters because they force them to concentrate more at bat. It's amazing how many players have discovered that they are better hitters with two strikes on them than with one or no strikes, probably because with two strikes they focus on making contact with the pitch rather than trying to drive it.

Now if we could just get our pitching staff stabilized we have plenty of time to make a good run for the flag. TJ and McDonald both tried to use Duke's pitching charts, but they found out it was impossible. Batters only have to remember a sequence of seven or eight pitches, but pitchers have to remember a lot more information than that for each batter. TJ tried it for two hitters, then reported, "I got so confused I couldn't even remember my own number. So I went back to the regular scouting report." We can't depend on the catchers to memorize all that material either; there's just too much of it. We probably could have Bill Lee or Yogi or Nettles signal the catcher from the bench, but I know Lou would be against that.

That means that Duke's charts are too good to use. They contain so much information that it takes too long to interpret them. Too bad, because after seeing how much they've helped improve our hitting, I'd like our pitchers to experiment with them. Right now I just can't figure out how to do it.

JULY 31 ★

Today, July 31st, in Atlanta, Georgia, Braves owner Ted Turner made baseball history. In the sixth inning of the Braves' only scheduled appearance on the CBS *Game of the Week,* manager Jim Beauchamp sent the first woman ever to appear in an official major-league game up to bat. The wire service story I saw an hour ago claimed it was the most significant event to occur in baseball since Jackie Robinson broke the color barrier in 1947. Although later in the same story the writer compared it to the day St. Louis Browns owner Bill Veeck sent a midget up to the plate.

Apparently it came as a complete surprise to everybody except Turner and Beauchamp. Believe me, I know baseball players, and if one of them had known about it, the entire Free World would have known about it. And, at least from what I saw on TV, a lot of them looked stunned and even a little embarrassed by her appearance.

According to the AP, yesterday afternoon Turner notified the National League office via teletype that the Braves had purchased the contract of a player named Julia Nevez from the Mexico City Reds in the Mexican League. I suspect that officials in the National League office assumed that that was a typographical error, because they approved the contract of Julio Nevez.

The Braves were trailing the Dodgers, 2–1, with two outs and nobody on base in the bottom of the sixth with pitcher Ryan Dusick scheduled to bat. There was a little commotion in the dugout, and all of the players started looking toward the dugout entrance. Just about everybody on the bench started moving down that way; several players even climbed up on the bench so they could see what was happening. Naturally, the CBS cameras focused on that doorway, and announcers Hank Greenwald and Tom Seaver speculated on who the Braves were waiting for. For a short time, everybody waited.

Just as home plate umpire Eric Gregg began walking over to the dugout to find out what was causing the delay, a small figure wearing a Braves uniform came out of there carrying a bat. At first, a lot of people in the stadium didn't notice that this player had a long black pigtail hanging out of the back of her Braves cap. "Ladies and gentlemen," the P.A. announcer droned, "for the Braves, batting for Dusick, number 36, Julia Nevez. Nev-ezz, number 36."

There was a smattering of applause as Nevez picked up the pine tar rag and wiped down the handle of her bat, then picked up the lead bat in the on-deck circle and started swinging it over her head to loosen up her shoulders. By the time she laid down the lead bat most of the people in the ballpark realized what was going on. I'd say there were an equal number of cheers and boos. She seemed oblivious to both.

On CBS, Hank Greenwald, told his viewers, "My oh my, you'd better go wake up Aunt Nellie, because you are not going to believe what you are about to see. Ladies and gentlemen, welcome to baseball's first *real* Ladies' Day. I'm not sure the crowd here at Atlanta–Fulton County Stadium has realized what's happening, but we're seeing major-league baseball history being made. Now stepping up to bat for the Braves is Julia Nevez. You heard me correctly, that's *Julia* Nevez, the first woman to ever appear in an official big league game. This is absolutely incredible. Tom Seaver, have you ever seen anything like this?

Tom Seaver was obviously shocked. "I'm shocked," he said. "I just don't see any reason to hit for Dusick at all. We're only in the sixth inning and he's been pitching a great ballgame. There's two out and no . . ."

"But what do you think about the girl at bat?"

"I don't have a scouting report in front of me, but I'd pitch her the same way I'd pitch any batter I hadn't faced before. Breaking pitches away until I've seen her swing. I'd try to get ahead in the count and make her hit my pitch."

On the field, Dodger manager Tommy Lasorda came out to discuss the situation with Gregg. Beauchamp immediately came out of the Braves' dugout with Julia Nevez's fully approved National League contract.

As Gregg examined the contract, Lasorda started getting angrier and angrier. He looked like he was rehearsing for an antacid commercial. Finally, he lost it. He started screaming and yelling, he took his hat off and threw it onto the ground. At one point he went stomach-to-stomach with Gregg, and Eric really had him outstomached there. Gregg finally threw him out of the game. But as Lasorda marched away, accompanied by the cheers of about half the crowd, he stopped and turned around, and yelled at Gregg, "You can throw me out of here if you want to, but I'll quit this game before I have to call somebody a baseperson!"

While all this was going on, Turner was standing up in his box directly next to the Braves' dugout, taking deep bows. Several women came over to him and kissed him.

Up in the press box, Braves public relations director Jim Schultz was handing out a press release. Greenwald told his viewers, "We've just been handed some information about Nevez. She's a little fel—lady, 5'8" tall, 135 pounds and . . . I don't see an age listed here. Believe me, this is just as much a surprise to all of us in the booth as it is to you at home, and we're passing along whatever information we get as soon as we get it. According to the Director of Player Development, Hank Aaron, Nevez is a native of San Pedro de Macoris, in the Dominican Republic and, naturally, she's a shortstop. She bats right, throws right and, if I may make a personal comment here, she looks all right too. . . ."

Gregg finally permitted her to bat. Dodger pitching coach Ron Perranoski went out to the mound to discuss the situation with pitcher Fernando Valenzuela. In the booth, Tom Seaver was telling viewers that Nevez was really at a disadvantage because a woman's body made it easier to define her strike zone. He started to say something about the way women hang over the plate, but Greenwald caught him in time.

Nevez stepped into the batter's box and dug in. The fact is that she really looked like she knew what she was doing. Fernando went into his windup, the crowd roared, and he pitched. He threw her a screwball, outside. She watched it. Ball one.

His second pitch was a fastball down the pipe. Strike one.

She stepped out of the box and glared out at Valenzuela. Who could blame her for being nervous? He threw again, another fastball. She swung and missed. Strike two. She really didn't have much of a swing. "After watching her swing," Seaver said, "I think I'd go right after her with fastballs. You don't want to play around with hitters you don't know. One lucky swing, and there's a run."

Fernando went into his windup again. Another fastball. She swung, and hit a little bouncer toward second baseman Willie Randolph. Willie fielded the ball as Nevez streaked down the line. She could really run, and she made it a much closer play than it should have been. Willie flipped across his body to first baseman Eddie Murray, nipping her by a step. Murray, instead of tossing the ball to the umpire as he usually does when the last out of the inning is made at first base, handed it to Nevez, then kissed her on the cheek.

She slapped him across the face. Then the whole crowd roared.

In the booth, Greenwald said, "Ladies and gentlemen, that's all she wrote."

Nevez trotted back to the dugout. About a dozen players came over to her and gave her high or low fives. Several of them had her autograph baseballs for them right there in the dugout.

Lasorda was still angry after the game. "I love women," he told reporters, "but the reason she was out there today was because she's a woman, not because she's capable of playing major-league baseball. That's what I object to. I don't have a problem with women eating at men's clubs and things like that, I've seen a lot of women who can eat as well as any man, but this is different. You guys saw her swing. That was a joke, and I'm against anything that turns this wonderful game into a joke."

After the game the AP reported that baseball memorabilia collector Barry Rosen had offered $5,000 for each of the baseballs she'd signed in the dugout, and $25,000 for her uniform.

In the clubhouse before our game tonight Nevez was practically the only thing anybody wanted to talk about. Verola and Mattingly were interviewing people for their books. Raoul Rojas told them he thought he played against her in a canefield game when he was growing up.

"But I never thought she make the big leagues someday," he said. "She no very good goin' to her right."

The pitchers spent a lot of time debating how they'd pitch to her. "Curves, curves, curves," Cadaret insisted. "You can see she can't reach the breaking ball."

Nicholson disagreed. "Bust her inside," he said firmly.

"Hey, c'mon," McDonald interrupted, "watch it with those sexist remarks."

Biondo was adamant. "You got to pitch her just like you'd pitch any woman."

Parker said, "I think Seaver was right, pitch her away. I wouldn't give her anything to pull."

Rosey Rogers happened to be walking by and heard Parker's comment. "I would," he said with a lewd smile.

During our game we heard that National League President Bill White had explained, at a press conference in New York, that Nevez had "a valid contract and a good lawyer, and was therefore an eligible player."

At a press conference in Atlanta, Braves' owner Ted Turner defended his decision to play her, saying, "Things have been stagnant around here too long, so I thought it was time to shake up some of our stags. I've never cared if a player's a man or a woman, as long as he can play the game." He also said he didn't know how long she would remain on the Braves roster, or whether she'd appear in another game.

After all that, our game was a little anticlimactic, but we managed to beat the Orioles, 6–4. TJ picked up his ninth win against three losses, and Taft got his 12th save. Mr. Cool really seems to be catching on. Harley-Davidson has already offered Taft a commercial deal, but both Suzuki and Kawasaki have guaranteed to top any offer if he'll ride in from the bullpen to save the game on their bikes.

The character is great fun. I'm just a little nervous that Tums is beginning to take the whole thing a little too seriously. He's now wearing his sunglasses all the time—in the clubhouse, at dinner, in the shower after the game. And he's starting to talk about Mr. Cool in the third person, telling reporters things like, "Mr. Cool wasn't the slightest bit nervous when he came in, that's why he's Mr. Cool." Or, "When the call goes out to the bullpen for Mr. Cool, the game is on ice."

The fact that he wears the sunglasses while pitching has upset a lot of people. I'm really surprised that nobody's ever done it before. The hitters seem to hate it, and a couple of teams have asked to have them banned, claiming they create an unfair distraction. The league has refused to take any action, pointing out that there is nothing in the rulebook to prohibit a pitcher from wearing sunglasses on the field.

A few others pitchers have worn them in games, figuring that anything that batters don't like has got to be helpful. Two pairs of sunglasses have been confiscated, though. National League umpire Joe West took a pair of red heart-shaped lenses from San Francisco Giants pitcher Scotty Garrelts, and American League umpire Dave Phillips took a pair from the Angels Chuck Finley because they had little plastic guns in the corners above the lenses. In both cases the umpires ruled that these were not standard sunglasses and did create an unfair distraction. Like any piece of confiscated equipment, they were sent to a testing laboratory for a complete analysis. The lab ruled that both pairs were sunglasses.

AUGUST 4 ★

Kenny Davis went public with his complaints last Tuesday, and it's created a problem. Davis told *Newsday*'s Marty Noble that he doesn't want to play in New York anymore, that he wants to be traded to a team "where my abilities would be respected." When Noble's story ran, Davis claimed he'd been misquoted, that he'd really said that he didn't want to *not* play in New York anymore. When Noble produced a tape of the interview, on which Davis can be heard saying clearly that he wanted out, Davis claimed that he'd been mistaped.

Noble released a copy of that tape to the TV and radio stations, which made the newspaper story the prime topic of TV and radio sports news. When Davis heard the tape played on the air he got really angry and announced that he was no longer going to be speaking to reporters. "People just don't realize how hard it is not to play in New York," he fumed. "The press just won't leave you alone. That's the problem with the New York media. You people are always so busy reporting the facts that sometimes you miss the whole story."

Piniella tried to defuse the situation. He called Davis into his office and asked him to reconsider his statement until he'd had a little time to cool down. That really set off Davis, who told Piniella that he couldn't tell him what not to do. "Maybe you've heard of the Bill of Rights?" he screamed so loudly that everybody in the clubhouse could hear him. "You know what Freedom of Speech means, don't you? It means I'm free not to speak to anybody I don't want to. And I want to not speak to those reporters.

"And lemme tell you something else. If I decide not to speak to somebody, I'll be the one to tell them that. That's my right as an American Leaguer."

I don't know if I should get involved in these problems. Lou decides who plays and who sits, and it's his job to handle the players. If I get involved, it'll look like I'm undermining his authority, which I don't want to do. Unless it becomes absolutely necessary. And believe me, it's never necessary when a .220 hitter with 6 home runs is involved.

We tried an experiment in the game tonight. We had Duke sitting next to our dugout with her computer, relaying signs to catcher Jim Sundberg. Ever since Nevez made her big-league debut, Duke has become a lot more confident. She practically demanded that I give her a seat next to the dugout from which she could operate her computer and pass the information to our catcher. When I spoke to Lou about it, he was furious. He stomped around my office and threatened to resign if I gave control of his pitching staff to a "dame with a computer."

Coincidentally, and certainly fortunately, at that exact moment I got a phone call from soon-to-be sophomore Pete Rose, who'd read about the dissension in the clubhouse and just wanted to tell me that "I been taking French lessons. I got it down paté."

By the time I'd hung up with Pete, Lou had calmed down. "We've got to do something about the pitching," I pleaded with him. Finally, we agreed to leave the final decision up to Bill Lee. If Lee approved of the experiment, we'd try it.

"So tell me, Bill," I asked, "how do you like working for the Yankees?" After hearing my argument, Bill agreed with me. Duke set up her computer right alongside our dugout. She was wearing a specially designed black sweater with white lines that divided her chest into 16 zones. After each pitch Sundberg would look at her chest—

everybody assumed he was looking into our dugout for the signal—and she'd point to the zone where the pitch should be thrown, then use, one, two, or three fingers to indicate what type of pitch to call.

Bruce McDonald pitched the best game of his brief big-league career, giving up only six hits and striking out ten in seven strong innings, beating the Tigers 4–1. After the game both Duke and McDonald were absolutely thrilled—it was a big game for both of them. There was nothing Piniella could do but agree to let any pitcher who wanted to use Duke's information do so. Lou isn't happy with the situation, but he hasn't been able to get the pitching staff straightened out, and, if this works, he's the one who'll get all the credit.

During the game, incidentally, Dave Winfield set another league record. In the fifth inning, he was way out in front of a Jack Morris changeup and his bat sailed out of his hand and spiraled into the second deck. That's a new bat-throwing distance record that's going to be very hard to beat.

AUGUST 5 ★

I had a phone call this morning from the Padres' principal owner, Roberto Satin who is serving on the Player Relations Committee. With less than two years left in the Basic Agreement with the Major League Baseball Players Association, a lot of the owners are starting to get nervous. Having now been convicted three times of conspiring to limit payments to free agents, I think we've learned our lesson. This time we're being much more careful to avoid getting caught. "I want to talk to you about the ee-fray agent-say," Satin said. It took me a minute to figure out what he was talking about. He was talking about exactly what the league attorneys have warned us not to talk about.

"Oh," I said, "the ee-fray agent-say. What about them?"

"The most amazing thing happened," he continued. "Six owners just happened to be visiting Phillipsburg, West Virginia, for the big strip mining festival—did you know that's where the Strip Mining Museum and Hall of Fame is located? Well, we just happened to run into each other in the lobby of the big Motel Six."

"That's some incredible coincidence," I said.

"Unbelievable," he agreed. "Who would've guessed we were all strip mining aficionados? But as long as we were all there, we decided to have dinner together, and you know what? Each of us, independently, acting alone, without discussing this with anyone else—just in case anybody should ask you—reached the conclusion that we weren't going to ign-say more than one ee-fray agent-say each this year, and that we weren't going to ay-pay more than oo-tay illion-may to any of them."

"Now that's another incredible coincidence," I said, "because that's exactly what I was about to think."

"Amazing," Satin said. "Of course, if this should ever come up, I want you to remember in the future that I've never spoken to you in the past."

"Naturally. And listen, it's been nice not talking to you." As I hung up the phone I felt a little like Kenny Davis.

Later this afternoon we discovered that Eric Plunk is missing. Well, he's not exactly missing, he's just been misplaced. We had planned to take him off the disabled list today, and he came into the clubhouse to get a final physical examination from Gene Monahan. When we notified the league office that we wanted to activate him, they told us that they couldn't find him. He wasn't on our active roster, but he also wasn't on any of their other lists: disabled, waivers, voluntarily retired. The last record we have is that we put him on the 15-day DL nine days ago, retoractive to the first date we put him on the 30-day DL, which has nothing to do with his transfer to the 60-day DL, which was retroactive to spring training. So, according to our records, he was eligible to return to the active roster today.

The American League office informed us that until they find him, he can't play. "What exactly does that mean?" Plunk wanted to know.

"It means that, officially, you don't exist."

He thought I was kidding. "But here I am," he said, laughing, and pointing to himself.

"Unofficially," I pointed out. "Officially," I shook my head, "you're nowhere. Look, it's just a little mix-up. I'm sure you'll turn up soon. It's something to do with a computer problem in the league office. Just start throwing, stay in shape, and as soon as they figure out what they've done with you, you'll be back in the rotation."

Plunk didn't believe me. He looked at me as if I was kidding, and said, "Bill Lee put you up to this, right?"

Meanwhile, we won again last night. Cadaret gave up nine hits, but got very tough with runners in scoring position and shut out the Tigers, 4–0. Mattingly had three hits, including his 12th home run, to raise his average to .345, and Reich had two doubles to bring his average over .200 for the first time this season. We're now 2–0 with Duke at work next to the dugout.

AUGUST 10 ★

It's almost two o'clock in the morning and I'm exhausted. I've been on the phone for several hours trying to get the whole story straight. But the reports I'm getting are almost impossible to believe.

What seems like about a year ago started out to be a normal day. This afternoon, Commissioner Vincent rejected the Dodgers request that Houston's Mike Scott be suspended for illegally defacing baseballs before pitching them. In what has instantly become known as Vincent's "Dreaded Scott" decision, the Commissioner found that although the 17 baseballs submitted by the Dodgers, each of them with the word "Mike" scratched into the cover, seemed to indicate something was going on, there was only circumstantial evidence to connect Scott with them. He said he had no choice but to dispense justice as it had always been done in baseball, "Everyone is entitled to a trial and error."

Then, maybe an hour after that, the Braves formally asked waivers on Julia Nevez for the purpose of giving her her unconditional release. Nevez has appeared in all five of the Braves' home games since making her big-league debut. She batted five times, with no hits and four strikeouts.

I don't think this whole thing has worked out quite as well as Ted Turner expected. Although he sold out his ballpark five times this week, the National Organization for Women has accused him of exploiting women for profit, and claimed that he was using Nevez as a "freak to attract attention and increase attendance."

Turner denied that completely. "I know all about exploiting women," he said, "and that's not what I'm doing. What I'm doing is using her!" I think what he meant to say was that he was using her the way any owner would use a ballplayer. The bottom line is that the Braves are leaving on a ten-game road swing through the west, and NOW threatened to put up picket lines around any ballpark Nevez appears in, and urged all female fans to protest "the continued exploitation of Julia Nevez by boycotting Braves' games." I suspect Turner got so much pressure from the owners of the teams they're going to play on this trip that he decided to let her go.

However, he's sold movie rights to *The Julia Nevez Story: Mom's a Big Leaguer,* for a reported six-figure guarantee. The rumor is that Lindsay Wagner's going to play Nevez and Richard Chamberlain's going to play Ted Turner.

And then our problems began. I was at home watching our game against the Blue Jays in Toronto on WPIX. TJ was pitching a great game, but it seemed like every close call went against us. Second-base umpire John Hirschbeck called Joe V out on a steal attempt when the replay showed he was safe. First-base umpire Al Clark rang up Sax on a half-swing third strike when he had clearly held up. Then Clark called Reich's long fly ball into the right-field seats foul when on the replay it looked like it might have been fair. Finally, with the Jays leading 1–0 in the eighth, Espinoza was on first base when Kelly hit a long drive into the right–centerfield gap. It looked like it was going to be in for extra bases, with Espinoza scoring the tying run. But Lloyd Moseby came out of nowhere to make an incredible over-the-shoulder catch, then in one motion whirled and threw toward first. Gruber cut off the throw and threw a strike to McGriff. To me, it looked like Espinoza had beaten the throw back to first base, but it was close. Clark didn't hesitate—he called Espinoza out to complete the double play. That's when Piniella erupted.

I don't think it was just that one play that did it. I think it was a whole season of frustrations culminating in that one play. I think everything got to him all at once: the inconsistency of the pitching staff, the arguments about Duke's charts, the injuries, the recent problems with Davis—the thousand petty annoyances that every manager has to deal with every single day.

I've seen Lou lose his temper before, but this time . . . It even made his famed eruption in the 1977 playoffs, when umpire Ron Luciano called him out at home plate—because, Luciano explained, Lou had slid over home plate rather than touching it—look like a lovers' quarrel.

Lou started by coming out and pleading with Clark for about a minute. But Clark just stood there, arms folded in front of him, not saying a word. I could see Lou's anger building. Finally, Lou exploded. He took off his hat and slammed it on the ground, then kicked the artificial infield dirt on Clark, then drop-kicked his own hat into the air. Clark turned around and started walking away from Piniella. Lou tried to follow him, but home plate umpire Mike Seeherman stepped in front of Piniella and held him back. Piniella must have shouted something at Clark, because Clark suddenly turned around and wound up his arm and threw Lou out of the game. I think that's probably when Lou lost it completely.

In a rage, he reached down, yanked first base right out of its mooring, and flipped it high into the air. Then he looked around for something else to grab, and headed for the Yankee dugout. When he got to the dugout the first thing he grabbed was the Gatorade cooler. He heaved it onto the field. Seconds later the plastic water cooler came flying out of the dugout. Then Piniella took the ball bag and dumped out twenty or thirty baseballs, which started rolling all over the field. Then he took our bats out of the bat rack, one by one, and threw them onto the field.

Clark had finally had enough. He started moving toward the dugout, and Piniella came out to meet him. Seeherman grabbed Clark, and Nettles, Winfield, and McDonald just barely managed to hold Lou back. For a few seconds, the situation seemed to have calmed down. Winfield and McDonald let Lou go. In retrospect, I'd have to say that that was their big mistake.

The recently installed artificial playing field in the Skydome, TundraTurf, is supposedly the state of the art in plastic surfaces. Not only does it look like real grass, it's actually been scented to smell like a newly cut lawn. The manufacturer has also installed plastic weeds in the outfield, and provided papier-mâché rocks for the imitation dirt infield. They've even created false worn spots around the coaches' boxes. It was a beautiful field.

When Winfield and McDonald released Lou, he straightened out his uniform, picked up his hat and brushed off the imitation dirt, and started walking back toward our dugout. Then some fan, sitting near the photographers' box just beyond the dugout, yelled something at him. That was about as smart as checking the gas tank with a lit match. Boom! Lou ran toward the stands. The photographers grabbed their cameras and retreated. The fan took off up the aisle, and stadium security moved in to protect him. By the time Lou reached the railing, that fan was probably halfway home. I'm not sure exactly what happened next, but somehow Lou found a loose edge of the TundraTurf carpet. He grabbed that end in both hands and started pulling. The turf came right up. It looked as if Lou were pulling up the carpet in a living room. The whole surface began pulling away from its brown rubber backing. Lou pulled it up all the way into right field, ripping up about a quarter of the playing field. Somehow, he must have ruptured a water line, because a stream of water suddenly spouted about ten feet into the air, and slowly began creating a new lake where first base had been only minutes earlier.

Meanwhile, Al Clark was trailing Lou, writing down everything he did on a pad. "I'm watching you, Piniella," he warned him. "I'm writing everything down."

I think Lou was probably running out of steam by this time, but he wasn't quite finished. The thing that makes the Skydome unique is that it has a roof that can be opened or closed mechanically. I guess, to be completely accurate, I should say that it *had* a roof that could be opened or closed mechanically. It seems that one of the major operating gears was located under the playing field, presumably to allow maintenance and repair people easy access to it. When Lou ripped up the carpet, the gearbox door sprung open, and water from the broken pipe washed into the controls, shorting out the system. The gears started turning; the roof started closing. Unfortunately, the water also picked up some of the bats and balls and carried them right into the gearbox. Believe me, I could hear that grinding sound on my TV set. Bolts started popping out of the gears. The roof stopped moving. Optimists would say it was half open, pessimists would say it was half closed. Insurance adjustors say it's completely broken.

"I'm writing all this down, Piniella," Clark warned him again. "You keep this up, you're gonna get into serious trouble."

Lou looked around for something else to attack, but by that time I think he'd gotten out most of his frustration. So finally he wiped his hands together and went directly to the clubhouse.

It was, without doubt, the greatest tantrum in the history of managing.

The ballpark was a shambles. A huge section of the TundraTurf had been ripped up, the gears to the roof had been stripped, and every once in a while another nut or bolt popped into the air. A small lake was growing into a large lake where first base used to be, and bats and balls were strewn all over the place. The grounds crew tried to restore the field to playing condition, but that was impossible. After waiting an hour and a half, the umpires ruled that the field was unplayable, and forfeited the game to the Blue Jays, 9–0.

I'll say this for Lou, he didn't deny a thing. "I did it," he told reporters in the clubhouse, "but it wasn't all my fault. The umpires have been sticking it to us all season, so I think they bear at least a little responsibility. I just think that every so often a man has to stand up and tell them, 'I'm mad as hell at the umpires and I'm not going to take it anymore. . . .' That's all I was trying to say."

It was obvious to me that he was going to be suspended for at least three days.

My telephone at home started ringing seconds after Piniella finished. Chicken wanted to know who I thought should manage the club during Lou's suspension. A music producer called to find out who controlled the video rights—with proper editing, he told me, Piniella's performance could be turned into an award-winning music video. Our insurance agent called to tell me that this would probably not be considered an Act of God, and warned that we might not be covered. Earl Weaver called me from Florida to offer his congratulations. Several reporters called to get my reaction. And Billy called to tell me that his chickens were pregnant again.

My wife, Mary, had the best suggestion. "If I were you," she said as we watched a replay of the Skydome being destroyed, "I'd find out if they paid for the thing with an American Express Card."

I asked her why.

"Well, you know they're always advertising that if you pay for something with an American Express Card and it gets lost, stolen, or broken they'll pay to replace it?"

"Yeah?"

"After seeing what Lou did to their ballpark, I sure hope they paid for it with an American Express Card."

Lou called about two hours later. "Jeez, Lou," I said, "I know you were angry, but the whole ballpark?"

"You saw that call, Spark. They've been doing that to us all year."

"But the whole ballpark?"

"Well, maybe I did get a little carried away, but . . ." He chuckled. "I guess we got their attention, huh?"

"But the whole ballpark?"

AUGUST 14 ★

We're still waiting for some sort of decision from American League president Bobby Brown on what's become known as "The Eruption of Mt. Lou." Brown can't take action until he receives an official report from the umpiring crew, and supposedly Clark's report is already seventy-two pages long and he hasn't even gotten to the gearbox yet. While we're waiting Lou has continued to manage the team.

Meanwhile, something good is beginning to happen. I can feel it. The club is starting to come together, like Jell-O in a refrigerator. Since Duke started working with the pitchers almost the whole staff has become more consistent; but it's more than that. For the first time all season we're hitting in clutch situations, our defense has been good, and we're playing smart fundamental baseball. The problem is that we're not gaining any ground on the league leaders. The Red Sox got hot at the same time we did, and moved ahead of the Blue Jays into first place yesterday behind Oil Can's 3-hitter over the Indians. So we're still ten games back. But hunches and feelings and guesses are an important part of baseball, and I've just got this feeling that we're about to make a run.

Yesterday morning, before our game against the Rangers, Joe V went to visit the children's ward at St. Vincent's Hospital in Greenwich Village. A hospital administrator called me afterwards to tell me how terrific Joe had been with the kids. He handed out baseballs and pictures and signed autographs. Sometimes, I think, because professional athletes live in such an insulated world, we forget that to a lot of people we're big heroes. Obviously that's ridiculous; we're not heroes—well, not big heroes, at least.

During his visit to St. Vincent's, Joe spent a lot of time with the cutest little seven-year-old girl whose leg had been broken in an automobile accident. When Joe was getting ready to leave, she looked up at him with her big, wide, innocent brown eyes and asked, "Joey, will you hit a homer for me tonight?"

"You can bet on it, Susie," he promised, then added, "but only in Las Vegas." When he came into the clubhouse this afternoon he was as pumped up as any player I've ever seen. He told everybody that he was going to take one deep. Unfortunately, sometimes things don't work out in real life the way they do in fairy tales. Nolan Ryan started for the Rangers, and he was throwing his new knuckleball that made his heater even more effective. Joe V struck out four times as Ryan notched career victory number 312, 4–1.

After the game Joe V was really upset. He just sat in front of his locker, in uniform, head bowed, not saying one word. Finally Nettles went over to him. Graig is just so good in sensitive situations like this one. He sat down next to Joe, put his arm around Joe's shoulders, and said loudly, "You know, maybe next time it'd be better if you let Nolan Ryan go see the kids."

AUGUST 15 ★

Just a typical day in baseball: Tommy John brought his arm into the medical carpenter for the regularly scheduled 100-inning checkup. A couple of small springs were slightly out of alignment, but the carpenter was able to straighten them right there in the office. I guess, in the world of medical carpentry, that's what's known as spring cleaning.

I have to remember to tell that one to Nettles.

Also today we were notified by the American League office that Eric Plunk has a serious disk problem: his soft disk is broken. "We're quite sure he's somewhere in our computer system," Chicken was told, "but we're having problems with his soft disk. For some reason our computer doesn't want to read it. So you see, there's a lesson in this for all of us. Whether it's on the ballfield or in the computer room, if you don't back up, you're going to get into trouble." They've guaranteed us that they would have Plunk up and on screen within two days.

In Chicago, platoon managers Carlton Fisk and Ray Miller got into a big fight when Miller, the defensive manager, tried to put Fisk, the offensive manager, into the ballgame for defensive purposes. "You can't put me in the game," Fisk told him, "I'm saving myself as a pinch hitter. I'm the offensive manager."

"I know that," Miller agreed. "But don't you know that the best offense is a good defense?"

"No, no, no," Fisk corrected him, "I think you've got that wrong. See, the way that saying really goes is, the best *defense* is a good offense. See, defense is offense. You just have it reversed, that's all."

Miller disagreed. "Excuse me, but no. Offense is defense. I had it right."

"Hey, Ray, ease up a little," Fisk told him. "Don't be so defensive. So you made a little mistake. . . ."

"The only mistake I made was agreeing to platoon with you," Miller snapped. "The only thing you're right about is that you're the most offensive manager I've ever known. . . ."

And that's when the fight actually started.

AUGUST 17 ★

They found Eric Plunk today. He's retired. Actually, he's not retired; his file is. The American League office found him on their Voluntarily Retired List. Chicken told them we wanted to activate him right away, then asked, "How'd he get on that list?"

"Well," the clerk, a woman named Iris Jacobson, replied, "I guess he didn't want to play anymore."

Chicken laughed. "No, wait, that was a mistake."

"Then I guess he shouldn't have retired. He should have made sure that that was what he wanted to do before he did it. Now he goes and changes his mind and it's nothing but a big headache for me."

"Miss Jacobson," Chicken explained politely, "he hasn't changed his mind."

"Then why do you want me to take him off the Voluntarily Retired List?"

"So he can play."

"I thought you said he didn't change his mind."

"I did; he didn't."

"Okay, let's start from the beginning. He retired . . ."

"No!" Chicken screamed.

"Okay, where do you want to start from?"

Eventually, Chicken thinks, he got the problem straightened out. Supposedly, Plunk will be returned to our active roster tomorrow, and will be eligible to pitch immediately. At least that's what Chicken is hoping for. "The last thing she said to me," he remembered, "was that she hoped Mr. Plunk's disk condition had improved."

AUGUST 19 ★

American League President Dr. Bobby Brown suspended Lou Piniella for ten days, starting today, and fined him $500. Official estimates of damage to the Skydome are now at $475,000, but still rising. Sort of like the way that lake rose on the field until they managed to get the water turned off. Chicken and I agreed that Yogi will take over the club during Lou's suspension. A lot of people don't remember that Yogi won championships with two different ballclubs, and since his hands softened up at first base our players have grown to respect him.

When Joe V heard that we'd named Yogi, he immediately asked for a new number for his cellular glove. Poor Yog; Joe really has been giving him a hard time. Yogi called him in the sixth inning the other night, and when Joe answered the glove he snarled, "I told you not to call me when I'm working," and hung up.

Lou's suspension comes at a bad time. For the first time all season we've got both our hitting and pitching in order, and we're playing with confidence. We go on the field knowing we're going to win.

About an hour after the league made the announcement, Duke came into my office to talk about tonight's game. She's really been doing a good job for us. She now sits in my box during the game, on the press level where the other teams can't see her, and communicates directly with Bill Lee in the dugout. After each pitch she feeds the new count into her computer, which responds by figuring out exactly what the next pitch should be. She tells Lee, who relays it to the catcher, who signals the pitcher. I don't know if it's the inside information she provides or just the confidence that comes from believing that you have inside information, but this new system has been very effective. Since Duke started giving the signals, our staff earned run average has been reduced by almost a run a game, enough to make the difference between a fourth-place club and a legitimate contender. It's beginning to look like a pretty young girl with a computer has been able to accomplish what dozens of pitching coaches, the most advanced video technology, chanting, vitamins, and even the legendary Cy Young have not been able to do—turn ten pitchers into a dependable staff.

So today Duke came to me with another idea. "I know I'm not supposed to be interfering," she said innocently, "but since Lou is out I thought maybe I could help a little. So I ran some information about the Tigers through the system, you know?"

"And?"

"And the computer says we should move Mattingly up into the number two spot in the batting order, start Rojas at shortstop, and try to go the opposite way against their relief pitching."

I didn't answer her right away. The truth is that I didn't know what to do with that information. This was Yogi's first game in charge and I didn't want to shake things up; but her computer had made a big difference in our hitting and pitching. "I'll mention it to Yogi," I said casually. "Can I at least tell him why?"

She frowned. "Oh, Spark, you know how secretive computers are. They just tell you what, they never tell you why."

Yogi was sitting at Lou's desk, filling out the lineup cards, when I walked in. "You know, Yog, I've been thinking," I said, "and I've got a few ideas . . ."

Yogi listened attentively. "How come?" he wanted to know.

"You and I have both been around this game for a long time, Yog," I explained, "you even longer than me. So you know how sometimes you get a zimmer, a feeling you can't explain, a feeling that says, just do it, whether it makes any sense or not?"

"Sure," he agreed, "I know. Last time I got that feeling was when George hired me to manage the club. While I was talking to him on the phone, I got this feeling that I should hang up, sell the house, and move someplace where he could never find me. But I ignored it and took the job."

I handed him Duke's suggestions. "Do it," I said firmly.

Without a word, Yogi dropped his lineup card into the wastebasket and started making out a new one. "You're the boss," he said. This time I didn't disagree.

We won the ballgame, 6–5, with Mr. Cool coming out of the bullpen to throw two more perfect innings. It was a pretty big day for

Tums: Not only did he get his 19th save, he also became the first player in Yankee history to be chosen to appear on the cover of *American Biker* magazine. Mattingly had two more hits and Winfield, batting in Mattingly's usual number three spot, hit a long home run. It was a great game for us—we scored three runs in the bottom of the ninth to win it, only the second time all season we've come from behind after the seventh inning to win a ballgame. Rojas knocked in Kelly with the game-winning run. With two out he tried to go to the opposite field against the Tigers' bullpen ace, "Big Time" John Ansell, and hit a routine grounder to second baseman Lou Whitaker. Whitaker moved over to field it, but just before the ball reached him it hit something and bounced over his shoulder into right field for the game-winner.

My question is this: How did that computer know that the ball was going to hit a rock?

I noticed after the game that Duke had a satisfied smile on her face. "That was some piece of good luck, wasn't it?" I asked.

"Maybe," she said, and walked away.

AUGUST 21 ★

We got some good and some bad news today. First, the good news. Judge Sklar threw out Denny Wilson's lawsuit against Ken Davis and Yankee Corp. this afternoon. What happened was that the laboratory testing the bat and ball discovered traces of K-Y Jelly on the cover of the ball. K-Y Jelly is used—illegally—by some pitchers to make the ball sink. It's a modern spitball. More specific testing enabled the lab to actually get a partial fingerprint off the residue. Our attorney, Glen Goldstein, petitioned the court to order Wilson to produce a set of his fingerprints. Goldstein pointed out to the court that if Wilson had, in fact, "doctored, defaced, or marked" the baseball in any manner before throwing it, the pitch would be considered an illegal act under the standard rules of baseball. Therefore, Wilson's illegal act preceded the illegal act that Davis is charged with, making Wilson guilty of contributory negligence.

Wilson's attorney, Elyce Hagouel, argued that the flight of the baseball toward home plate was not pertinent to the flight of the ball after it had been struck by the illegal bat. Additionally, she argued, forcing Wilson to produce a set of his fingerprints would violate his Fifth Amendment right not to be compelled to give evidence against himself. "I strongly object, Your Honor," she strongly objected.

Judge Sklar briefly considered her objection. Then he put his thumbs in his ears, wiggled his fingers, and stuck out his tongue. "Too bad for you," he said. "Either produce the prints or withdraw your suit."

After a long conference in the judge's chambers, Wilson agreed to accept an apology from Davis, and Davis signed a stipulation in which he didn't admit any guilt, but swore he would never do it again. "I've never knowingly used an illegal bat," he told reporters on the court-house steps after the hearing, "and I've agreed never to do it again."

Later in the afternoon, the league notified us that Davis was suspended for three games, starting immediately, for using an illegal bat.

But the really bad news came after our game tonight. Way after. It seems like every sports season has to have at least one good scandal. They've become as much a part of America as Japanese cars—players trading wives, fathering illegitimate children, using drugs, traveling with a mistress—but baseball hadn't had a single scandal this season. Until tonight. I was at home, asleep, when the phone rang at about four o'clock in the morning. It took me a few seconds to recognize Rosey Rogers's voice. "Sorry to wake you, Spark," he said, "but I called to ask you an important question. Okay, here it is. How would you like to read a story about two of your players being arrested in a barroom brawl with the husbands of their dates in the middle of the night?"

"I don't think I'd like to read about that at all," I told him.

"Well, in that case," he said, "maybe you'd better not buy the morning paper." Then he started laughing.

"Rosey, where are you?"

"Let me answer that this way—how familiar are you with the New York City penal system?"

It was just after dawn when Chicken and I bailed out Rogers and Biondo. After they'd signed autographs for just about everybody in the stationhouse, we went for breakfast at a Greek diner on 23rd Street and they told us the whole story. "First thing is, it wasn't really our fault," Rosey began.

"That's true," Biondo agreed. "They told us their husbands were out of town on a fishing trip."

"I'm gonna tell you exactly what happened," Rosey continued. "After the game we went to McMullen's for a drink. We just wanted to relax, that's all. And we were sitting there minding our own business when these three women came over and sat down. . . ."

"That was one for me," Biondo said.

"And one for me," Rogers said.

Then they looked at each other and said in chorus, "And one for good luck."

And then they started laughing. Biondo stopped suddenly, and put his hand on Rogers's arm, stopping him. "Now that I think about it, we shouldn't have taken her at all. She sure wasn't good luck." Then they started laughing again.

"Uh," Chicken suggested, "maybe you guys have had a little too much to drink, huh?"

"No way," Rosey protested. Then he looked at Biondo and started laughing again. "We've had a lot too much to drink."

To make a scandal short, when McMullen's started emptying out, the five of them decided to go downtown to one of those popular new safe-sex singles bars in the East Village, a place named "Deep Thought." "We wanted to go someplace quiet," Biondo said. "Someplace where nobody would know us." Then he winked at me.

They'd just sat down when the girl with Rosey looked across the room and saw her husband, who was supposedly on a fishing trip, sitting in a booth with a blonde girl in an all–black leather outfit. "So," Rosey continued, "this girl tears across the room and screams at her husband, 'What are you doing here?' The whole place got real quiet. He stood up and screamed right back at her, 'Me? What are you doing here?' By this time I'd caught up with her, and she sort of wrapped herself around my arm and screamed proudly, 'I happen to be here with Mr. Rosey Rogers of the New York Yankees!' "

Biondo interrupted, "That's when I introduced myself. But they didn't want to shake hands."

Rosey continued his story. "So they kept shouting back and forth at each other, and the other girls went over and, sure enough, their husbands were there too. So then everybody was screaming and shouting and me and Frankie were standing there and these guys' dates were just sitting there and we started looking at each other . . ."

"These were real foxes, Sparky," Biondo said. "Real foxes. So I had this idea about how we could settle the whole thing. I told the guys that we should just trade dates and everything would be okay." He looked at Rosey and asked, "That's when he hit me, right?"

Rosey shook his index finger from side to side. "No. First he stood up and . . . he was a little guy, but real tough, you know; he had an earring in his nose. And he said to Frankie, 'What's the matter? My wife isn't good enough for you?' "

"So I tried to be very polite, see," Frankie explained. "I said. 'Oh, no, but she's married to you.' And then he said, 'You saying there's something wrong with her because she's married to me?' And then . . .' "

"And then I tried to play peacemaker. I told him, 'Listen, there's nothing wrong with your wife and there's nothing wrong with you, see?' "

"And I agreed with that," Biondo said, "I told him, 'That's right. Both Rosey and I have gone out with lots of women much worse than your wife.' "

"I think that's when he hit you," Rosey said.

Frankie looked a little confused. "Then when did her blouse get ripped off?"

"Oh, much later," Rosey told him. "That was after that big guy . . . Remember? The guy dressed like a German officer? That was just after he threw one of the husbands into that real old mirror behind the bar."

Frankie shook his head and sighed. "Was that before or after the jukebox got thrown through the window?"

"Way, way after. Right around the time that big wine rack crashed down."

"Gee," Biondo said in a bewildered voice, "I don't know where I was when all of this was going on."

It was some brawl. Rogers and Biondo both suffered some minor scrapes and scratches, but no serious injuries. And apparently nobody else was badly hurt either. But the place was wrecked. We didn't find out the most amazing part of the story for a few more hours, until a reporter from some local TV station in New Jersey called me. It turned out that these three men were business partners—they owned the largest marshmallow producing and packaging plant on the entire East Coast! Marshmallow makers! Just like the guy Billy had had a fight with. That's the absolute truth. If this book wasn't nonfiction I wouldn't dare write something like that, because I know most readers wouldn't believe it. But they owned the Soft Touch Marshmallow and Caramel Company, in Fort Lee, New Jersey.

After breakfast Chicken and I decided that Rosey and Biondo should go up to the Stadium and get a complete physical checkup. As we drove up to the Bronx I told them, "You guys are going to have to pay for the damage you did to the bar, you know. And I'm going to have to fine you a big number."

They agreed.

"The problem now," Chicken said, "is what are going to tell the papers?"

Nobody said anything for a few minutes, then Rosey snapped his fingers, "Let's make up some really good truth for them," he said. "Let's tell them that we were just having a quiet drink after the game, and we began talking about how nice the beat writers covering the team have been all season, and we decided it was time we did something for them, just to show them how much we appreciated their work. We wanted to do something that would get their bylines moved from way in the back of the paper right up to the front page where they belong. So we thought about it for a while"—his voice got louder with enthusiasm as he figured out the end of his story—"and then we went out and got in this fight just to help them with their careers!"

"That's right!" Biondo yelled, "that's great. And then we'll give every one of them an exclusive interview!"

I looked at Chicken questioningly. He shook his head. I shrugged. "They are gonna sell a lot of papers, you know."

AUGUST 23 ★

Rogers and Biondo were right. The beat writers certainly did get front-page bylines, and the story sold a lot of newspapers. We fined both of them $5,000. That wasn't the end of it, though. In Kangaroo Court after our fourth straight win, Judge Jackson really came down hard on them. Pointing out that they had tarnished the Yankee tradition by buying many drinks for these women, and got nothing out of it except some ugly bruises and a large bill for damages, he fined them an additional $1,000 and sentenced them to three days in jail. After the bailiff, Mattingly, reminded Jackson that he couldn't do that because the Yankees didn't own a jail, he reduced the sentence to six hours in the mood room watching Billy Idol music videos.

Rosey pleaded for jail.

The league also suspended Rogers and Biondo for two games, which happened to coincide with Davis's suspension. That just goes to prove the old baseball adage, you can never have too many big, slow, left-handed–hitting DHs.

Incidentally, during that session of the Kangaroo Court, prosecutor Winfield, in an unprecedented move, brought charges against the judge. It seems that during his broadcasts Reggie has begun referring to home runs as "reggies," as in, "Kelly had a long reggie his last time at bat," or "That was Mattingly's 18th reggie this season." The official charge was Excessive Reggieism, and circuit judge John, sitting in for Jackson, ruled that "Since bunts are never legally referred to as rizzutos, there is no reason to call blasts, clouts, dingers, tankers, circuits, 'taters, bangers, or bag-cleaners reggies, and therefore I'm fining you $15 for this offense and an additional $5 for any further illegal use of 'reggie.' "

Today was a travel day for us. A long travel day. The team flew down to Baltimore to start a three-game set tomorrow, and I think this trip proved how much the players have come to like Duke, or "The Duke," as they now refer to her. The trip to Baltimore normally takes a little more than an hour, but Duke booked us onto a commuter flight which made brief layovers in Philadelphia, Norfolk, and Washington, D.C. before finally landing in Baltimore. The flight took four hours, but enabled us to pile up almost 10,000 extra frequent flyer miles, including bonus miles. Now, if another traveling secretary had done this, the players wouldn't have hung him in effigy—they would have hung him in Baltimore. But since Duke had made the arrangements they took it good-naturedly. As Suarez said, "That Duke, she sure put the sex in the word traveling sexretary."

Duke has been accepted as a valuable member of the team. Before each game she runs around the clubhouse handing out her charts and answering any questions about them. Then during the game she sits upstairs and works with Bill Lee on pitch selection. And in the last few days she's made a point of giving me several "Strategic Models" suggested by the computer a few hours before each game. These are based on statistical analysis and provide information like the highest-percentage starting lineup against a certain pitcher, which teams are particularly vulnerable to what plays, which pitchers are particularly easy to bunt against in late innings. The thing that surprised me was how willingly Yogi accepted these suggestions. When I asked him how he was able to adapt so easily, he shrugged as if it was no big deal and told me, "It's like Casey used to say, 'You can push all the buttons you got, but if you don't have the right ones anyway your shirt looks very silly and you can't get into the best restaurants which is very important to a young man today, but if you have the right buttons all you have to do is touch them and people think you invented the button, which is also silly, but you can still get into the best restaurants and sometimes they pick up the check for you, which is not such a terrible thing, but the important thing to remember is that it's the buttons that keep the shirt closed anyway, and without them you might as well get a sweater,' and I've always believed Casey knew what he was talking about."

And I agree with Yogi.

Of course, The Duke is not even the most important woman in baseball today. That has to be Julia Nevez. As soon as she cleared waivers the Seattle Mariners signed her, and she makes her debut at the start of their nine-game home stand tonight. "We think it's a very good deal for us," Mariner manager Chad Johnson said. "It's pretty obvious she never got a real shot in Atlanta. But we're in the process of rebuilding the franchise here and we're going to give her a real chance to find out if she can play with the big boys. . . ." When a reporter asked Johnson if the Mariners had signed Nevez just to sell some tickets, he reacted angrily, "If giving a human being an opportunity to move forward in life is exploitation, then I guess you could say we're guilty of that. But I'll guarantee you one thing, when Julia Nevez takes the field at shortstop for the Seattle Mariners in the Kingdome tonight at 7:30, and becomes the first woman to play in the field in the history of major-league baseball, you'll find out whether we're taking advantage of her. Personally, I'd advise all baseball fans in the Pacific Northwest to come out to the ballpark during this nine-game home stand and decide for themselves whether she can play."

I still agree with Yogi.

AUGUST 26 ★

This season is beginning to get very interesting. Earlier tonight Suarez and Madden hit home runs and Eric Plunk hurled six strong innings in relief of McKeever as we beat the Orioles, 8–6, to complete a three-game sweep and move to within eight games of the league-leading Bosox. It was our first series sweep in Memorial Stadium since 1987. I wouldn't say we're exactly in the middle of the pennant race yet, but we're on the fringe. I don't know if the Red Sox and Blue Jays are looking over their shoulders yet, but I think they may be hearing spikesteps.

TJ, Cadaret, and Kline have all made several consecutive quality starts, and Parker has been pretty dependable since returning to the rotation. I still think Dotson can win in Yankee Stadium. The only problem is McKeever, who's been hit hard his last few outings; I've asked The Duke to consult with her IBM and find out if we should replace him in the rotation with Plunk. McDonald has looked good in his few spot starts and long-relief appearances, and the bullpen, with Tums "Mr. Cool" Taft, Big John Nicholson, Chuck Cary, and Frank Biondo has been dependable. Chicken and I sat around for maybe an hour yesterday thinking about Tsumi, but we never heard from him, so obviously he's still not 100 percent. Even without him, though, I still think we're "well armed" for the pennant wars.

Maybe I should have been a sportswriter.

The sad news in baseball today came out of Oakland, where the A's announced that Jose Canseco may have had a nervous breakdown. He was found at dawn this morning, driving in large circles in the parking lot of the Oakland Police Department, at speeds up to 110 mph. A police sergeant managed to contact Canseco on his car phone and talked him down. When they finally got him stopped, all he could do was mutter, incoherently, "They keep calling, day and night, night and day, the phone never stops ringing, it never stops, it never stops. Ever since I had that 900 number put into the house it never stops ringing and I have to tell them the same thing over and over and over and over . . ." The arresting officer described him as in a state of "total exhaustion," and said he kept repeating, "I tell them why I don't use steroids. I tell them why I was carrying that gun. I tell them what I had for breakfast, but it's still not enough, it's never enough. They keep calling and calling. The phone rings all night long, it rings all day long. I just can't take it anymore. Do you hear me? I can't take it anymore. Don't you understand? Doesn't anybody understand? That's why I have to speed. I have to get away from that ringing, I have to go so fast they can't call me." He grabbed the officer by his jacket lapels and pleaded, "Please, please, arrest me and take me to jail where it's quiet. Where the phone won't ring and ring, and I won't have to tell them why I was speeding and tell them why I don't use steroids and ringing all the time and they keep calling 1-900-WHY JOSE? and don't you see . . ."

Apparently they managed to get him calmed down, and everything was fine until they booked him and told him he was entitled to make one phone call.

Even in the middle of the pennant race I have to find time to run the store. Big John Nicholson's agent, an attorney named Tyler Lee, came in to talk to me about extending Nicholson's contract an additional year.

Tyler started going through the numbers. I was sort of aware that Nicholson was having a good year, but until Lee showed me the statistics, I hadn't realized he's been the second most effective long reliever in baseball history. "I know you're a busy man, Mr. Lyle," he said in a soft Southern drawl. "I just want to remind you that next year is John's walkaway season. He wants to give you every opportunity to retain his services, but if you don't want to begin working on it soon, he'll probably choose to remain unsigned and test the free-agent market. I think you know how much a proven long reliever is worth in today's market."

Maybe I did. The real truth is that I've never been very good with numbers. "Mr. Lee," I said politely, "this is all very interesting, but I'm afraid you've come to the wrong person. Chick—Mr. Stanley is our general manager, and he's in charge of contracts. I have nothing to do with contracts and I don't want anything to do with contracts. Nothing. I don't negotiate any contracts; I don't sign any contracts. Contracts are not my field. Nada. Nothing. When it comes to contracts, zero. So?"

"I understand," he said calmly, "but I have just one question."

"What's that?"

"Who negotiates Mr. Stanley's contract?"

I sat there in silence for a few seconds, hearing that question bouncing around my mind, then I looked at Lee and thought how much I'd like to have him at bat with two strikes on him and throw him a great slider in the dirt. Finally, I said, "That's a good question. I'll have to get back to you on that one."

Incidentally, a nice thing happened right after the Orioles game. The game was broadcast to the Dominican on the Armed Forces Network, and when Suarez hit his home run his pregnant wife got so excited she went into labor. He left right after the game to fly home to be with her and their first baby. Since tomorrow's an off day, Felipe can get home and still meet the team in Kansas City in time for Friday night's game.

AUGUST 28 ★

I've just finished watching the CBS Movie of the Week, *Mr. Perfect: The Story of Tommy McKeever*. Ironically, it was shown the same day that Yogi put McKeever in the bullpen to "look for his good stuff." Of course, there are some people who think McKeever doesn't have "good stuff," that now that the other teams have seen him once, they're adjusting to his "regular stuff," and hitting him hard. In the big leagues a pitcher who doesn't have "good stuff" can't get by with "nothing," so I think we're going to find out pretty quickly how good McKeever's stuff really is.

I've asked Bill Lee to start working with him on a new pitch, maybe a hard slider. And if that doesn't work, maybe McKeever should think about learning how to load up the ball. For some pitchers, the substance they put on the ball, like K-Y Jelly, is their good stuff. Personally, although I never did it, I never saw anything wrong with putting something on the ball or scratching its cover. Batters scratch themselves; why shouldn't pitchers scratch baseballs?

The movie was very well done. I have to admit that before I saw it I didn't know that Tommy McKeever had actually started life as a poor black kid with one leg, growing up in a ramshackle sharecropper's hut just outside the small town of No Fork, Georgia. The people in this town were so poor they could only afford one road, no forks. But this brave little kid had a big dream, and that was to play in the big leagues. And he fought to make that dream come true, and some-where, during those years of long bus rides down the dusty roads of minor-league baseball, he became white and grew another leg and married Lindsay Wagner, a nurse who'd served in Vietnam and still suffered from the case of bulimia she'd caught there. Unfortunately, she'd lost her memory, and because Tommy was only making a minor leaguer's salary they couldn't afford to have it replaced, so she'd left him. But miraculously, he'd made it to the big leagues the same day his 101-year-old grandmother, a former slave, was dying from "a bad case of too much life." The last thing she heard before closing her eyes forever was her Tommy pitching his perfect game. And after the game Lindsay Wagner, who'd heard the game on the radio and been shocked into remembering him, raced to the ballpark and met him outside with her brand new memory.

Maybe I'm exaggerating a little. But the movie had almost nothing to do with real life. The truth is, I didn't like the way Raymond Burr played me.

I certainly hope Judge Reggie Jackson didn't see the film. Because if he did, we're going to find out if a Kangaroo Court can impose the death penalty.

AUGUST 30 ★

"I'm a manager, not a programmer—and I'm not about to let any machine take the man out of managing!" With that declaration, Lou Piniella finished his suspension and returned to the dugout today.

Yogi did an excellent job filling in for Lou. As usual, Yogi was very lucky, catching the team just as it got hot. We won eight of the ten games he managed. During Yogi's last few games he was personally communicating with The Duke from the dugout. She sat up in my box, or, when we were away, in the scout's box, feeding the pitch-by-pitch progress of the game into her computer. The computer would then decide which of the available options was mathematically the most desirable in a given situation: It told Yogi when to sacrifice, when to hit and run, when to try to steal a base, when to replace a pitcher or to pinch-hit. It even advised him which player was the most likely to be successful at that point in the game. Yogi followed The

Duke's advice in almost every instance. The result was eight out of ten.

Lou didn't want anything to do with The Duke's system. Before his first game back I told him all about her new "Strategy Options Program." He started screaming about machines taking the "human" out of "humanity," and the "man" out of "managing."

When he said that, I reminded him that when you take the "man" out of "managing" you're left with "aging," and that one of the things that happens to some people when they age is that they become inflexible—they refuse to accept new ideas, and progress passes them by. "In this case, Lou," I said, "I think you're aging."

I finally convinced him to read The Duke's pregame analysis, but he absolutely refused to take advice from her during the game. Chicken tried to talk to him about it too, but he was really adamant. "No machine's going to tell me what to do," he said, "and she can put that in her program and print it."

We lost to the Indians, 3–1. Kelly and Sax were both thrown out stealing, we failed to sacrifice what would have been, at the time, the tying run into scoring position, two pinch-hitters both failed to get the ball out of the infield, and Biondo gave up the third run in relief in the eighth inning. Afterward Lou spent twenty minutes in the frustration room banging away at the bag. The only good news is that both Boston and Toronto lost, so we stayed eight games out.

I think The Duke could have used some time in the frustration room too. When she came into my office after Sundberg had struck out to end the game, her face was a very attractive blush red with anger. "He did everything against the system," she fumed. "Doesn't he understand? The computer isn't telling him what to do, it's just answering the questions he hasn't asked yet?"

"Lou is Lou," I said.

She looked at me coldly. It was a look I'd never seen on her face before. "Yes, he is," she agreed, "and maybe you'd better start thinking about the fact that Lou is the first sound of the word 'lose.'" Then she spun around and marched out the door.

Human, humanity. Man, manager. Lou, lose. The real problem with all of this is that when I tell the whole story in my book, nobody's going to believe it actually happened this way.

On top of everything else, I had a phone call this morning from Dan Hunter of United American Holding Company. It took me a minute to remember who he was; then I realized he was the man who'd given me Yankee Corp. Since I hadn't heard from him all season, I assumed he was calling to congratulate me on how well we were playing. And at first, that's exactly what it sounded like. "You've been doing a splendid job, Mr. Lyle . . ." he began.

"Thank you, Dan," I said, "it took us a little while to put it together, but . . ."

". . . until now," he finished.

"Excuse me?"

"Mr. Lyle," he explained, "I'd like to give you a brief education about the world of big business: Buy low, sell high. Would you like me to repeat that?"

"No, that's okay," I said. "I've got it. Buy low, sell high. Makes sense to me."

"Good. I'm glad we understand each other. Now, we sold Yankee Corp. to you at what we considered to be a very fair price. Precisely nothing."

"That was pretty fair," I agreed.

He ignored me. "Naturally, we expected some appreciation in the value of the principal asset, but lately . . . I must admit I'm not much of a sporting fan . . . but lately the company seems to be winning matches. Is that a fair appraisal of the situation?"

"We've started playing well, if that's what you mean. What's this all about?"

"Mr. Lyle, we did not give you the business to improve it. You were not supposed to win baseball games."

I banged the receiver on the desk, figuring that there must be a problem with the line. "Sorry," I said. "I thought you said we weren't supposed to win games."

"That's precisely what I said. You see, we bought Yankee Corp. at what we considered to be a fair price, considering the fact that attendance has been declining, leisure-time options are being expanded, and, perhaps most important, due primarily to the actions of your predecessor, enthusiasm surrounding the corporation has been substantially reduced. All of which affects the value of a concern. Now, with your limited business background, we had a reasonable expectation that you would be able to maintain that low standard. In other words, we expected you to keep up the bad work." His voice dropped into an extremely serious tone. "Mr. Lyle, I'm afraid you're letting us down."

I was stunned. Again. "Let me get this straight. Are you saying you really didn't want Yankee Corp.—the Yankees to win this year?"

"Mr. Lyle, I understand that you're not particularly sophisticated in matters relating to business, so let me try to make this as clear as possible. Our experts in this field warned us that success on the playing field would make the principal asset of the corporation more valuable, and since it is our intention to repurchase the corporation under the terms of our agreement, it's in everyone's best interest to keep that value as low as possible. If our objective had been to increase the value of the asset by succeeding, we would have hired an expert and done that. Instead, we hired you. The truth is that you were specifically selected primarily for your complete lack of experience in the management area."

I was beginning to understand what this whole thing was all about. I was never supposed to turn the organization around. I was supposed to make sure the corp—the Yankees—continued losing, so its value would be less, so they could buy it back from me at the lowest possible price. "Well," I said, "this is . . . this is some surprise."

"No, Mr. Lyle, this is business."

"Let me ask you something. If the corporation becomes more valuable, when you exercise your option you'll have to pay me more money, right?"

"So far."

"So that means if the team wins, I make more money?"

"Technically, that's correct. But any accountant worth his bottom line would tell you that there are certain situations in which the more money you earn the less money you make. I, personally, have known people who have earned a fortune yet can't afford to have their Ferraris properly serviced. And this is one of those situations. Through skillful use of capital gains taxes, loss equity, investment credits, simple shelters, and what we in the world of high finance often refer to as 'Loco wacko,' which means, basically, 'What the law doesn't yet know it allows,' you're in a position to make a lot more money by earning substantially less."

"So what you're saying is that it's going to cost me money if the team wins and becomes more valuable?"

"I didn't make the tax laws, Mr. Lyle, I just take advantage of them. Let me put it this way: This is the United States of America. If Yankee Corp. lost every match, if you didn't sell one ticket, you could become a very wealthy man."

"But . . . but what if I didn't care about the money? What if I just thought that winning mattered? You know, just because I wanted to win?"

He laughed in staccato bursts, sounding a lot like a string of firecrackers exploding. "They did warn me that you had a sense of humor," he said between bursts. "But I must admit, I did doubt them." His laughter finally wound down, like a battery-operated toy running out of power. "Mr. Lyle, you're a reasonably intelligent man. So I think you'll understand me when I tell you that winning is an abstract principle. What is winning, really? Take World War II, for instance. I suspect there are some people who would still argue that Japan and Germany lost that war, yet United American is presently involved in a limited partnership with the Murashimi Group of Tokyo in which we're negotiating to purchase the White House mortgage. Would it still be accurate to claim that Japan lost the war if a Japanese corporation held the mortgage on the White House? Certainly not.

"Now, in your case does winning mean scoring more points than the other boys? Or does it mean maximizing your investment to provide lifetime security? I think the problem is that you still hold to that long discredited theory that baseball is a game rather than a business. Potentially a very lucrative business, I hasten to add. You would do well to read Peter Ueberroth's recently published revised autobiography, *Baseball Was My Business.* And after that, if you're still interested in playing games, try the stock market. Now I'm terribly sorry, but I must go. . . ."

He said something that sounded slightly threatening, like, "Our agents will be watching your matches with great interest," then hung up. I was so surprised, so angry, so frustrated about the call that, for the first time all season, I went to the mood room to try to relax. I put on an environmentally soothing video titled, *Walking the Winter Woods,* accompanied by a cassette of the Philadelphia Symphony Orchestra conducted by Eugene Ormandy performing Beethoven's "Broken Concerto," but it didn't help at all. So finally I stood up and punched out the video machine. That helped. Then I locked myself in the flotation tank for an hour, where no one could hear me, and I started screaming.

After we'd lost the game to the Indians I got a fax from Hunter. "Congratulations," it read, "I knew you were a winner."

SEPTEMBER 2 ★

I've always thought a baseball season is a lot like great sex: It starts out slowly and gently, as if it might last forever. Positions change frequently, and those involved who expected to be on top often find themselves on the bottom, as they feel each other out, probing for an opening. The pace gradually quickens; they struggle to be on top, changing positions less frequently, until they find the rhythm of the season, which moves faster and faster, as one game goes into another and another and another. Then, nearing the end, the tension begins to grow and it swells and the pressure builds and builds. The days get longer and longer and it seems like the season will never end until suddenly . . . the climax: The pennant race!

There is absolutely nothing in sports like a great pennant race. We're making our move on the league leaders, six and a half games out and closing. There's a feeling in the clubhouse, everywhere in the organization, that we can win this thing—that we're going to win this thing. I think the players are beginning to appreciate what it means to be a winner in New York City: "Plug" told me he hadn't paid for a restaurant meal in so long he was beginning to think he was a politician. Rosey Rogers's ex-girlfriend called, he told me happily, to ask if he had one extra ticket for Sunday's game against Toronto. "And," he added, "she said that in my honor she was going to wear my favorite kind of lingerie to the game." He paused, smiled broadly, then winked and yelled, "NONE!" And Raoul Rojas told me that three months ago nobody had ever heard of him, and now people were offering him $5 for his autograph.

Chicken and I spent the last few days solidifying the roster for the stretch run. Yesterday, September 1st, the roster limit officially expanded to forty players and we immediately made some moves. We started by recalling several minor leaguers, including legitimate prospects like Bernie Williams, Kevin Maas, Chuck Calandros—who had a great year at Albany—and Jesse Reichler, an infielder with great hands, as well as pitchers Kevin Mmahat, Rod Friedperson, and C. Ron Riley. The "C" stands for curveball. Several of these kids'll be playing in the big leagues next year, and might be ready to help us right now. But we also purchased the contracts of several players who'd spent five years or more in the bushes and are never going to make it. They're not prospects; they're no longer even suspects. They just fill out some minor-league rosters. But a long time ago I promised myself that if I were ever in a position to do something about it, I was going to reward these players for their dedication, their sacrifices, and their love of the game of baseball. I vowed that I would bring them up to the big leagues and get them into at least one game so they could earn a place in the *Encyclopedia of Baseball.* So at the end of their careers, when they left the game with nothing more than some old spikes, a well-worn glove, and a lot of memories, they would have something to point to that proved they'd made it to the big show. Maybe just for one game, one at bat, one inning, but they'd made it. So I brought up Georgie Kaufman, Tom Dyja, Lyn Arany, Juan Riveria, and Andy Smith.

I knew how grateful they'd be. In fact, when Smith got here from Columbus, he came right into my office and said, "Now that I've made the big leagues I'd like to renegotiate my contract."

The moves made The Duke very unhappy. "I don't have any of their records," she yelled at me. "I don't know any of their tendencies. How am I supposed to deal with people who have no statistics?"

Then, late yesterday afternoon, Chicken traded Raoul Rojas and Mad Man Madden to Houston for veteran starting pitcher Mike Sanderson. We hated to give up on a 22-year-old prospect like Rojas, but my baseball committee agreed that we needed another dependable pitcher if we wanted to win this thing. The only reason Sanderson was available for a prospect and an aging veteran is that he hasn't had a good season at all, winning only 5 of 15 decisions, and his contract expires at the end of this year. But three years ago he was 12–1 at the All-Star break, and if we can correct the flaw that Bill Lee found in his delivery he can win the three or four games that make the difference in the stretch. Rojas was very disappointed when Lou broke the news to him. With tears in his eyes, he asked Lou, "How much you think my autograph be worth in Houston?" Madden, on the other hand, was thrilled at the deal. He told reporters, "I think the record I've compiled during my career in pinstripes speaks for itself. I leave New York as one of the most successful players in Yankee history. I mean, how many players have hit .500 over their entire Yankee career? Of course, the fact that I only had two at bats as a Yankee may prevent them from honoring me with a plaque on the Wall of Fame, but years from now, when I look back on my weeks here, I'll know I sat on the same bench as Babe Ruth, Lou Gehrig, and Hector Lopez.

"The fact is, though, I never understood why they got me in the first place, I never understood what my role was supposed to be while I was here, and I don't understand why they got rid of me. But other than that, I enjoyed sitting for Lou Piniella."

So, with the addition of Sanderson and the players we've recalled and purchased, and with Sundberg going back on the 10-day disabled list with frayed nerves, our roster now stands at thirty-two players.

I think. We started with twenty-four players on the active roster. We brought up twelve; that's thirty-six. We traded two; that's thirty-four. We got one back; that's thirty-five. We're taking Tsumi off the disabled list; that's thirty-six. But we're putting Sundberg on the DL; that's thirty-five. That's correct. We now have thirty-five players on our roster.

That's not right. Calandros isn't supposed to report until spring training, and Kaufman has a bad ankle, so, although we brought him up to get him into one game, he probably won't be able to play. That means we've got exactly thirty-three players on the roster, give or take a player. As I've admitted, I've never been very good at statistics. But we're definitely ready for the stretch run.

SEPTEMBER 4 ★

Six games out. Four behind second-place Toronto. We beat the Blue Jays this afternoon, 4–3, on Keith Reich's sacrifice fly in the bottom of the ninth. Mr. Cool got the win. Mattingly and Sax each had three hits. And, to the amazement of every one of the 39,675 people in the stands, as well as Piniella and his entire coaching staff, with one out in the ninth Andy Smith, making his big-league debut as a pinch-runner for Alvaro Espinoza, suddenly took off from second base and stole third without a throw. That allowed him to score the winning run on Reich's fly ball. It also cost him $100 in the Kangaroo Court.

The only problem I faced today was that I was informed that we can't get liability insurance on the bullpen motorcycle, meaning that if Taft has an accident, we're totally responsible. For example, if he should lose control and drive into section 38, some fan could end up owning several acres of left field. I've asked Chicken to speak to Tums about either driving a little slower or trading in the bike for something a little safer. Like a station wagon. "Tell him he can be Mr. Comfortable," I suggested to Chicken.

We had the final meeting of the season of the Yankee Advisory Committee at breakfast this morning. I personally thanked each member of the panel for his or her time and gave each of them an assortment of Yankee souvenirs, including wristbands and beautiful facsimile signed baseballs, and promised all of them that they could keep their seats for the Playoffs and Series.

Then each of them gave their final report. Joe Maresca, Sr. suggested that ushers wear numbers so fans could report them for extorting money for wiping off clean seats with dirty dust mitts. "I finally figured out what Yankee Stadium ushers do in their spare time," he revealed. "They're exactly the same people who extort money from drivers by insisting on wiping the clean windshields of their cars with dirty water and oily rags. Yankee Stadium is where they do their basic training."

Maresca also wanted us to add a "short persons section" to our special seating plans so that a person under 5'5" would not have to sit behind somebody 6'3" and miss the entire game "except when the big ape went to the refreshment stand or bathroom."

Geri Simon interrupted and told him to forget about short people. "It's the senior citizens you should be concerned with." She wanted us to establish a special senior citizens section so that older fans could sit together safely and "reminisce about how wonderful it used to be to be able to come to the ballpark and feel safe enough not to have to sit with a bunch of old people and reminisce about how wonderful it used to be to be able to come to the ballpark and feel safe enough not to have to sit with a bunch of old people and reminisce . . ."

She might have gone on for a long time if Joe Maresca hadn't offered a compromise, suggesting, "How about a special section just for short senior citizens?"

Geri Simon had to leave before we were finished, she explained, because she'd just received a table from Macy's "that I waited six months for. And when it finally came, wouldn't you know it, there was a bad scratch on one of the legs. This I don't pay that kind of money for. What am I? A fool? But that's why I shop at Macy's, they're very good about this type of situation. So I called them up and the man from Macy's is coming to my house at noon, I mean, who knows if he's really going to show up. But my sister Vera is home alone and I want to be there." Before she left she had several pretty good ideas, none of which involved scratched table legs. She wanted us to put up suggestion boxes around the ballpark and reward people who made suggestions that we adopted with free tickets. "I'm telling you, somebody would have suggested suggestion boxes a long time ago, but how could they when you don't have any suggestion boxes for them to put the suggestion in."

Joe Maresca looked at his watch and asked, "Isn't it about time for that Macy's man to arrive?"

Geri Simon ignored him, and suggested that we set up a Yankee Complaint Line, so that people who have had a bad experience at the ballpark or have had trouble getting tickets could call and complain. "Listen to me, please. If you do this, you have to have more than one or two lines. Because I worked for a company who did this and they only had one line, so by the time people got through, they spent most of their time complaining that they couldn't get through to the complaint line." Ms. Simon offered to come to work for the Yankees as Complaint Line Supervisor, claiming that, "I've lived in New York for so long that, when it comes to complaining, I'm the expert."

"You know, that's not such a bad idea," Maresca agreed. That was the first thing the two of them had agreed upon all season. "You could even make it a 900-number," he suggested, "I know lots of Yankee fans who would be glad to pay to have somebody to complain to. You'll get so many complaints that you could take the money and go out and buy yourself a decent starting pitcher. Complaints about the ushers alone could buy you a decent reliever."

Lou DiGiamo announced that he had lost twenty-eight pounds since being named to the Yankee Fans Advisory Committee and going on the Tommy Lasorda diet. "No fats, no starches, no proteins, but most of all, no food," he explained. He wanted us to sell Weight Watchers products at the ballpark. "And if you don't want to do that," he continued, "sell something you call 'Dieter's Delight,' or whatever you want. All you have to do is give people the same foods they can buy at other stands, but smaller portions. You can even charge a preparation premium for them. It's the perfect marketing situation. You can actually charge people more money for giving them less and make them happy by doing it."

I looked at Chicken. I think at that moment both of us realized we were in the presence of a genius.

Alex Langsam had celebrated his thirteenth birthday in August, he told us, and he wanted to have a big party at Yankee Stadium. That's when he discovered we didn't have a party room. "You should have one," he said, "and maybe you could even get players to stop in, and then everybody at the party could watch the ballgame. I really wanted to have my bar mitzvah here"—he frowned—"but my parents made me have it at the temple."

Alex also thought we should take a photograph of every name that appears on the message board, so that people and organizations would have evidence that their name was up in lights at Yankee Stadium. This is some clever kid. He also suggested that we make videocassette copies of the roving camera shots that we show on the scoreboard between innings—the pictures of people waving to the camera so that they can see themselves waving to the camera—then make them available to the fans for a few dollars. "Then you can take that money," he finished, "and go out and buy the team some pitching."

I made a note to make sure I sent him an extra wristband.

Joan Silver made a similar suggestion. She wanted us to use the scoreboard to run a video dating service, showing the available person and giving his or her vital statistics. "Just like you give the ballplayer's statistics."

She also wanted us to run personal ads on the scorecard. "All my friends think it's a great idea," she said. "See, that way fans with the same interests could meet each other at the ballpark. You know, the ads could be like SMHF, that means, single Met-hating female, desires to meet YF, that's Yankee fan, with the grace of DiMaggio, the sense of humor of Sparky"—she looked at me and I smiled—"the dependability of Richardson, and the loyalty of Billy, for future ballgames. Objective: A Hall of Fame family. See Joan, section 104, row B, seat 7."

I wondered if I could take away Joan's wristband.

I went back to my office after the meeting and heard on the radio that the Mariners have given Julia Nevez her unconditional release. In nine games with Seattle, she batted nine times, with no hits, one walk, and six strikeouts. "We feel we gave her every opportunity to show that she can play with the boys," Mariner manager Chad Johnson said, "and she was simply unable to take advantage of that. But we were certainly pleased to have had her with us and wish her well in the future."

After getting her release, Nevez announced that she had agreed to become the first major leaguer to pose for a *Playboy* centerfold. Nettles stopped by the office to suggest that maybe we should sign her. "You know," he said, "every team can use a good centerfolder."

SEPTEMBER 7 ★

Some days are good days, some days are bad days, and then there are some days like today, days that are so bad that they make the regular bad days seem like good days. The best thing I can say about today is that in a few hours it'll be yesterday. It started first thing this morning when we received an emergency notification from Bio-Pitch Inc. informing us that Tommy John's arm was being recalled for repairs. I couldn't quite understand the technical jargon in the notice, but I think it said that one of the fluids used to lubricate his new arm may contain traces of asbestos and has to be replaced immediately. If I understand this correctly, TJ's arm has become a toxic waste dump and has to be cleaned up. "Patients are advised to avoid putting severe strain on their devices until this procedure can be completed," the notice warned, meaning that TJ had to miss his regularly scheduled turn while his arm is in the shop for repairs.

Then, in the early afternoon, The Duke came into my office crying hysterically. "Somebody's gummed up the works in my computer," she managed to blurt out between tears.

I handed her a handkerchief. "Blow your nose," I ordered. "Now, what do you mean?"

"I told you," she said. "Somebody put gum in my hard drive."

Gum? In her hard drive? That was difficult to believe. Obviously it was done intentionally. Gum doesn't just fall into somebody's hard drive. The implications are frightening: Somebody is trying to sabotage our computer system! "Is everything gone?" I asked. If the computer had swallowed her data, our pennant chances were just about gone.

She shook her head as she blew her nose. "No," she eeked out between sobs, "I've got everything backed up on floppy disks. I've ordered a new hard drive, but it'll take me a few days to copy everything."

After everything else that has happened this season, I thought, this was the one thing I never expected: Our IBM was going on the disabled list.

When The Duke had finally caught her breath, she looked up at me with the most innocent eyes and asked, "Why, why would anybody want to do that to us? To me?"

"I don't know," I said, shaking my head. "I just don't know," But as I sat there, mentally listing the people who had the most to gain by us losing the pennant, it became clear that there were several candidates—including every player on every other team in the American League East. "Duker," I asked softly, "I'm sorry, but I have to ask you an important question. You have any idea what kind of gum it was?"

She exhaled. "I do. It was my favorite when I was growing up." Somehow I knew what her answer was going to be even before she said it. "It was Juicy Fruit."

Once again, I felt that chill doing laps up and down my spine.

And then finally, later in the day, we played the game. Oh, the game. There are a few games in every season that never stop hurting. Games that when you look back on them, even many years later, cause your shoulders to tense up and your mouth to go dry. Games like tonight. A lot of games are "if" games: If so-and-so had just advanced the runner, if that pitch had been called a strike, if that ball had been an inch higher it would have gone out—and tonight we played the "if" game of the season.

Piniella decided to start McKeever against the Royals in TJ's place. Because the IBM was on the DL, Lou just played a hunch. I think he'd like to have that hunch back. Kansas City jumped on "Mr. Not-So-Perfect" for four runs in the first inning before Lou could get him out of there. Nicholson, Biondo, and McDonald then shut them down completely, and we knocked around Gubicza and relievers Tio Lemke and Shane Ehrman for seven runs. We would have scored even more runs if Kelly's drive down the line with Geren and Espinoza in scoring position in the seventh inning hadn't landed foul by about an inch, and if Sax hadn't been thrown out stealing the pitch before

Mattingly launched number 22, but I still figured a three-run lead going into the ninth with Taft on the mound was going to be enough.

After Mr. Cool retired the first two batters, he walked Kevin Seitzer on a 3–2 pitch that was close enough to be called either way. Then Jim Eisenreich, trying to hold up his swing, hit an "excuse me" dribbler between the mound and third base that neither Taft nor Reich could field. That brought Danny Tartabull to bat. Piniella went out to the mound to remind Taft to keep it away from Tartabull, but make sure he got ahead of him in the count. "Throw strikes," he told him, "but don't give him anything good to hit."

Taft's first pitch was low and inside and Tartabull yanked it into the upper deck in right field to tie the score.

It gets worse. Taft was obviously shaken up. He accidentally hit Bo Jackson with his next pitch—it had to be an accident because no sane pitcher would intentionally throw a baseball at Bo Jackson. That was enough for Lou. He pulled Taft and brought in Tsumi. This was Hanko's first appearance in almost two months. He got ahead of Walt Tice 0–2, then threw him an absolutely beautiful curveball. The kind of pitch that should be framed and hung in the Museum of Modern Baseball. Tice was bailing out and the ball hit his bat and blooped over Mattingly's head into short right field. By the time Winfield chased it down, Jackson was rounding third base. He was coming all the way. Dave threw a rocket toward home plate—it would have easily nailed Jackson—but the throw hit one of the pigeons that lives in the ballpark eaves, and went off line. The pigeon dropped straight down onto the mound, and the ball landed in foul territory behind third base. Jackson and Tice scored. We went out one-two-three in the bottom of the ninth, losing a game we should have won, a game we couldn't afford to lose, 9–7.

The Duke was really upset. "It's all my fault," she cried. "I should have been on line. I could have made a difference."

I laid a comforting hand on her shoulder, and said sympathetically, "Listen, kid, when you've been around the game as long as I have, you know that there are just gonna be days like today."

As her eyes welled with tears, she said softly, "Not too often, I hope."

SEPTEMBER 10 ★

The Duke got her hard drive working last night, but we didn't need it as we moved to within five games of the Red Sox by beating Cleveland 9–2. Toronto also won, so they're only half a game back. We're closing in on the leaders, and I think some of our players are beginning to feel the pressure. And there's no way of predicting how a player who hasn't been through a pennant race before will react to the pressure. Some people can't sleep; others lose their appetite. I knew a pitcher who bit his fingernails so far down that he couldn't properly grip the ball and lost the movement on his fastball. Some players blossom, like Reggie; other players wilt. And sometimes, when a blossomer meets a wilter under the pressure, there's an explosion.

Biondo and Suarez got into a fight in the locker room before the game tonight. Fortunately McDonald was able to separate them before anybody got hurt. I know how dangerous fights can be at this point in the season—I was with the Yankees in 1974 when Bobby Murcer got hurt breaking up a fight between Rick Dempsey and Bill Sudakis and missed the last few games of the season, maybe costing us the pennant.

Biondo started it. The truth is that sometimes he doesn't really seem to understand what he's doing. All season long he's been watching Mattingly and Taft give people hotfoots, so he decided he was going to play a practical joke—he was going to give Suarez a coldfoot. It probably wouldn't have escalated into such a big deal if he hadn't picked on Suarez, but Felipe has been struggling badly at bat and he's very sensitive to the whispers that he's folding under pressure like a paper bag in a monsoon.

Biondo dumped half a tray of ice cubes in Suarez's spikes while Felipe was in the trainer's room getting a rubdown. When Suarez put on his shoes, his feet nearly froze. He went tearing around the clubhouse until he found the empty ice tray in Biondo's locker. "Hey," Biondo told him, "cool down, man, I was just kidding." Things might have ended right there if Biondo hadn't added, "Besides, what's the big deal? Haven't you ever heard of somebody getting cold feet before a big game?" That's when Felipe went after him.

In Kangaroo Court after the game, Judge Jackson refused to fine Biondo, pointing out that there are laws to protect juvenile offenders. "And Frankie is the most juvenile person we have on this team."

As if that wasn't enough, about an hour before game time, Piniella burst into my office screaming. "That's it, I've had it, Lee's got to go, he's finished."

"Calm down, Lou," I said. "What are you talking about?"

"I didn't mind the chanting," he said. "You know that. And I didn't mind the vitamins and the health. I didn't say a word about the exorcism, and . . . and I thought it was a little crazy, but I didn't even say a word about the seance. But this . . . this . . ." He looked at me and asked calmly, "You were a pitcher, Sparky. You ever hear of National Pitchers' Day?"

That was when I found out that Lee had declared today a pitcher's holiday. It had something to do with that Leeism cult he started in spring training. He's been trying to convince the staff all season that, "The game begins and ends with the pitcher; the pitcher is the giver of the pitch. Without the pitcher, there is no game." Until this moment, I didn't believe anybody took it seriously. Apparently they do, because several pitchers told Piniella they couldn't pitch tonight.

I went right down to the locker room to talk to Lee. "What do you mean they're taking the game off?"

"Nobody works holidays," he explained. "Mailpersons don't deliver on Easter, meterpeople don't give tickets on Christmas, so pitchers don't pitch on Pitchers' Day. It's that simple."

"It's also crazy," I pointed out. "Pitchers' Day is not a legal holiday anywhere in the United States, and it's also completely illegal under the Basic Agreement and the standard player's contract."

"Look," Bill admitted, "I never expected it to get to this point. It started as sort of a joke, a way of getting everybody rowing in the same direction. I wanted to create an improved sense of self-awareness, which is proven to help build self-confidence. I wanted them to realize how special they were to have developed the skills necessary to perform at this level of competition. I know the concept seems to be an extension of reality into less than factual areas, but if you can go along with it for one day, I believe it will help build a camaraderie and confidence that will sustain us down the stretch."

"We are down the stretch," I reminded him. But I could see his point. Fortunately, Sanderson happened to walk into the clubhouse at that very minute. I grabbed him and asked urgently, "Are you a Leeist?"

He took a step backwards, then eyed me warily, as if I might be threatening him. "What do you mean?"

"I mean, do you believe in Leeism?"

"Nah," he said, "I'm a Buddhist."

"Great," I told him. "You're starting today."

He looked very surprised. "How come you want to start a Buddhist today?" I explained the situation to him, then sold the idea to Piniella. Convincing Lou to go along was about as easy as selling surfboards to Eskimos, but eventually he agreed. This has been a rough year for Lou, but he's done a terrific job. I wonder where we'd be without him.

Then Sanderson made us all look very smart by pitching his best game in several seasons, beating the Twins, 6–4, on a neat nine-hitter. He did the things he needs to do to win; he threw strikes, he kept the ball in the Stadium, and he gave up fewer runs than we scored. Sax led the offense with three RBIs and two stolen bases, his 44th and 45th of the season. The only bad news was that once again Suarez went hitless in three at bats. After striking out for the second time he went back to the dugout and took a big swing at the back wall, shattering his bat and sending everybody scattering. The only person who didn't move was batting instructor Jon Boswell, who just looked up at him and nodded approvingly. "Now that was a nice level swing."

"Maybe," Suarez agreed. "But that's only 'cause there's no such thing as curvewalls."

Both the Red Sox and Blue Jays also won, so we're still five out. We leave tomorrow morning on our last road trip of the season, three games in Milwaukee and three in Chicago. When we come home for the final run, we'll know if we're contenders or pretenders.

On the late news after the game, sportscaster Jerry Girard announced that the Phillies had signed Julia Nevez. Phillies GM Joe McShane said that "In this great city, the cradle of democracy, we believe in giving every person, regardless of race, creed, color, or sex, an equal opportunity to play the most American of all sports. So it is indeed fitting that the fans who have made this great city what it is today will finally have an opportunity to see this great American sports pioneer in action. The principal beneficiary of this signing is the Phillies fan." Coincidentally, the Phillies, who were mathematically eliminated from the pennant race two days ago, have just begun their longest home stand of the season.

SEPTEMBER 15 ★

It finally happened. I was working alone in my office this evening, waiting for our game to start in Milwaukee, going over the long list of manufacturers who have applied for a license to market products under our new "Yankee" logo. When we set up the licensing department earlier this season we decided to limit the products to be marketed under our logo to those things that have some relationship to athletics and are of provably high quality. Among the items I approved before it happened were biodegradable disposable diapers—players have children, too—typewriter ribbons, "Yankee" blue jeans, gum, and cereal.

As I was studying a proposal from General Motors to put out a special edition "Yankee" Pontiac Grand Prix, I thought I heard a noise in the outer office. "Who's there?" I yelled. No answer. I got up and opened the door. The office was empty. So I went back to work. A few minutes later, I heard the same rustling sound. Again I got up, and walked as quietly as possible to the door. And just as I put my hand on the doorknob, the door was suddenly pushed open from the outside. There he was, just standing there, staring at me. "Boss," I said. "What a nice surprise. Where you been?"

Then I noticed he wasn't alone. Standing behind him, partially hidden in the shadows, were three very large men. Each of them was wearing sunglasses, and that made me very nervous. I knew from a lifetime of watching bad movies that people who wear sunglasses in dark rooms are never up to anything good. I tried to hide my anxiety with a little joke. "Hey," I said to them, "I like your 'Mr. Cool' imitation."

I never said it was a good joke. The Boss ordered his boys into the office. "Secure the telephones," he ordered. "Nothing goes in or out." Then he looked at me and smiled just a bit triumphantly. "It's nice to see you again, Spark. Why don't we go back into the office and have a chat."

"I was just going to suggest that." I turned around and went to my desk, trying to figure out what this was all about.

The Boss took two steps inside the office and stopped. He looked around approvingly. "You have excellent taste," he said. "You haven't changed a thing."

"Well, you know, I've been very busy." One of his men came around the desk and wordlessly yanked the telephone line out of the wall. "So," I asked as casually as I could, "what brings you around tonight?" I snapped my fingers. "Tickets, right?"

"Keep quiet," he snapped. He paused to straighten out the photograph of Billy hanging on the wall. I thought I heard him whisper something like "Hi, kid." Then he glanced at me. "I've been around all season," he began. "I've been watching you. You haven't done too badly. Perhaps you stayed with your manager a little too long; but overall, not bad, not bad at all."

"What is this?" I finally asked. "What are you doing here?"

"This?" He laughed, a laugh that came from deep in his throat, and seemed to have just a hint of hysteria around the edges. "Have you ever heard of a hostile takeover? Why, this is the ultimate hostile takeover." Then he laughed once again.

I'd been expecting something like this for a long, long time. The mascot mugging, the computer sabotage, the dozens of smaller incidents throughout the season that added up to . . . to this moment. "What do you expect me to do?"

He was staring at a photograph of Reggie. He whispered something that sounded like, "We really had some times, didn't we," but I couldn't be sure. Then he said loudly, "You? You are going to sign over the controlling interest in this organization to me. You didn't really think I was just going to be dragged away from all this, did you? The Boss? Not very likely."

"And if I don't?"

"You will, you will." He signaled to one of his men, who produced a briefcase and laid it on my desk. The Boss twirled the numbers on the lock, and the briefcase popped open. He took out a thick contract and put it in front of me. "This explains the whole thing. Don't bother to read it; it's just the usual legal formalities. Doesn't make any difference."

"You can't get away with this, you know. Nobody'll believe you."

"I can't, huh? Once again you've underestimated The Boss. They told me I couldn't get away with it when I signed Catfish Hunter. And they told me I couldn't get away with it when I signed Reggie. And they told me I couldn't get away with it when I gave an illegal campaign contribution to Richard Nixon." He paused and reflected on that for a moment. "Well, two out of three will win the pennant every season. But enough about me; let us come to you. Sign. Now."

I had one chance. The doctors I'd spoken to in anticipation of this situation had suggested that I try the "Star Trek Defense." This is the unproven, and extremely controversial, theory which postulates that a perfect machine, when confronted by its own imperfection, will self-destruct. In this case, it meant that a megalomaniac faced with his own failed megalo would not be able to deal with it, and collapse. The doctors warned me that it might not work, but I had nothing to lose. The bases were loaded against me in the bottom of the ninth with nobody out, and all I had left was a 75-mph fastball.

I reached into the top drawer of my desk and took out the file I'd prepared so many months ago. "Maybe I'll sign it," I said. "But first I want you to look at . . . this!" I held up a photograph of Don Gullet, taken when he signed with the Yankees as a free agent, just before he came up with the sore arm that ended his career. "Look at this, Boss," I demanded. "Look. How many millions did he cost you?"

The Boss was momentarily thrown off guard. "It was . . . I made a little mistake. . . ."

Then I held up a photograph of Rawley Eastwick. "How many millions, Boss?"

I could see him wavering. "But . . . he was so young. . . . I thought he'd be another Catfish. . . . So young . . ."

I held up a picture of Dave Collins. "Two million, Boss? Three million? Is that what you paid him?"

He took an involuntary step backward, almost falling, but braced himself against the armchair, then threw his hands in front of his face. "But I . . . he . . . they. . . . He could run. . . . Why are you doing this to me?"

I held up a picture of Steve Kemp. "Four million, Boss? Maybe five million? Look, Boss, look. You signed him!"

"Stop this!" he screamed, desperately trying to shield his eyes from the truth. "Don't do this!"

I knew I had him. So I skipped right to the end. "One more, Boss. Look at this." And I held up the picture of Ed Whitson.

His scream echoed through the long, lonely corridors of the empty ballpark, bouncing from wall to wall, down the silent ramps, from section to section, until it caught the wind and was lifted out of the ballpark, fading into the Bronx night. When I looked at The Boss again his eyes, stone cold only moments earlier, seemed to be pleading for understanding. His shoulders had dropped and one corner of his mouth hung limp. "I tried . . ." he whispered. "I tried . . . I just wanted to win . . . for my fans. . . . They love me, you know. . . . They say . . . they say they don't, but they do. I know they do. I hear it in their thoughts. . . ." His voice became so soft I couldn't hear a word, although his lips were still moving. I looked at one of his men, who was standing helplessly waiting for orders.

"Take him away," I told him. Two of the men went to The Boss's side. "See that he gets whatever help he needs." They led him out of the office very carefully, as if he were a fragile object they were worried about damaging. I stood at the door and watched as he walked down the ramp, into Yankee history.

I went back to my desk, but the office suddenly seemed too big, and very empty. I was satisfied I'd solved the mysteries of the season, and could now concentrate on winning the pennant. I turned around in my chair and shut off the air conditioner that was right behind me—and it was then I realized that the chill that had been running down my spine had finally disappeared.

SEPTEMBER 17 ★

Kenny Davis's pinch-hit home run in the top of the eighth inning off Ash DeLorenzo provided the only run we needed as Eric Plunk shut out the White Sox, 1–0. It was our fourth straight win, moving us 4½ games behind Boston, 2 behind the Blue Jays. Toronto comes into the Stadium this weekend for a three-game showdown, and then a week later, the Red Sox come to New York to finish the season. Davis's home run wasn't much more than a high fly ball that got up in the wind and carried into the second row of the stands. But as far as I was concerned, it was the greatest home run I'd ever seen.

During the game Yogi phoned Verola in left field to move him a little deeper. When Joe V answered he told Yog, "I'm on my other glove. I'll call you back." Two innings later Yogi suddenly stood up in the dugout and asked, "What other glove?"

At Shea Stadium this afternoon, the Mets actually reached a new

low in baseball superstitions. The Mets, who invented the rally cap—
which consists of turning up the peak of the cap and sticking a
baseball between the peak and the rest of the hat—and who perfected
the curtain call for hitting a fly ball, created a new sort of rally . . .
bottom, I guess. They were losing to the Reds, 4–1, in the eighth
inning when Darryl Strawberry hit a titanic solo home run to make it
4–2. When he got back to the bench, somebody noticed that the
fly on his uniform was unbuttoned. Kevin McReynolds figured that if
it worked for the Straw Man it would work for him, so as he went to
bat he unbuttoned his fly. When he homered, every player in the
dugout unbuttoned their fly. The Mets came back to win, 6–4, and a
new baseball tradition was born.

Nettles called me from Chicago to tell me that everybody was
talking about it in the dugout, and the thing that surprised most
people is that it wasn't done first by the Montreal Expos.

SEPTEMBER 20 ★

Today was the most difficult day of my owner career. We beat the
Blue Jays, while Boston was losing to Detroit, to move to within three
games, but before the game I had to fire Lou Piniella.

By the time I got to the ballpark this morning The Duke had already
been waiting for me more than an hour. I don't think I'd ever seen her
any more excited. "The system has never been more certain of anything in its entire functioning existence," she said. "I've never seen it
react like it did when I fed in all the pertinent data."

"Now just relax," I said, "and tell me about it."

"We have to bunt today."

I waited for her to elaborate. Bunt? We'd been bunting all season.
What was so important about bunting? "Okay," I finally said. "We'll
bunt if the situation calls for it."

"No," she insisted. "I don't mean just bunt once in a while, I
mean every player has to bunt every at bat. I mean an entire bunting
game."

"Just wait now . . ."

"Honestly, Sparky, I've never seen anything like it. It was like I'd hit the jackpot. The system blinked on and off. It made noises I'd never heard before. It . . ."

"Maybe it's broken," I suggested.

"No, no, this is for real. Statistically, teams that have bunted against the Blue Jays have had an unusually high rate of success. And . . . and you know as well as I do that most big-league teams don't field bunts very well. They're always throwing the ball into right field or making the play to the wrong base or just mishandling the ball. Don't you see the genius of the machine? What could possibly be more unexpected?"

At first I didn't think she was serious. "I don't know, Duke, somehow it just doesn't seem right. Even if it works, think how embarrassed the Blue Jays'll be."

"Why? Because they can't handle the most fundamental play in baseball? Sparky, this is the most important game of the whole season and the system is telling us how to win it. Are you really going to worry about hurting Toronto's feelings when the pennant's at stake? You owe it to those people who've played their hearts out for you to do whatever you have to do to win."

She was right, of course. As the season had progressed, the system had become more and more important. The hitters were relying on her charts to work the count in their favor, the pitchers were following her readouts, even Piniella was occasionally incorporating her statistical analysis into his strategic decisions. It had all worked very well, and this was as certain as the system had been all year. Why not, I wondered; why not?

I knew Lou wasn't going to be pleased when I handed him the Duke's readout. I think it would be fair to say that "not pleased" is an understatement. He tore up the pages in tiny pieces and tossed them into the air. As they snowed down upon both of us, he said, "This is what I think of that garbage. I'm telling you right now, Sparky, I've had it. That's it. No more interference from her, no more batting charts, no more calling pitches, no more nothing. Baseball isn't a game that some jumble of tubes can . . ."

"Chips," I corrected.

"Garbage as far as I'm concerned, 'cause I've had it. Listen to me, Sparky, don't you see what you're doing? Even with hundred-million-dollar TV deals and domed stadiums and huge player contracts, baseball is still the most human of all the sports. It's a game in which normal people can star, a game that was created to be played in the fresh air on sunny summer afternoons and balmy evenings. It's a team game that tests an individual's character with the whole world watching. There isn't a computer in the world that really understands baseball. Sure, maybe for one play or one game; but the reason the season is so long is because the team with the best starting players, the team with the best statistics, doesn't always win. Because baseball is still the game in which a simple little thing called heart can make the difference between a world champion and an also-ran.

"Now you . . . you and your machine there, do you really think you can reduce it all to numbers? You really think that by feeding numbers into a machine you're gonna find out who has the guts to hang in there at second base to complete the double play with Don Baylor bearing down on him? Do you honestly believe you can reduce Babe Ruth to a few pages of data? You think some machine's gonna be able to tell you that a crippled Kirk Gibson is going to hobble off the bench and hit a game-winning home run? If that's the game you want to play, count me out. I don't want any part of it."

"What are you saying, Lou?"

"I'm saying it's either me or the computer. You've got to choose between us, and you've got to do it right now. Maybe I won't win the pennant, but if I lose, I'm going to lose proudly, and I'll lose fair and square, the way the game is supposed to be played."

"You're really serious about this?" I couldn't believe it.

"Never been more serious in my life. It's me or IBM."

I didn't even have to pause to think about it. "Gee, Lou," I said, "we're really gonna miss you around here. You've done such a great job this season . . ." I didn't think I had any choice. Lou was willing to lose to prove his point. I wanted to win because winning is much better than losing. The success of the corporation depended on it. I think Lou was just refusing to face the facts—the game that he claimed was created to be played in the fresh air of sunny summer afternoons was now being played in the fresh air conditioning of frosty fall nights to accommodate fans in all the time zones. I told Lou to pack up his things and vacate his office. No matter what he believed, I wasn't breaking any rules by using the information provided by The Duke's computer. As far as I was concerned, the computer was simply the advance scout of modern technology.

So, two hours before the most important game of the season, ten games before the end of the regular season, I was without a manager. Before I could make a decision, the phone rang. "Good news," Pete Rose said, "I got all A's and B's. They told me I'm on a roll."

"That's honor roll, Pete," I said, "honor roll." Of course I knew why he was really calling. "I'm sorry, Pete," I told him, "but in this situation, when the chips are down, there's really only one man who can run the ballclub." I knew I had to give the job to the best damn interim manager in baseball. So what if people said he was just lucky—right at that moment I needed baseball's luckiest charm.

"I'd rather be the needed than the needee," Yogi said.

I sat with him in Lou's former office as we made out the lineup card for the all-bunting game. I was trying to help Yogi by filling in the starting lineup, so I opened the top drawer of Lou's desk to look for a pencil and . . . and I stopped. What I found there stunned me. My hand hung suspended in midair. Nestled in a corner of Lou's top drawer, were two opened packs of Juicy Fruit gum. Six sticks were missing. More than enough to gum up the works.

Lou? I couldn't believe it. I had been certain it was The Boss. This certainly wasn't real evidence. It wasn't the "smoking gun," but it seemed to be the "missing gum." In all the years I'd known Lou, through all the seasons of our adult lives, never once had I seen him chewing Juicy Fruit gum. "Yog," I said, holding up the pack, "look at this."

"Oh, good," Yogi said, reaching across the desk. "Let me have a couple of sticks."

Sax led off the game by beating out a bunt on Jimmy Key's first pitch. Espinoza, batting second in the bunting lineup, laid down a perfect sacrifice. With the Blue Jay infield playing deep, Mattingly beat out his bunt, sending Sax to third. Toronto's infield still refused to come in, so Winfield also beat out his bunt, Sax scoring. Gruber made a nice play on Davis's bunt to nip him at first, but Mattingly and Winfield moved into scoring position. Then, Key fielded Joe V's bunt and, in his hurry to throw him out, threw it over McGriff's head into right field. Mattingly and Winfield scored. By this point the Blue Jays were badly shaken up.

Toronto just refused to believe that we would continue bunting the entire game. I could see the frustration on their faces; Cito Gaston had to be thinking that we were just waiting for him to bring in his infield so we could slash away—and he wouldn't do it. So we kept bunting. And we won easily, 7–2, on eight bunt singles, four walks, four stolen bases, two hit batsmen, a major-league record ten sacrifices, three Blue Jay errors, and at least two other misplays that could have been scored as errors.

By the ninth inning it was obvious that we'd won more than one game; we'd broken their spirit. They were confused, angry, and beaten. They just wouldn't believe that we would have every batter bunt—every batter, every at bat. When Mattingly beat out his second bunt single of the game—and his career—in the sixth inning, Key got so upset that he decked Winfield, then walked him, decked Verola, and walked him too, and finally nailed Geren with a fastball in the back, forcing in a run. When he hit Geren umpire Jim McKean threw him out of the game, and Key tried to start a fight. But nobody would fight with him. I think we all sort of accepted the fact that we were provoking him. And I don't think anybody blamed him.

After the game Gaston said, "I never thought I would see the day that the once powerful Yankees would be reduced to bunting. It makes me very sad." Almost as sad as losing would have made me.

The one thing we have to remember to do is change our bunt signal. By now I think every player and coach in the major leagues must know what it is.

SEPTEMBER 22 ★

We finished off the three-game sweep of the Blue Jays yesterday, charging past them into second place. With eight games left, we're still two back of the Red Sox. Next weekend they come into the Stadium for a three-game showdown. If we can pick up just one more game before then, I know we're gonna win this thing. I know it. I think, on that historic day when General Abner Doubleday didn't actually invent the game of baseball in Cooperstown, next weekend is what he had in mind—the Yankees vs. the Red Sox, the greatest rivalry in professional sports, three games, winner take all. I wish today was already tomorrow.

We were officially given permission by the American League office to start printing playoff tickets. Twenty minutes after we announced that, a sports memorabilia dealer called and offered to buy all of the tickets we printed if we *didn't* make the playoffs. I guess that's how big the sports memorabilia business has become—tickets for events that didn't even take place may become more valuable than tickets for actual events.

Yogi and I had a long meeting in my office in the morning to discuss the details of his contract. Before I gave it to him to sign, we discussed the Duke situation. I told him that I felt she had made a significant contribution to the success of the team and that I expected him to continue using the information she provided. "I can live with that," he said. "Where's my contract?"

Yankee fans were thrilled to have Yogi back in charge. The Boss had been so smart to realize that only a Yankee could replace a Yankee. No matter how much the fans loved Lou, Yogi was baseball's unbooable man. Banners welcoming him hung from every deck: "Notice to the Red Sox—Yogi's Back and You're Gonna Be Sorry," "New Hyde Park, N.Y. Luvs Yogi and Ice Cream," "Mom—send money," "No. 8 is No.1."

It was clear from the very first pitch that the Blue Jays were still confused. They played tentatively the whole game. We bunted two or three times, just to keep them anxious, and won, 5–2. TJ threw a six-hitter to win his 15th game, and had absolutely no problems with his certifiably detoxified arm.

The Piniella story has shaken the baseball establishment the way the fans shook the Stadium. I think the whole thing has been blown way out of proportion. According to some of the stories that are being printed, The Duke was supposedly running the team. The *News* wrote that, according to an "informed source," "Lyle is under her spell. She dictates who to play, she calls every pitch during the game, even 'manages' the team from her queenly perch in Lyle's private box." I wonder who that informed source might be: Lou Piniella?

I decided to become an "informed source" too. I called Ira Berkow at the *Times* and introduced myself as a "highly informed source particularly close to Sparky Lyle." "In response to the unfounded rumors," I told Berkow, "all we're doing is using the analytical material she provides in conjunction with the scouting reports and other information we've developed. And we combine everything to determine our strategic options."

"Sparky," Berkow said, "isn't it true the all-bunting game was her idea?"

"How'd you know it was me?"

"I spoke to you yesterday, remember?"

"Oh. Well, officially, I'm not Sparky right now, I'm an informed source. So this is all off the record, not for attribution, just deep background from a usually reliable source. The answer to your question is a simple yes and no. She suggested it, but we only agreed to try it after long and serious discussions with our baseball committee. Lou just couldn't go along with the program, so he asked to be relieved." In less than one season I'd gone from being a retired pitcher to Henry Kissinger.

Obviously, this was the biggest story in baseball since Steve Garvey's sex-change operation was revealed, when he claimed he wanted to be both a father and a mother to his children. Commissioner Vincent was quoted as saying, "If this story about the Yankee situation is true, there is apparently nothing illegal going on, but it certainly changes the world of baseball as we have known it." The Sporting News, in a brief editorial entitled "Baseball's Benedict Arnold?" asked if any computer could really understand the meaning of "a sense of fair play," and compared the use of computers in baseball to programmed trading on Wall Street. Several other teams have called for a complete investigation into the allegations, and suggested a reexamination of the rules applying to electronic surveillance. People called to request photographs of The Duke "in action." The National Enquirer has offered her $25,000 for her exclusive story about "Life on the road with twenty-four virile young men." News crews from all the networks and local channels and CNN have been camping outside the Stadium since the story broke, waiting for a statement from me and pictures of The Duke. I've asked her not to speak to them, but if she can't avoid it, to try to be completely honest and just deny everything.

SEPTEMBER 23 ★

We lost a heartbreaker to the Brewers tonight, 2–1, as Teddy Higuera beat Gene Kline on B.J. Surhoff's suicide squeeze in the top of the ninth. I guess the team that lives by the bunt cries by it too. We had a lot of chances to win, leaving seven men in scoring position. When Suarez struck out with one out and the tying run on third base in the bottom of the ninth he finally lost control. He pulled a Double-Bo, breaking his own bat over his head. Of course, the difference between Bo and Suarez is that Bo hit himself with the handle, or thin end, of the bat, while Suarez hit himself with the barrel.

Everything turned out all right though; the doctors said he could probably leave the hospital in the morning. And once again it proved how loyal Yankee fans are—when Suarez was being carried off the field on that stretcher they gave him a standing ovation, even while he's in a terrible slump.

Oakland clinched the Western Division title today, their fourth division championship in the last six years. Dave Stewart pitched the clincher, notching his 23rd win of the season. Unfortunately, it looks like he isn't going to win his first Cy Young Award again this season. Stewart's gotten more publicity for not winning the Cy Young Award than anybody who ever won it. But Nolan Ryan, with only 15 more strikeouts in the final two starts of the season, will reach the magical 6,000-strikeouts mark to go with his 24 wins, 21 losses, one no-hitter, and two one-hitters. Ryan, "The First Wonder of the Baseball World," has to be the sentimental favorite, so even though Stewart has won 20 games for six consecutive seasons, he still won't have a Cy Young to show for it.

In the National League Easy, the Cubs, Mets, and Cardinals are bunched within a game with a week to go. Whitey is still confident that if he can get Chris Carpenter off the DL for one start, the Cardinals can win it. The Mets' Darryl Strawberry vowed yesterday that he is going to lead the team to the pennant with "a monster week." And the Cubs' Don Zimmer continues to confound the experts by playing bizarre hunches and winning ball games. Two days ago he decided to use a defensive alignment that consisted of five infielders, a short fielder behind second base, and a single "roamer" in the outfield against the Phillies. "When that wind blows in from center field in

Wrigley Field," he explained, "you really don't need any outfielders." The Phillies were so overanxious to hit balls into the vacant outfield that they kept popping up to the infield, and the Cubs won a Wrigley squeaker, 10–5, to keep pace with the Mets and Cardinals.

In the NL Best, the Dodgers magic number is one—any combination of Dodgers wins and Giants losses totalling one will give them the division title. Meanwhile, the Hired Guns have already announced a price increase for next year, and have hinted they may ask at least one pitcher to join them.

SEPTEMBER 24 ★

Yankees 4, Brewers 3. A great, great win. It felt just about as good as a heart transplant with six breaths to go. We were losing 3–2 in the bottom of the ninth, when Winfield beat out a chopper to short with one out. Rosey Rogers flied out to medium center field for the second out. Winfield crossed up everybody, including Yogi and Duke's system, by stealing second base. Then Felipe Suarez pulled reliever Sid Spanier's fastball into the left-field bleachers for the game-winner.

Two back of the Bosox. And closing.

Suarez broke out of his slump tonight with a single and a double in addition to the home run. The only thing wrong with that is that he thinks he's Don Mattingly. Somehow, that blow on his head gave him a minor case of amnesia. The doctors ran all kinds of tests and cleared him to play, telling us that these aftereffects are quite common and will clear up in a few days. Meanwhile, as far as Suarez is concerned, he's Don Mattingly.

It started this morning when he came into the clubhouse. He seemed a little confused, so Nick Priore had him lie down on the big lounge chair that Mattingly keeps in his locker. Suddenly Suarez seemed to snap out of it. He sat up and looked at the nameplate above the locker that read "Don Mattingly," and his face lit up with recognition. Nick was smart enough to hang Suarez's uniform in the locker, and Mattingly was more than willing to dress in Felipe's locker. Nobody wanted to risk upsetting him by telling him who he wasn't. I think a lot of people thought he was faking, but they thought it was pretty funny, so they played along. Yogi told him, "Mattingly, you'll bat in Suarez's spot tonight and start in left field."

But the most unusual thing was that when Suarez came to bat, instead of hitting out of his own stance in which he keeps the bat cocked right behind his ear, he got down in Mattingly's crouch and held the bat back at shoulder level like Mattingly does—and got three hits. So now we've all got to keep going along with this, and hope that his amnesia doesn't clear up for the next few days. I'm afraid that if he wakes up and remembers who he is, he'll go right back into his slump.

Mattingly, the real Mattingly, said that the only thing we have to do is make sure Suarez doesn't sign any checks.

We held a team meeting before the game tonight to vote on distribution of shares in whatever prize money we receive. The first four teams in each division get a lump sum payment to be divided any way they want to divide it. Usually, teams break down the payments into full shares, half shares, quarter shares, and cash awards. The value of a full share is determined by where a team finishes in the standings and the total amount of money in the World Series pool. In the old days players really needed this money to supplement their salaries, and they used it to do things like get the car repaired, or finish the playroom, or even make a down payment on the sporting-goods store or bar. Today, with the salaries most players are making, these shares allow players to keep up with their alimony payments, make the IRS happy, or buy their agent a new car.

The voting went pretty much as expected. The players who've been with the team all season each got a full share, while other players got shares or cash awards based on the amount of time they spent with the club. The team also voted to donate a half share to the American Leeist Society to Build a Better World, and to give a cash award to the estate of Cy Young.

As the meeting was about to break up, TJ said, "I got a great idea. Let's give a quarter share to Kenny Kaiser."

A few people laughed, assuming he was kidding; but TJ was serious. "Hey," Big John Nicholson asked, "why in the world would I want to give my money to an umpire?"

"No reason at all," TJ admitted.

"We can't do it," Nicholson said. "If we do, the reporters'll go absolutely bananas trying to figure out why we did it."

TJ smiled mischievously. "I know."

SEPTEMBER 27 ★

This is getting very interesting. If it gets any more interesting, I may never sleep again. We're one game behind Boston after beating the Tigers while the Sox were losing to the Orioles. One game. Just one game. Right now, right this minute, it seems like a huge number. I just can't help remembering all the games this season that were decided by one bad pitch. And all the games that turned on one call by the umpire. And I can't help wondering how many games we lost by one step at first base, or by one line drive that landed two inches foul, or one fly ball that ticked off the fingers of an outfielder's glove. A team plays 162 games; that's a long, long season, and we're either going to win or lose the division by a single game. Maybe even by a single pitch.

The tension in the clubhouse is so thick I'm surprised that somebody hasn't tried to slice it, wrap it, and market it. It's been so bad in there that Rosey Rogers hasn't complained about his girlfriends in a week, Keith Reich has finally relaxed for the first time all season, and Nicholson is talking about breeding bugs instead of catching them. When "Mr. Cool" came in to relieve against the Tigers he was so nervous that he took a wrong turn at third base and ended up driving right onto the pitcher's mound with his bike. In fact, the only player who seems really calm is Suarez, and he doesn't even know who he is. The doctors say he's maintaining his composure because he thinks he's Mattingly, and he believes Mattingly would maintain his composure. So I guess it would be accurate to say Suarez is maintaining Mattingly's composure.

Nettles told me that the real Don Mattingly is so nervous that he put his socks on the wrong feet yesterday. I asked him what was wrong with that. "Nothing," he told me, "except the feet were Sanderson's."

I don't think the Red Sox are any more calm than we are. The rumor going around is that Wade Boggs hurt his hand in a locker room fight with utility infielder Tony Thomas. Supposedly, the fight started when Boggs told Mike Greenwell that he'd broken out of his recent batting slump by sleeping with his Louisville Slugger, and Thomas asked if that meant a litter of little sluggers was going to be delivered in nine months. It would be awful if Boggs was really hurt and couldn't play at full strength. Sure it would. The truth is that that would be my second greatest wish, right behind peace on earth—but not that far behind.

The Duke Schneider story seems to be getting bigger and bigger. Computer experts all over the country are claiming that it would be impossible to develop a really effective program to manage a baseball game because there are too many variables, and too many optional responses to each variable.

Meanwhile, Nintendo announced that they intended to have "The Super Mario Brothers Winning Baseball Game Game" ready for Christmas, and several other companies have made substantial offers to The Duke for the rights to her "Yankee Baseball Program." If it exists. At least one company doesn't even care if the program actually exists. They've offered to buy the name and create a program to go with it. When Duke asked one of their executives how they could do such a thing, he told her proudly, "Marketing."

As long as the team is winning, I don't think our fans care how we're doing it. Most of them probably feel like the fans who put up a banner last night, reading "Freehold, N.J., Luvs the Yankees, Don Mattingly, ESPN, and IBM."

SEPTEMBER 28 ★

TIED! TIED! After 159 games, after 1,455 innings, after 428 pitching changes, after 5,883 at bats, we're absolutely even. We're tied with the Red Sox. Knotted up. The New York Yankees: 97 wins, 62 losses. The Boston Red Sox: 97 wins, 62 losses.

I spent the entire night sitting in my box simultaneously watching our game with the Tigers on the field and the Red Sox—Orioles game on ESPN. Both games finished within minutes of each other. We beat the Tigers, 7–3, and the wonderful, lovable Baltimore Orioles beat the Bosox, 5–1. From the first pitch the Stadium was in an uproar that never quieted down one decibel. I don't know that I've heard that much noise in this old ballpark since Horn Day. In fact, in the sixth inning, two policemen from the local precinct showed up to say that the resident of an apartment eight blocks away had called to file a noise complaint about "a party in the vicinity of Yankee Stadium."

"You've got three innings to quiet down the crowd or we're going to have to issue a summons," one of them explained. Then they sat and waited.

When I told Nettles about it after the game he laughed, and said that was the silliest thing he'd heard since Toronto was here last week and the same two cops had tried to give TJ a ticket for Jay walking.

Blame Nettles, he said it.

Suarez is so hot people are afraid they'll get burned if they touch him. He had three more hits, and three RBIs, tonight. Since becoming Mattingly, he's hit .750 in 24 at bats. He's so hot that when Duke feeds his statistics into the computer her program rejects him as being "improper information."

Everybody has been terrific about his problem. The media is treating it like a joke, reporting that Suarez is "pretending" to be Mattingly because he's on a tear. Maybe he is pretending; but if he is, he doesn't know it, and that makes his pretense even more believable. The real Mattingly continues to take the whole thing very well, saying, "This is as hot as I've ever been without being me."

The three-game, winner-take-all, for the jackpot, the marbles, and the pennant begins tomorrow night. Several dozen fans are camping outside the ticket booth to make sure they get some of the bleacher seats we're putting on sale at 10 A.M. We've had requests from 130 newspapers and television and radio stations for credentials, and the phone hasn't stopped ringing in a week. After the game tonight Yogi told the press, "To me, it seems like the season started just a few days ago. But it's been a long, tough year and it's coming down to this: two great teams fighting it out for the flag. I'm just glad I have a good seat for these games."

I can't help thinking about the playoff game between the Yankees and Red Sox at the end of the '78 season. That was exactly the same situation, except it was one postseason playoff game rather than three regularly scheduled games, and it took place at Fenway Park rather than Yankee Stadium. But other than that, it was exactly the same. The thing I remember most about that game is how confident we all were that we were going to win it. Just like this year, we'd come from so far back in the standings that it didn't seem possible we wouldn't win. Before that game Dirt Tidrow told me he was experiencing "future déjà vu." He said that that meant in the future he was going to be able to look back on the game and remember being positive we were going to win.

Yogi and The Duke have worked out our pitching rotation for the three-game set: TJ is pitching the opener, Cadaret is scheduled to go in the second game and, if the third game means the division title, we'll start Eric Plunk. Everybody else is in the bullpen.

In my office after the game tonight Duke said her system had figured that the odds are heavily in our favor that we'll win the first two games to clinch.

Chicken told her that his system was indicating that he had had too much to eat at dinner.

It's unbelievable how well everybody is getting along. There's usually a little dissension on every team; it's natural when so many competitive people live together under tremendous pressure for a long period of time. But there just doesn't seem to be any on this team. Yogi deserves a lot of credit for that. In the Kangaroo Court tonight, Reggie brought charges against him for letting Espinoza swing away with a 3–0 count. Espinoza popped up. Yogi demanded a lawyer, so they gave him Hanko Tsumi. Yogi wasn't sure he wanted a lawyer named "Sue me." "Since this is only a first offense," Judge Jackson decided, "I'm going to go easy on you. The fine is $10,000." Tsumi thanked him very much.

Yogi immediately pleaded temporary insanity. Reggie rejected his plea, saying that everybody knew it wasn't temporary. Yogi offered to throw himself on the mercy of the court. Rosey Rogers offered to throw himself on the first woman who walked into the clubhouse. Finally Reggie reduced the fine to $1. Yogi said, "That's a fine with me." Reggie then fined him $10 for misuse of an Italian accent.

In other baseball news, Julia Nevez asked the Phillies for her release so she could sign with the All-California Raiders of the National Football League. Raiders managing partner Al Davis said that he had decided to break the league's conspiracy against female football players, and that Nevez would be in uniform kicking extra points for the Raiders in this Sunday's opener against the Steelers.

SEPTEMBER 29 ★

There is a certain magic about the game of baseball that can never be explained. It just is. There are nine batters in the starting lineup, yet somehow, when the game is on the line, the best hitter on the team will have a shot to win it. Great players make great moments happen. It's McCovey batting against Ralph Terry, Reggie against Bob Welch, Yaz against the Goose, Will Clark against Mitch Williams, and tonight, Don Mattingly against Phil Grann.

Yankees 4, Red Sox 3. The champagne is on ice.

With two out and two on in the bottom of the eighth, the Red Sox leading by a run, Mattingly fouled off six consecutive strikes from Grann, then pulled a double down the right-field line for two RBIs and the ballgame. At this moment we're the first-place New York Yankees. Our magic number is one—one win and we're the Eastern Division champions. One win in two games. I can't believe it.

It was a great day. When I got to the ballpark this morning I found out that Mattingly had actually spent the night sleeping in the batting cage so he could get up early to get in some extra batting practice. It paid off; his three hits raised his average to .361, putting him a point ahead of Wade Boggs and three points ahead of Kirby Puckett in the race for the batting title. Suarez, who had two more hits, also came in early this morning, but he spent an hour in the video room watching tapes of Mattingly hitting.

Obviously, we were helped by Boggs's injured hand. Watching him try to hit with only one hand was really very sad. He was so crippled, we were able to hold him to two hits.

TJ was magnificent. His heater got up to 97 mph, the fastest he's been all season. When he was in the medical workshop for that toxic waste removal they also oiled his springs and increased the tension, and that seems to have helped. Sanderson came in to get an out in the seventh, then Taft finished with two perfect innings for the victory. Right now, right at this moment, I think I'm as high as I've ever been in baseball. I can't wait for tomorrow.

SEPTEMBER 30 ★

Tomorrow turned out to be a bad today, so now I'm waiting for another tomorrow. If we lose tomorrow, there is no tomorrow, and we'll just have a lot of yesterdays to look back on. Right now, right at this moment, I think I'm as low as I've ever been in baseball. I think the saddest of all words in sports must be these—the champagne is getting warm.

Red Sox 5, Yankees 1.

It began as a perfect day. The sun was shining in a cloudless sky, there was no traffic on the Deegan, and there were no lines at the newspaper store when I bought my lottery ticket.

My telephone was ringing when I walked into my office at 7:30 A.M. Cliff Campion of the Meadowlands complex was calling to congratulate me on our great win yesterday, and to tell me that if I insisted on staying in Yankee Stadium, they would be willing to dismantle the Stadium brick by brick and reconstruct it in the Meadowlands. "Like they did with London Bridge. That way," he explained, "you can stay in Yankee Stadium *and* move to the Meadowlands at the same time."

As soon as I hung up with him, Fred Rappoport of the Mayor's Council for Economic Development called to congratulate me on our great win yesterday and told me that the city had decided, in honor of the wonderful season we've had, to name an elementary school after me. "How does 'P.S. Sparky Lyle' sound to you?" I told him how much I appreciated that, then mentioned that the only other thing I've had named after me was a Stage Delicatessen sandwich consisting of bologna and tongue, with relish. "You're a lucky man," he said, then asked, "as long as I've got you on the phone, is there anything else we can do for you?"

"Well," I told him, "there's no such thing as enough pitching."

I was just hanging up when The Duke came into my office waving a sheet of paper. She was about as excited as she'd been the day she programmed the all-bunting game. "Look at this," she said. "Look at this." I looked, and saw the usual rows of numbers that made no sense to me. She explained, "According to the program, Bruce McDonald should get the start today."

"What?" I couldn't believe that. McDonald had started four games since we'd recalled him, compiling a win, a loss, and two no-decisions.

He done all right in several long-relief appearances, but nothing to indicate he should start the most important game of the year. "Are you sure it says that?"

"Here it is," she said, shrugging. "Based on yesterday's game, the system believes that Boston is particularly susceptible to right-handed fastball pitching. McDonald is the choice. He's right-handed, he's got a live fastball, and they've never faced him before. That gives him a big advantage."

"You're absolutely sure of this, right?" It just seemed so hard to believe. She was sure. I had no choice. A long time ago I had committed myself to this path. It had led me to the brink of a championship. It was too late to turn back.

"That's incredible," Yogi said when I told him about it. "I was just thinking the same thing myself. They'll never expect this. In a game this important, they'll expect us to start one of our best pitchers. We'll really fool them. The Red Sox will never know what hit them."

Actually, it was the Red Sox that hit McDonald. Hard, and often. He lasted only 2 innings, surrendering all five runs on seven hits and five walks. As it turned out, the only people who were fooled were me and Yogi.

I was getting ready to leave the ballpark when I saw the lights still on in The Duke's office. I found her feeding the computer. "That was a big surprise tonight," I said. "I've never seen the program be that wrong."

She shrugged, and said nothing.

"It was the program, right?" She wouldn't look at me. Instead, she kept punching numbers into the system. So I said it again. "It *was* the program that wanted us to start McDonald?"

She slowed down, and finally stopped and looked at me. "You knew?"

"I guessed."

"What are you gonna do about it?"

"I don't know yet. I know we probably wouldn't have gotten here without you, but I don't understand how you could have done that. I mean, we're so close . . ."

She lowered her head. "I couldn't . . . I just . . . You know, we . . . Bruce is so . . ." I knew exactly what she was trying to say; she did it all for love. She believed in Bruce McDonald; the starting assignment in the most important game of the year was her gift to him. "I'll never do anything like that ever again, Sparky, I promise."

I looked at her. Sitting there in the reflected green light of her monitor, she looked particularly vulnerable. "Let me ask you," I said softly, "what does . . ." I pointed to the computer, ". . . what does it say I should do?"

She forced a smile. "Sixty-four percent chance of forgiveness."

I nodded. "But when this is all over, we're gonna have to talk about it."

As I left the room she called to me. "Do me one favor, please," she asked. "Don't ever tell Bruce, okay? Let him think it was the computer that named him."

Driving home I heard on the car radio that the Cubs had clinched the National League East title. Zimmer had put three pitchers in his starting lineup, Rick Sutcliffe on the mound, Greg Maddux in left field, and Mike Bielecki at first base. Throughout the game he'd change pitchers on every Pirate hitter, so no batter saw the same pitcher twice. Maybe he's working with an Apple Macintosh, because the Cubs won, 4–1.

The baseball season is now nine innings long.

OCTOBER 1 ★

To paraphrase the late baseball commissioner Bart Giamatti, the game of baseball is designed to break your heart—especially if you're a Boston Red Sox fan.

Yankees 2, Red Sox 1. Game, season, championship.

I'm having a difficult time writing this because the champagne is dripping from my hair onto the paper. A few hours ago the Yankees and Red Sox played one of the greatest games in baseball history, a game that baseball fans will be reading about forever. Plunk started for us against Roger Clemens, and it was clear from the first pitch that both of them had their best stuff. Over the first four innings Ellis Burks was the only Red Sox to get to second base, and Roberto Kelly's single was our only hit. Nobody even threatened to score.

Meanwhile, another drama was taking place in our dugout. While were at bat in the third inning Winfield hit a long foul ball into the upper deck in left. Suarez turned to Kenny Davis and said admiringly, *"Ay caramba."*

"Shit," Davis said, then shouted to everybody in the dugout, "Felipe's normal."

"Oh, no," Yogi said. It couldn't have happened at a worse time. Batting third that inning, Suarez went back to his old stance and struck out on five pitches. He came back to the dugout muttering in Spanish.

The game moved briskly through the fifth and sixth innings and into the seventh with neither team mounting any real threats. Suarez was scheduled to hit third in the seventh, and Nettles came up with a plan. "It's a long shot," he told Sundberg, "but maybe our only shot." At the end of the top half of the inning, as he was trotting out to the third base coach's box, Nettles went past Roger Clemens, who was walking out to the mound. "You hear what Suarez said about you?" he shouted.

Clemens was in a state of complete concentration, but that snapped him out of it. "What? What'd he say?"

"Nothing much. Just something about you being afraid to come inside because you've lost your fastball. But so what if he said you're a yellow-bellied, no good, mother-sucking pig's innards."

There were two outs when Suarez came to bat. Coaching third base, Nettles yelled to him, "Don't worry about him coming inside, he's afraid of you." Clemens's first pitch hit Suarez flush on the side of the helmet and bounced away. By the time Suarez stood up, he was Mattingly again.

Geren followed with a single, sending Suarez to second. That was a problem—if Suarez had still been himself, who can run, he would have made third easily. Unfortunately, he's much slower as Mattingly, so he stopped at second.

But then veteran "Plug" Reich, playing the game of his career, lined a base hit to right field, scoring Suarez. We were winning, 1–0.

We held the lead until the ninth. The September shadows were creeping across the infield; pieces of wax paper that had once been wrapped around hot dogs—still covered with mustard—were blowing across the Stadium. In the clubhouse, the champagne was on ice. In my box, The Duke was feeding data into the system. Three outs from the division title. The toughest three outs in baseball.

Boggs, leading off against Plunk, reached out and poked a base hit into left field. Duke did some quick figuring, then called down to the dugout. Yogi came out to give Plunk the hook. Out of a cloud of bullpen dust, Mr. Cool appeared. The first hitter he faced was Marty Barrett, with Boggs on first, nobody out.

Barrett hit a tweener into left-center. Kelly, Espinoza, and Suarez all had a shot at it, but it landed between them for a hit. Boggs had held up to make sure it dropped, so he had to stop at second.

First and second, nobody out, Burks the batter. Taft, working very carefully, got ahead in the count, 1–2. Duke signaled slider. Taft threw a beautiful slider in the dirt that Burks went after and missed. Strike three! Strike three!

Still first and second, but now there was one out. A double play would have gotten us out of that mess. Mike Greenwell was the batter. Ball one, high and away. Ball two, again, high and outside. I was sitting upstairs thinking, you can't pitch from behind to a hitter like Greenwell, when Taft tried to throw a fastball by him. Greenwell scorched a line drive into right-center. Boggs scored the tying run. Barrett rounded third and held.

The lead run, probably the division-winning run, was 90 feet from home plate. I couldn't sit still. Half the people in the Stadium were on their feet; the other half were yelling at them to sit down. Dwight Evans was the batter. The great Dwight Evans, maybe a future Hall of Famer, a crafty veteran, a man who'd been in this situation before; one of the fine clutch hitters in the game. That Dwight Evans. Taft threw him a slider away. Called strike one. Taft came inside with his second pitch, it was a little low. Ball one. One and one. Taft took something off his next pitch. Evans swung and was way ahead of it—foul ball, strike two. One and two. Taft walked behind the mound, took off his sunglasses, and wiped the perspiration off them. Maybe he was saying his mantra; I couldn't tell.

He climbed to the top of the hill and got Duke's sign from Geren. The runners led off first and third. Taft swung into his windup. Evans tensed. Curveball, away, it was supposed to be a waste pitch—it just hung out there over the plate. Evans swung fluidly and hit a routine fly ball to medium center field. Routine every other time the entire season; this time it might be the division winner. Kelly came in four or five steps. He waited a little behind the ball, so he could be moving forward as he caught it to get his whole body behind his throw to the plate. Barrett went back to third base to tag up. Greenwell went to first to tag up. In Boston and New York, millions of hearts were thumping marching tunes. The ball started coming down.

Kelly made the catch as Barrett took off from third. Kelly made a great throw toward the plate. Greenwell saw the throw going home and took off from first. Kelly's throw looked like it was going to be a split second too late, but . . . but Mattingly cut it off and fired back to second base. Sax put the tag on Greenwell. Second base umpire Steve Palermo called Greenwell out at second, but umpire Davey Phillips, behind the plate, immediately signaled that the run counted, that Barrett had scored before the third out was made at second base.

Red Sox 2, Yankees 1.

Sax casually flipped the ball toward the pitcher's mound and started trotting off the field. We still had three outs left, but I could see that the fight had been drained out of the team. In my box, The Duke sat staring at her monitor screen as if the computer had betrayed her. Chicken just shook his head from side to side, saying nothing. A game we were sure we were going to win, the most important game of the season, was getting away from us. It looked like fate had taken a wrong turn at the crossroads.

Then, suddenly, Yogi burst out of our dugout, waving his arms and shouting at somebody on the infield. At first I couldn't figure out what he was doing. Taft, Sax, Reich, and Mattingly had all crossed the foul line into foul territory, but Espinoza was still one step away from the line. He stopped, and his momentum carried him forward, right to the line. He teetered, on the verge of falling over the line, but maintained his balance. Then, as the Red Sox ran onto the field, he raced to the mound and picked up the ball before Clemens could get it. Then he ran over to third base and leaped on it with both feet.

Third base umpire Dale Ford gave the out call of his career. He threw his right hand high up into the air and shook his fist. Out! The most unusual play in baseball had been called—the fourth out. Barrett had left the base too soon. His run didn't count. That's what Yogi had been screaming about—according to the rules, Barrett's run didn't count officially until every infielder, including the pitcher, had crossed the foul line. Espinoza never crossed the line. The run didn't count. The run didn't count. Red Sox 1, Yankees 1.

Players and coaches poured out of the Red Sox dugout like oil out of a supertanker. Manager Don Baylor led the charge. But Dale Ford, bless his tiny little umpire's heart, stood firm. It took almost twenty minutes for the umpires to get the field cleared so we could resume play. So we could win the title.

The replay showed that Ford was correct. Barrett had left the base at least 1/100th of a second too soon. Those umpires have amazing vision when they're right.

Clemens didn't seem to be rattled by the incredible turnaround. He knew what he had to do. As they were saying in the SportsChannel booth, he was a real professional; he'd come to play. If someone watching him warm up to pitch the most important half inning of his career didn't know that this was the bottom of the ninth of the deciding game of the season, they could have assumed from his demeanor that this was just another game in mid-June. That's how confident he looked out there.

Winfield led off the inning by trying to pull an outside curveball and bounced a harmless grounder to short. That brought up Suarez. Just about every Yankee player was on the top step of our dugout, shouting encouragement to Felipe. "C'mon Donnie, baby, you can do it!" or something like that.

And so he did it. Clemens tried to be too fine with his first pitch and missed away. His second pitch was a slider up, up around the eyes. The moment he let it go he knew it was a bad pitch. Pitchers know that. Bad pitches are pitches that batters see very well; no matter how fast a bad pitch is thrown it seems to take forever to reach the plate. When I hung a slider I'd have a whole series of thoughts—like a dying man seeing his lifetime passing in front of him—before the ball reached the batter.

Clemens's slider seemed frozen in midair, like wet wash on a clothesline in January. As the ball reached the plate, Suarez uncoiled, a snake snapping at a fat toad. When a ball is hit as hard and solidly as he hit that pitch, the sound is more a dull thump than a crack or whack. And this was a deep, resonant thump. Clemens didn't even bother turning around. He just dropped his chin onto his chest and started walking off the field. Burks at least made the gesture of going back to the wall, but there was nothing he could do except look up and watch it sail far over his head into the bleachers. Suarez had pulled a Munson—he'd hit the longest home run of his career at the most critical moment. He hopped and skipped and leaped around the bases, baseball's magical tour. Some fans ran onto the field, but security guards nailed them before they could get near the plate.

The Stadium was raining programs. Up in my box Chicken came over and we hugged each other. I looked over at The Duke, who was furiously typing something into her IBM. Later, I found out, she was writing "We did it! We did it!"

The entire ballclub was waiting for Suarez at home plate. Maybe he touched the plate, maybe he didn't. When he rounded third base Nettles leaped into the air and started clapping joyously and ran home alongside him, until Suarez disappeared into a pinstriped sea.

Holy cow.

OCTOBER 2–9 ★

When they sell the history of this season on videotape, the playoffs will pale by comparison to the regular season finale. The playoffs seemed anticlimactic. The great Oakland A's, with Jose Canseco, who'd recovered from his breakdown minutes after his phone was disconnected, and Mark McGwire and Rickey Henderson and Walter Weiss and Carney Lansford and Dave Stewart and Dennis Eckersley, with a rested pitching staff, with the experience of having been in the playoffs four times, with all that, they had no chance against us. Any team with two Don Mattinglys in the lineup is very tough to beat, and until the collision at second base in the fourth game, we had two Mattinglys. But we also had fireballing Tommy John, Steve Sax, who played the greatest series of his life, "Mr. Cool" Taft, Duke Schneider and her program and, most importantly, fate.

Sitting here now, putting all this down, the playoffs seem like a great blur. The clubhouse celebration after winning the division title went on through the night. I think they're still trying to get that champagne out of the flotation tank. I can now tell you from experience that you can't really float on a sea of champagne. And believe me, the mood room was not made for Madonna tapes.

I discovered the next morning that one of the toughest things about making the playoffs is getting tickets for everybody in New York who needs them. Tickets to major sports events have become very important business status symbols, and there are more people in New York who need business status symbols than anywhere else. I think I read a survey which showed that New York was the capital of insecure executives—and every single one of them was only four box seats behind first base away from security.

Obviously, every politician in the state had to be there. The difference between the demands of politicians and the demands of business executives, I discovered, is that executives need seats they can see from, while politicians need seats in which they can be seen. Of course, celebrities want both; serious celebrities, like movie stars and network newscasters, want seats where they can be seen, and at the same time look as if they really care about the game.

The truth is that the only thing a lot of these people know about baseball is that tens of millions of people are watching the games on television. The president of a major corporation was irate when we offered him seats behind third base; he demanded seats behind second base. A Bronx union leader was upset when he picked up his tickets. "The playoffs?" he complained loudly. "I thought these were for the payoffs."

Somehow, we managed to shoehorn 57,566 people into the ballpark for each of the first two games. Without question, the key to our success in the playoffs was The Duke's strategy readouts. If we could have picked our Most Valuable Person after the playoffs, our unanimous choice would have been Duke Schneider. "Baseball's New Psychout King," as *Time* dubbed her after the playoffs, ignored the dozens of reporters who constantly hounded her for a story, ignored the hundreds of proposals that poured into the office for her, even ignored the fact that CBS had a camera trained on her at work throughout the playoffs, and managed to create a strategic plan that won the playoffs for us.

Before the first game she decided—actually the program decided—that we would walk Jose Canseco every time he came to bat. Whatever the situation was, two outs and nobody on base, runners on first and second and no outs—we were going to walk him intentionally. The only exception, of course, was if the bases were loaded with less than two outs. So we did. Every time. Jose Canseco hit .000 for the five games—unless you count the water cooler in the A's dugout; he hit 1.000 against that. He had 18 walks, two very frustrated strikeouts, three stolen bases, four runs scored, and, most important, no RBIs. I'd guess those walks were responsible for the A's scoring another four runs—walking Canseco forced runners into scoring position. But what it really did was take the A's most explosive weapon out of their arsenal.

Before the series started everybody knew that the A's put a better team on the field than we did. Vegas made them an 8–5 favorite. Nettles summed it up best when he said, "We can't strike 'em out, so let's psych 'em out." And that's exactly what we did. Once the A's realized that we were going to walk Canseco every time he came to bat they lost their composure. It upset their rhythm; it changed the whole balance of their lineup. Canseco's job in the heart of the A's order was to drive in runs, not get on first base. We gave him first base and took away their power. Obviously the key to the success of the plan was that McGwire had a terrible series. Maybe he was pressing, maybe he wanted to punish us for walking Canseco to get to him, but he hit .178 with only three harmless RBIs. If he had been hitting . . . but he wasn't.

Our strategy drove Canseco crazy. At one point during the third game he stood at home plate and laid his bat on the ground, then challenged Plunk to throw a strike. He stood there screaming at Plunk, calling him all kinds of names, daring him to throw just one strike. Plunk paid absolutely no attention to him; he just threw four wide ones.

By the fifth game it was obvious that Canseco was ready to snap. Throughout the series, after each walk, he'd toss his bat away and trot to first base muttering to himself. This time he angrily flung his bat toward the dugout, took two steps down the first base line, then lost it. He whirled and ran right at Chuck Cary. Cary gave a great feint to his right and Canseco missed him, and by the time Jose had stopped and turned around, Bruce McDonald had raced to the mound and snapped an El-Haiku submission hold on him. Canseco was thrown out of the game. Actually, he was dragged out of the game. That was when he blasted the water cooler.

The Duke's offensive strategy was even more brilliant. Before the first game she explained that the program strongly recommended that we not swing at a single pitch from Dave Stewart for the first six innings. "Don't even take the bat off your shoulder," she said. I expected to hear some loud complaints about that, but the players have such confidence in her that not only didn't they complain, they loved the idea.

Stewart struck out the side in the first inning on twelve pitches. By the second inning he realized that something was going on. Again, he struck out the side, but this time it took him sixteen pitches. If it's possible to see someone thinking, I could see Stewart thinking. He'd lost his natural rhythm. It took him nineteen pitches to strike out the side in the third inning. In the fourth inning he was throwing very tentatively, constantly looking into our dugout, trying to figure out what we were doing. He started missing badly with some of his pitches. He went to a 3–2 count on both Sax and Kelly before striking them out, and after a record-setting 11 consecutive strikeouts, he walked Mattingly. By the fifth inning he was becoming unraveled. He started missing consistently, fighting himself, and he took something off his fastball just to get it over the plate. He began aiming his pitches, and once a pitcher does that it's just a matter of time until he's finished. And still, nobody swung the bat.

The fans were a tremendous help. At first, when they realized we weren't swinging, there were a lot of boos. But once they realized we weren't swinging intentionally, they became very supportive. They jumped all over Stewart every time he threw a ball. I think he became conscious of the crowd early in the game and, instead of just concentrating on what he was doing, tried to throw harder to shut them up.

We were trailing 2–0 in the bottom of the seventh. Stewart was pitching a no-hitter. A no-swinger, in fact. But I could almost feel the confidence bursting out of our dugout. Joe V told me after the game that when they came in to hit in the seventh no one said a word about starting to swing because they didn't want to alert the A's. Suarez led off the inning by taking two balls. Stewart's third pitch was a medium fastball right down the pipe. Felipe laced it cleanly to left field for a base hit.

After that it was like the floodgates opened to let in the cavalry. Genen singled. Reich tripled. Espinoza hit a long sacrifice fly. Sax walked. Kelly singled. And Stewart was out of there. A parade of relievers followed him, but no one could shut us down. I think, in that game, we got more out of nothing than any team in the history of baseball, winning 8–1.

The confidence we'd gained by beating one of the best pitchers in baseball in the first game carried right over to the second game. We won that one easily, 6–3.

The A's were starting to panic. They'd been so confident going into the playoffs that they figured beating us was just a formality. We were nothing more than a stoplight on the way to the Indianapolis 500. They were looking past us to the World Series. Things had changed pretty quickly. We hadn't just beaten them on the field, we'd psyched out the side—they were playing defensively rather than aggressively, wondering what kind of stunt we were going to pull next.

The series shifted to Oakland for the next three games—nobody even complained when we stopped in Miami to pick up an extra 12,000 bonus miles—but the results were just about the same. We were like a steamroller going downhill without any brakes—and they were like Sylvester the Cat trying to stop us. We rolled right over them; we flattened them thinner than a pancake, 9–3. Winfield was the hitting star with two home runs and five RBIs.

In the fourth game, Suarez, who'd hit .385 for the series—ironically exactly the same as the real Mattingly—tried to take out Walt Weiss at second base on a double play and smashed into his knee. Weiss had to be carried off the field. Suarez was out for a few seconds and, when he regained consciousness, he was Suarez again. "Well," Nettles reflected after the game, "it could've been worse. He could've woken up and been Biondo."

The A's rallied to win that fourth game behind Stewart, 4–1. Maybe if we hadn't swung at any pitches we would've scored more runs, but I think that by that point we were confident we had the series won, so we treated the game as a minor irritation.

The fifth game was probably the best game of the whole series. Cadaret started for us and, with IBM calling the signals, pitched into the seventh inning of a 2–2 game. With two down in the seventh he gave up a couple of hits and Yogi yanked him. Big John came in to get the final out of the inning, ending their last real threat. In the ninth we had runners on second and third with one out, but Eckersley walked Mattingly intentionally and induced Winfield to hit into an inning-ending double play. We went into extra innings. Neither team threatened in the tenth, or the eleventh, or the twelfth. Finally, in the top of the thirteenth, Espinoza led off by fouling off seven straight pitches before walking, then went to third on Sax's perfect hit-and-run ground ball through the right side. Then Kelly, with a count of no balls and two strikes, laid down a perfect suicide squeeze bunt to score Espinoza with the go-ahead run.

IBM named McKeever to pitch the bottom of the thirteenth. Tommy was making his first appearance on the mound in almost three weeks, and for those three outs he was the old "Mr. Perfect." When McGwire popped up to the infield with Canseco on first, we were the new American League Champions.

In the raucous clubhouse after the game reporters asked Yogi why he'd brought in McKeever to pitch the thirteenth. What was he going to tell them, "My pitching computer told me to do it?" Instead he explained, "Tommy hadn't pitched in a long time so I figured he'd be strong."

Listening to that, Nettles whistled softly, then whispered to me, "Based on that, we should've pitched Whitey Ford."

So this incredible, unbelievable, improbable season is going to last just a little longer—we're going to the World Series.

OCTOBER 12 ★

The World Series will open in Los Angeles this year. The Dodgers' "Hired Guns" made sure of that when they beat the Cubs four straight games. Zimmer tried everything against Lasorda and his Guns: in the first game he installed a "slugger shift," putting all of his fielders on the left side of the field and challenging right-handed hitters to try to go the opposite way. Instead, they went over the fielders, hitting a playoff record seven home runs. In the second game he tried to ruin their timing by ordering his pitchers to throw nothing but off-speed stuff—the Dodgers broke their own record, hitting eight home runs. In the third game Zimmer, after seeing how successful we'd been by not swinging, decided to try it the National League way. He had his batters swing at every pitch. Every single pitch. The Dodgers' Anthony

Herrara struck out 19 batters, and surrendered only two hits en route to a 9–0 victory. In the fourth game Zim used his three-starting-pitcher starting lineup and his slugger's shift. He tried to hit and run with the bases loaded, and crossed up both the Dodgers and his own team by trying to hit and run with nodody on base. Nothing worked. The Cubs were just outgunned, 7–1.

So it's just like old times all over again, the Yankee vs. the Dodgers for the World Championship. All's right with the baseball world.

OCTOBER 14–21 ★

By now everybody thinks they know the whole story of the World Series. They don't, not at all. Mattingly's book and Joe V's book and, for those people who can read Japanese, Tsumi's book, will tell what happened on the field, but the real story of this World Series took place off the field. And nobody except me, The Duke, and Mike Applegate know that story.

There is only one World Series. Oh, there's a World Series of Golf, a World Series of Auto Racing, a World Series of Bowling, a World Series of Poker, even a World Series of Rapid Accountants; but when somebody says, simply, the World Series, they're talking about baseball.

I was in five World Series. I'd like to be able to claim that playing in a Series was a dream come true for me, but the truth is that not having to carry china plate molds from the batter-out to the jigger-man at the Jackson China Company in Reynoldsville, Pennsylvania, was a dream come true for me. The rest was a big bonus. But playing in the Series was great fun and tremendously exciting. Most players react to being in a Series in one of two ways: Either they think, 100 million people are going to be watching me, this is my chance to be a hero; or, they think 100 million people are going to be watching me, I'd better not screw up. The team that has more heroes than screwups is the team that wins.

I don't think anybody knows how he's going to react until the first pitch is thrown. On our flight to the Coast—I figured The Duke was getting soft; the only stop we made was in Phoenix—everybody seemed relaxed and confident. McDonald spent part of the flight entertaining writers by eating baseballs. He got a mild case of cork poisoning and couldn't have pitched in the opener if we'd needed him. I sat down next to Mattingly, who was holding two bats in his lap while reading the *Reader's Digest Condensed Books* version of Buddy Harrelson's book on power hitting, and asked him how he was going to handle the whole Suarez story in his book. "I'm not," he said. "Nobody'll believe it anyway."

"You're probably right," I agreed. "I wouldn't mention it either if I was writing your book."

Maybe the only person on the plane who was nervous was Keith Reich. "I guess this is it for me, huh?" he said when I sat down next to him. "Soon as the Series's over you'll be handing me my unconditional release. Well, maybe it's time, I've been up here eight years, and . . ."

"Hey, 'Plug', slow down a little, okay? We haven't even thought about that yet."

He looked at me evenly. "You're trying to tell me something, right? You're trying to tell me if I don't have a great Series it's all over for me? That you'll think about it then?"

"No, no way. I'm telling you that when the season's over we're gonna sit down and look at everything and make some decisions. But you had a good year; you started over 100 games, you hit what, two-sixty-something. My guess is that if we can work out something with your agent, we'd like to have you back."

His eyes lit up. "You mean that?"

"I do, yeah."

And then he leaned over and kissed me. That was the first time I'd ever been kissed by a third baseman. Although Nettles did hug me a couple of times.

As I started to get up he said with satisfaction, "That's just great. Now I have a whole 'nother season to worry about it being my last season."

It was eight o'clock in the evening, and the last beautiful rays of the smogset were fading by the time we got to the hotel. Mary was flying in the next day with the players' wives and girlfriends, so I was just going to have a little bite with Chicken and Nettles and Yogi. I was still hanging up my clothes when there was a knock on the door. I opened it, expecting to see Chicken or Graig or a bellperson. Instead, a very well dressed man, very distinguished looking, sort of like a foreign diplomat from an old black-and-white movie, was standing there. He even had a mustache and beard, and was holding a black bowler in his hand. He certainly didn't look like he lived in Los Angeles. "Mr. Lyle," he said, "I'm Michael Applegate . . ." He offered me his hand.

I shook it tentatively. "Yes?"

"Oh. I'm so sorry, I thought you were expecting me. Didn't . . . didn't Miss Schneider tell you I'd be stopping by? I'm her rep . . . her agent."

I was very surprised. "No. No, she didn't." We stood there staring at each other, and suddenly I realized he was waiting for me to invite him in. After we'd settled down in the two-chair anteroom of the suite I asked him, politely, exactly what he wanted.

"Before we get to that," he said in a voice as smooth as Kansas City's artificial infield, "let me offer you my most sincere congratulations on your success this season. However, I think it's important to point out that my client certainly is responsible for at least a small portion of that success."

"Absolutely," I agreed, "and we're very pleased to have her with us."

"I'm sure you are. I'm sure you are. But . . . Mr. Lyle, you really don't know very much about her, do you? Where she's from, for example?"

I thought about that. There was something in the back of my mind. "The Midwest somewhere, I think." Actually, I couldn't remember what she'd told me.

"Let us just say she's from the South," he said. "The very deep South. Now, the reason I'm here . . ."

As he spoke certain things about him began to seem vaguely familiar. The beard and the mustache. Some of the words he used. And finally, his name. Applegate. Applegate. I'd heard it before; I just couldn't remember where. His reason for coming to see me, he explained, was to discuss "proper compensation for Miss Schneider's services. As I'm sure you realize," he continued, "since this . . . arrangement has become known to the public, my client has received several interesting inquiries about her availability, and before we initiated discussions with those interested parties, we felt obligated to meet with you."

"Mr. Applegate," I asked, "how come right now? I mean, doesn't two days before the start of the World Series seem like a bad time to negotiate?"

He smiled at that. "On the contrary, Mr. Lyle, I can hardly conceive of a better time. I think the answer to your question depends on the importance of winning the World Series."

I stood up. I wasn't sure, but it sounded suspiciously like he was threatening me. "Thanks for stopping by," I said coldly. "I think you've made your point. But let me remind you of a few things. The Duke is under contract to the New York Yankees until the end of the season. And after that, Mr. Chicken Stanley will be delighted to sit down with you and discuss her future."

He started to say something else, but I cut him off, telling him I had to meet some people for dinner. "So be it," he said, standing, "but it behooves me to point out that whatever happens beyond this point shall be your responsibility."

His presence stayed in the room a lot longer than he had. I told the story at dinner and we all had a good laugh. "Agents," I said. "They're worse than lawyers." But something about him continued to bother me; I just couldn't figure out what it was.

Time went by faster than a Ryan heater, and before I knew it, Sandy Koufax and Don Drysdale were throwing out the first balls to open the World Series. I hadn't said a word to The Duke about Mr. Applegate's visit, and she acted as if absolutely nothing had changed. She worked the clubhouse before the game, telling batters what to expect from Fernando, and when the game started she took her seat in front of her computer in our private box.

We scored in the first inning. Sax singled and went to third on Mattingly's base hit, then came home on Winfield's sacrifice fly. After that Valenzuela and TJ traded goose eggs for six innings. TJ had no problems working through the Hired Guns twice. Then, in the bottom of the seventh, he went into his windup—and sprung a spring. It was really a pretty terrible thing to see. His arm was bouncing back and forth like a pendulum gone berserk: backandforth, backandforth, backandforth, faster . . . faster . . . faster. Finally Gene Monahan and his assistant, Steve Donahue, stuck a bat in the crook of TJ's arm and jammed the spring. TJ walked off the field to a standing ovation.

The Duke's program decided on Sanderson to relieve, but he didn't have anything. Joe Carter broke it open with a three-run moonshot. The final score was 6–2. The Dodgers were one game up. After the game

Monahan confirmed my fears about TJ. "There's no spring left in his arm at all. We're gonna need a carpenter."

Mary and I were in our suite that night when the phone rang. I recognized Applegate's voice immediately. I had had a strange feeling that he was going to call. "I was just calling to commiserate with you," he said.

"I don't need your commis," I told him.

"Of course not, forgive me. I was just wondering if perhaps you'd changed your mind about negotiating with my client. It seems like you're more in need of her services right now than you were at this time yesterday."

I told him again that I didn't intend to discuss anything with him.

"So be it," he said.

The next day was unusually gloomy; a black cloud hung over the whole city. It never rained, though, and the Dodgers, behind home runs by Eric Davis and Mike Marshall, beat Cadaret, 5–1. That was the game in which Willie Randolph made the spectacular dive into the second row of seats that they've been replaying over and over on the news. He landed in Walter Matthau's lap, and somehow still managed to reach up and catch Geren's foul pop.

After the game The Duke sat in front of her terminal for a long time, furiously punching numbers into the computer. Everything looked absolutely normal; but somehow it was different.

We flew back to New York nonstop, which made me very uneasy. I tried to start a conversation with The Duke on the plane; she was very polite, but distant. Something had definitely changed.

I couldn't get to sleep that night. I couldn't stop thinking about all the little moves we'd made in the first two games that didn't seem right. Small things, like telling Joe V to take an 0–1 pitch that put him in a deep hole; like telling Nicholson to throw fastballs to Brett; like pitching to Marshall with first base open and two outs. Individually, I think, each move probably could have been defended by a good baseball strategist; but lumped together, it was almost as if someone wanted us to lose those ballgames.

Mary and I had decided to stay at the Regency Hotel rather than driving all the way back to Jersey. I sat up into the early hours of the morning mindlessly changing channels on the TV. And then I found it. On Channel D. It was the Yankee uniform that caught my attention. It was an old movie, a musical, and it took me a little while to realize it was *Damn Yankees*, the show based on the novel *The Year the Yankees Lost the Pennant.* I settled back and watched.

When that picture had been made, in the late 1950s, I think, the Yankees rarely lost a pennant. That was the joke in the book's title. You couldn't make a picture like that today. Unfortunately. As I watched the movie, Ray Walston, "Uncle Martin" from the series *My Favorite Martian,* came on screen. I didn't remember the story too well, just that the Yankees lost the pennant. Apparently, Walston was playing the Devil. And he was going under the name . . . Mr. Applegate!

Bells started clanging in my head. Sirens whined. Whistles whistled. Mr. Applegate. Suddenly everything began coming together. Mr. Applegate equaled Michael Applegate. Therefore, Michael Applegate was working for . . . the Devil.

I forced myself to calm down. At five A.M., after a long flight, those kinds of thoughts are possible. Then reality set in. The Devil posing as an agent? Well, that part made sense. But the Devil in Los Angeles today? Well, that part made sense too. But the Devil? Not too many people believe that the Devil assumes a physical form to bargain for souls these days. I watched the end of the movie, then turned off the set and sat there in the dark. I knew I would hear from him soon, and when I did, I wanted to be ready for him.

He reached me at my Stadium office early the next morning. The sound of his voice on the phone snapped me out of my stupor faster than a line drive back through the box. "I was thinking about what you said," I told him, "and I think maybe we should sit down and discuss this situation very soon."

Seconds after I'd hung up, Chicken poked his head in the door. "Good news," he said. "The carpenter thinks he can repair TJ's arm today. He can pitch in two days." The timing seemed to be quite coincidental. But was it, I wondered?

With Applegate temporarily satisfied, we won the third game, 5–3, behind a strong performance by Eric Plunk. I think the Dodgers were a little unnerved by the incredible din of the crowd and our creative use of the message board. We had a whole set of notes ready for the Dodgers—things like, "Eric Davis has never lived up to his potential," "Brett has had offers to play in the Senior Baseball League," and "Tony Young's nickname is Ax-fight-loser." Maybe it wasn't good sportsmanship, but it got the fans excited and might have caused the Dodgers to press a little.

I met with Applegate the following morning. "Exactly what is it you want?" I asked. As if I didn't know the answer to that question.

He began outlining a three-year deal. Including several options, the whole package was worth approximately $1.25 million, "plus several other minor items that we can discuss once the basic compensation issue is settled."

I suspected I knew exactly what those "other items" were, but I didn't say a word. My plan was to try to drag out negotiations right through the end of the Series. If I could do that, I knew, it would be too late for him to get what he really wanted. "Obviously I'll have to analyze this package," I said as our meeting concluded, "but I guess you'll agree that negotiations are proceeding smoothly."

"Certainly. And I'm sure my client will be glad to know that."

We won the fourth game too, 5–4, as Rosey Rogers came off the bench in the seventh inning to deliver a two-run pinch single, and Mr. Cool, "the best reliever in Yankee history since Sparky Lyle," except for Dave Righetti, according to the message board, came in from the bullpen to shut down the Dodgers. The Series was tied at two games apiece. All the newspapers were filled with feature stories about the stars of the Series—Mattingly was the leading batter, Joe Carter had three home runs and eight RBIs—but I knew that the real story of the Series was taking place in my office.

I decided to try to play hardball with Applegate, or whatever his name really was. He tried to continue the negotiations, asking to meet with me before the fifth game. I told him I hadn't had time to even look at his proposal.

Trailing 3–0, The Dodgers came back to win the fifth game, 8–5. Somehow, that didn't surprise me. The key play was a ground ball in the sixth inning that we couldn't turn into a double play. Eric Davis followed with a two-run triple, then scored on Doc Cronson's pinch-hit single. The Dodgers were up, three games to two, and we were going back to L.A. It was tough to be optimistic.

I slept on the flight back to California, and I dreamed I was outside Yankee Stadium in the pouring rain. The water was rising around me and I was trying desperately to get into the Stadium, where I knew I'd be safe. I ran from gate to gate, but Applegate was standing in front of each one, blocking it. And as I watched, Applegate's face slowly dissolved, like plastic melting, to reveal his real face—it was The Boss. When I woke up, the back of my shirt was drenched in sweat.

I met with Applegate in the coffee shop of the hotel. After some small talk, he started to hand me some typed papers. I put my hand on his wrist, stopping him. "Let's just cut the crap, Applegate," I said. "Let's get right down to it."

He looked very surprised. "What are you talking about?" he asked.

"All this stuff about money and bonuses. I know what you're after."

"Oh? And what's that?"

"You want my soul."

His eyes narrowed into slits as he considered that. "Do you know what you're talking about?" he asked, without a trace of emotion in his voice.

"I know who you are. I know who you really work for."

"And who might that be?"

I took a deep breath. "I know you're representing the Devil."

"What?" He was momentarily stunned, but then he started laughing. "Well, I do represent a lot of people, some punk-rock groups, several television actors, a few athletes. And, while I admit that some of them may lack certain . . . social graces, I'd hardly call them the Devil."

I licked my lips slowly as I tried to figure out what his game was. "So you're saying you don't want my soul?"

Two elderly women sitting at the next table overheard my question and looked at me. And smiled politely. I guessed that they were tourists, and were thrilled to hear a real California business deal under discussion. "Mr. Lyle," Applegate said, "what in the world would I want with your soul? Even if you were capable of deeding it to me, a possibility I find highly dubious, the State of California has very strict laws as to what kind of commission an agent can receive. Additionally, there really isn't much of a market in souls these days. I want cash, and I want it guaranteed for three years. And I want a signing bonus, options, and a buyout clause. Those are the things I want for my client."

"And what about those 'other items' you mentioned?"

"The right to use the Yankee logo in the movie version of Duke's story and sale of her computer program. Reduced responsibilities as traveling secretary. The right to purchase a percentage of your frequent flyer miles at a discount. A tax-free loan. . . . Shall I go on?"

"Then . . . then you're not in league with the Devil?"

"I'm an agent, Mr. Lyle."

"Don't evade the question. Are you, or are you not, partners with the Devil in this deal?"

"Certainly not." He smiled knowingly. "Is that really what you've been thinking?"

I had a difficult time believing him. "Let me get this straight. You're telling me that if I get up and walk away from this table you're not going to cause us to lose the World Series?"

He opened his mouth as if to speak, but no words came out. Finally, he coughed some sounds into his throat and said, "Mr. Lyle, when this season is over, perhaps you should consider seeking professional help about your problem."

I just couldn't believe an agent was telling me the truth. I'd convinced myself that he was working for the Devil. Now there was nothing to prevent us from winning the World Series. Except the Dodgers. "I'm going to get up now," I said, "and I'm going to leave. And I'm not going to talk to you anymore until this is over." I waited for his response. He just stared at me. "Okay?"

"I think at this point that's probably appropriate."

I stood up and walked out of the place very slowly, looking over my shoulder to see what he was doing. He sat there sipping his coffee, watching me leave. I was free.

When I saw The Duke at the ballpark I told her, "I'm glad your agent's not the Devil."

Several hours before the sixth game was slated to begin, Chicken found me in the small office the Dodgers had given us for the Series. He had several things he wanted to discuss. Among them the fact that Biondo was $1/3$ of an inning away from qualifying for a $50,000 bonus. "He's worked $74 2/3$ innings." He showed me. "According to his deal, he gets the bonus if he pitches at least 75 innings." He frowned. "That could be the most expensive third of an inning anybody's ever pitched."

I didn't respond to Chicken, but in the clubhouse I took The Duke aside. "Do me a favor," I said. "Let's not use Biondo these next two games."

"Is he hurt?"

"Um, sort of. I just have a feeling he's not gonna be that effective." Cost-effective was what I really meant, but I didn't say it.

"You're The Boss," she said, going back to her charts.

I stood there thinking about that. I guess, during the year, I'd learned that it isn't easy being any boss, but it's even tougher being

The Boss. I had a lot more sympathy for him than I'd had when I first bought the team. People just don't appreciate how difficult it is to run a corporation as complex and as public as Yankee Corp. Looking back, I'd agree that The Boss made some mistakes while he owned the team; but as I've always said, let he who has never wanted to trade a ballplayer in anger cast the first stone. At least I've always said that recently.

The sixth game was probably the best game of the whole Series. TJ, had been given a clean bill of repair, and he was overpowering. But Mike Morgan matched him inning for inning. Espinoza led off the seventh inning with a walk, then went to second on Reich's sacrifice. Because the game was being played in a National League park there was no designated hitter, and TJ was scheduled to bat. I looked over at The Duke, whose eyes were riveted on the computer screen. I figured the computer would decide that Rosey Rogers should be the pinch hitter. Finally, The Duke picked up her direct line to the dugout and said clearly, "Jorge Burns."

Burns? Jorge Burns? Our third-string catcher pinch-hitting with the lead run on second? That had to be some kind of joke. It made no sense at all. The only possible explanation I could come up with was that pinch-hitting Rogers now would set off a chain of lefty-righty switches that would end up with us having to pinch–hit for the pinch hitter, costing us Rogers's bat. It was a stretch, but maybe pinch-hitting Burns against Morgan was the high-percentage play. I didn't say a word. The Duke's system had helped us get into the sixth game of the World Series. I wasn't going to start telling it that it didn't know how to program. So I just sat there watching as the badly overmatched Burns went down on strikes.

Something seemed wrong. In the bottom of the inning Kirk Gibson came up to pinch-hit for the Dodgers, and I heard her tell the dugout to feed him a steady diet of fastballs. Fastballs to Kirk Gibson? In the seventh inning of a tied ballgame? Gibson eats up fastballs the way McDonald eats up baseballs. Nicholson threw his 85-mph heater and Gibson swallowed it whole, then spit it deep into the right-field seats. He hobbled around the bases on his crutch with the run that put the Dodgers ahead, 1–0.

It stayed that way until the ninth. The Dodgers were just three outs away from the World Championship. Rosey Rogers, hitting for Geren, led off the inning with a seeing-eye base hit up the middle. The tying run was at first base with nobody out. I glanced at The Duke, expecting to see her naming a pinch runner, but she never touched the phone. That was crazy. Any computer worth its chips knows that Rogers can't outrun a statue.

I decided I'd better take a closer look. As Dodgers pitching coach Ron Perranoski walked slowly out to the mound to talk to Morgan, I got up as casually as I could and wandered toward the refrigerator in the back of our skybox. I popped open a beer; but instead of returning to my seat, I stood in the corner. From that spot, if I leaned over to the side just a little, I could read The Duke's screen. She was working much too hard to notice me.

I waited to see who the computer picked to hit for Reich. Perranoski left the mound and went back to the dugout, leaving Morgan in the game. That meant Morgan had to face at least one more hitter. I figured the computer would analyze the data and decide that left-handed-hitting Kenny Davis should bat against the right-handed Morgan. Duke punched the situation into the system. Within seconds the computer responded just as I'd thought it would: K. Davis. The Duke picked up the phone and I heard her say clearly, "Verola."

My whole body started shaking. It hadn't been any Devil after all. It had been a woman. The Duke was trying to sabotage the World Series! But why? What possible reason could she have? What could be more important to her than the New York Yankees?

I looked down on the field. Joe V stepped into the batter's box. Morgan swung into his windup and missed with a fastball. Joe V stepped out of the batter's box and wrapped the bat around his shoulders. He looked down at Nettles in the third base coach's box, took a few practice swings, then stepped back in. Morgan threw another fastball. Joe V was fooled, but managed to get a little piece of it. He dribbled a slow roller between first base and the mound. Willie Randolph, playing in double-play position, charged in and made a great barehanded scoop . . . but juggled the ball and lost the play. Joe V was safe.

The pitcher's spot was next. I watched as The Duke fed a big meal of numbers into the system. Traditional strategy called for a pinch hitter who could lay down a sacrifice bunt. Mentally, I went down our roster. Sundberg, I figured; it had to be Sundberg. I glanced at the computer screen: J. Sundberg. Once again, The Duke picked up the phone. As she did I moved quickly. "Kenny Dav—" she started to say;

but I got there in time to grab the phone. "Sundberg," I ordered. "It says Sundberg."

I held the phone in my hand, looking at her. She didn't say anything. I couldn't even read an expression on her face. Down on the field, Sundberg was loosening up, swinging two bats over his head. I very gently replaced the receiver in its cradle. Then I leaned down and pulled the computer plug out of the wall. The screen went blank.

My thoughts were interrupted by the cheer of the crowd. Sundberg had laid down a perfect bunt. Brett fielded it, took a quick look at third, then wheeled and flipped to Randolph covering first for the out.

I had nothing to say to The Duke. I just shook my head and went back to my seat. The tying run was ninety feet away from scoring; the go-ahead run was at second, one out. Steve Sax the batter. Morgan went to a ball and a strike. I could see Yogi peering out of the dugout up toward our box. Yogi had had a tough year on the phones. Morgan went into his windup. The runners took their leads. Morgan threw. . . .

As effortlessly as a snake gliding on silk, Sax reached out and stroked a soft line drive into right-center. Davis and Joe V scored easily. We were back in the Series.

Sax died at second. I figured Taft would pitch the bottom of the ninth. The Dodgers had prohibited use of the bullpen motorcycle, citing insurance problems, so Tums had had to walk in when he made his previous appearance in Dodger Stadium. This time though, the bullpen gate opened and I could see Tsumi using a broom to sweep up a cloud of dust. It wasn't much of a cloud of dust, actually, more like a spray of pebbles, but suddenly, out of it came Mr. Cool—riding a bicycle! The crowd loved it. Even the Dodger fans couldn't resist laughing. That broke all the tension of the moment, and I knew that Taft was going to shut them down. That's exactly what he did. The Series was going to the seventh game.

And it was going there without Duke Schneider. It was almost one o'clock in the morning when I found her, sitting alone in a dark corner of the hotel lounge. Just staring off into space. When I sat down next to her she looked at me sort of blankly, and forced a smile. "Congratulations," she said coldly.

"You want to tell me about it?"

She frowned. "There's not much to tell," she said in a voice no louder than a whisper. I'd never seen her looking so vulnerable.

"I just don't get it, Duke. What was that all about?"

"I couldn't help myself, Sparky. I tried; I swear I tried. I just couldn't stop."

"But why? You'd done such a great job all year. We wouldn't be here without you. Your whole future was ahead of you. What happened?"

She blinked. "You really don't know?"

"No, I don't."

She bit her lip, then closed her eyes and lowered her head. Finally, she told me the truth. "I'm a Dodger fan, Sparky. I've been a Dodger fan my whole life."

"Wha . . ."

She was like a closet stuffed with secrets, and once she opened the door they all came pouring out. "Don't you see? Don't you get it? Who'd you think I was named after, Willie Mays? You"—she practically sneered—"you were a player your whole life; you don't have any idea what it really means to be a fan. To live and die with your team. To have all your moods change depending on whether your team won or lost. But I did, and my father did, and his father before him. In my house, when the Dodgers lost nobody would feel like eating dessert. The next day my father wouldn't buy the newspapers because he couldn't bear to read about a loss." She laughed at a small memory. "Do you know that on the Fourth of July my father flew his Dodger pennant right under the American flag. . . ."

"But I still don't . . ." I waved my hand helplessly through the air, looking for something that made sense to grab on to.

"Being a fan isn't a sometime thing, Sparky. It's something you do with all your heart and all your soul. It's a lifetime commitment, a relationship you never outgrow or forget about. It's a love affair, full of hope and joy and pleasures and disappointment."

"But what about loyalty to the Yankees? And to me, and Bruce?"

"You aren't kidding, are you? You really don't get it? Loyalty isn't like a sweater you can change when you get a better sweater. Loving a baseball team is one of the most passionate relationships anyone can ever have. The more you put into it, the more you get out of it; the more pain you feel when your team loses, the more pleasure you experience when your team wins.

"I tried to be fair with you, Sparky; you have to believe me. I did. And, for a while, I thought I could resist it. I thought . . . I hoped, really . . . that I could beat it. That I was stronger than it was." She inhaled and shook her head again. "But as soon as I saw those beautiful Dodger-blue uniforms I knew it was hopeless. I knew it was stronger than I was. So I prayed that the Dodgers would be able to win without my help. And for the first two games it looked like they would. And then . . . then it all started falling apart for me. I couldn't help myself." Her eyes locked onto mine. "You must really hate me."

"No. No, I don't hate you," I said honestly. "Maybe I don't understand you, but I don't hate you. See . . . I just don't understand . . ." I couldn't find the right words. "I could see, maybe, if you felt this way about the Red Sox. Or even the Cubs. But the Dodgers? No, I'm afraid not, I don't understand."

"What are you going to do about all this?"

"I don't know yet. Obviously you're not working tomorrow. I have to think . . ."

"Maybe if I can get some help, Sparky; if I can just stay away from the Dodgers . . ."

"It's too late for that, Duke."

The next morning I told the whole wild story to Mary. She couldn't believe it. "You really thought her agent was the Devil?" she said, laughing hysterically. "That's about the most ridiculous thing I've ever heard you do."

I called a closed-door team meeting an hour before the seventh game was scheduled to begin. "We've come a long way together," I said as I walked around the silent locker room, "and now we're on the verge of winning it all. But one of the people who has been with us on this long journey won't be with us today." I bowed my head. "This morning, I gave Duke Schneider her unconditional release." There was a loud murmur throughout the room. I paused in front of Nicholson's locker and watched as a California centipede struggled to climb out of a bottle. When the complaints finally quieted down, I continued. "We all know that Duke did a great job for us this year. But you know what? I don't think we really need her."

A chorus of protests rose from every corner of the room.

"Wait. Wait a minute," I shouted, holding up my hands. "Look around this room. What do you see?" I paused, then continued. "I'll tell you what you see. You see the New York Yankees, the greatest team in the history of baseball. And the Yankees, the real Yankees, have never needed any machines to tell them how to play the game. Did George Herman 'Babe' Ruth need a computer to tell him how to hit 714 home runs?" I waited for an answer. No one said a word. "Did he?" I shouted loudly.

A few people muttered, "No."

"Did Larrupin' Lou Gehrig, the Iron Horse, need a computer to tell him how to play in 2,130 consecutive games?"

Several more players said, "No."

"Did Joltin' Joe DiMaggio, the Yankee Clipper, need some barrel of bolts to teach him how to hit in 56 consecutive games and play the best center field this side of heaven?"

A ragged chorus agreed, "No."

"And how about Mickey Mantle? You think the Commerce Comet had to have some hunk of plastic tell him how to wrap his knee and go out there and win the Triple Crown?"

"No."

"And what about Roger Maris? Did some silly computer tell him how to hit 61 home runs?"

"NO!"

Mattingly stood up and shouted, "And what about the Gator? Did Ron Guidry . . ."

Reggie stood up. "What about me? Did I need a computer to . . ."

It was a magnificent sight. One by one the players rose and shouted a name, a highlight, from the glorious Yankee history. And when they were finished, they were ready to go out there on that field and meet the hated Dodgers in the seventh and final game of the World Series.

They stormed out of the locker room with a great roar, charging off to battle. I grabbed Yogi and took him aside. "You're on your own tonight, kid," I said. "There's no machine in the world that can help you."

"There's no tomorrow tonight," he said meaningfully.

He was absolutely right. I put an affectionate hand on his shoulder. "One more thing," I added. "Don't use Biondo. He can't get loosened up." Then, with a whoop, Yogi ran out of the locker room.

That seventh game will go down as one of the proudest moments in Yankee history. Sax opened it with a single, his fourteenth hit of the Series, and before the inning was over we'd scored a record-setting 11 runs to break it open. I knew the Dodgers weren't going to catch us. I knew we were going to be World Champions.

It had been such a long year, an incredible year, and somehow this was an appropriate ending to the season. By the seventh inning we were ahead 14–3, and I sat there, high above the field, looking down upon my team, savoring every moment. It seemed like just a few hours ago that Mary and I had been watching the *Jeopardy* All-Housewives Tournament and the phone had rung. I'd been so naive then; things had seemed so simple. I thought about all the things that had happened since that day—how much I'd learned, how much I'd changed. In many ways, I knew, I'd become that thing I once feared most—The Boss.

It was an odd feeling, sitting there alone, watching my team play. Suddenly, I had a strange and irresistible urge. For one brief second I think I experienced just a little bit of what The Duke had been talking about. I picked up the line to the dugout and waited until Yogi answered. Then I said, "This is The Boss. Put in Biondo."

OCTOBER 25 ★

I doubt I'll ever be able to get all the scraps of paper from the ticker-tape parade out of my hair. I keep finding little pieces in the strangest parts of my body.

The party started when Eric Davis bounced back to Taft, who threw him out, and lasted three days. We went through six cases of champagne in the clubhouse alone. All I remember about that part of the celebration was getting the World Series Trophy from Commissioner Vincent and the phone call from President Bush congratulating McKeever on his perfect game and telling him that he hoped he did it again soon.

There were about 11,000 people waiting at Kennedy Airport at six in the morning when our plane finally landed. The parade down Broadway and the ceremonies at City Hall took place the next morning. Fittingly, in the middle of the parade, the car carrying Chicken broke down. The Stanley Curse had struck one last time. At one point things actually got so raucous that even Reggie had to admit, again, "I'm not 100 percent sure I could have done all this."

When I got to my office this morning everything seemed so quiet. There is nothing sadder than a baseball stadium in winter. There were at least 200 telegrams and messages waiting for me, more than I could ever return. But on top, I noticed, was a note from The Duke. She'd entered a Dodgers Anonymous program, it said, and she would contact me when she was released.

I was thinking about her, trying to decide what to do, when Annie buzzed me. "Spark," she said, "there's a Mr. Hunter for you on line three."

I picked up the phone. "Congratulations," he said tonelessly. "Now, to more important things. I believe we have a business situation to discuss. . . ."

And that's just the way it happened, no matter what Mattingly and Joe V write in their books. So help me Abner Doubleday.